**An illustration of the original Globe Theatre,
Bankside, Southwark, London, England**

Praise for
SO POTENT

Art

"Brilliant, practical, witty, and accessible, Carding
gifts great insight throughout, sensitively introducing
the reader to Shakespeare, magic, and the creative
light that can shine from and through all of us."
—Ben Crystal, author of *Shakespeare on Toast*

"This is a glorious book—and long overdue. There have been
other works that looked into Shakespeare's magical life but
nothing as thorough or enlightening as this. Emily Carding is
to be congratulated for her work and for opening the doors to a
magical realm."—John Matthews, author of *How to See Faeries*

"'There are more things in heaven and earth, Horatio...' and
Emily Carding explains it all to you in this practical and
informed new book. With a lovely wit and Shakespearean
expertise, Carding shows how two seemingly unrelated
subjects—magic and Shakespeare—are inextricably
entwined and extraordinarily powerful."—Austin Tichenor,
artistic director of the Reduced Shakespeare Company

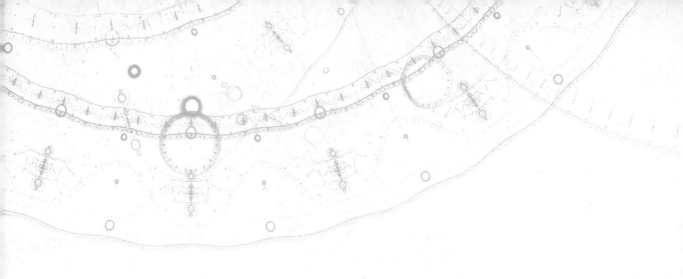

Emily Carding

holds a BA (hons) in theatre arts from Bretton Hall and an MFA in staging Shakespeare from the University of Exeter. She is an initiate of the Alexandrian Wiccan tradition and has been working with tarot for over twenty-five years. Emily is the creator of several tarot decks, including *The Transparent Tarot* (Schiffer), and she's the author of *Faery Craft* (Llewellyn). Additionally, she is the illustrator of *Gods of the Vikings* (Avalonia Books). As an actor she is best known for her international tour of the award-winning one-woman show *Richard* III by Brite Theatre. Emily lives in Hastings, East Sussex, England.

SO POTENT

Art

THE

Magic

OF

SHAKESPEARE

EMILY CARDING

FOREWORD BY CAITLIN MATTHEWS

FIRST EDITION
First Printing, 2021

Cover design by Shira Atakpu
Edit and book design by Rebecca Zins
Interior artwork from Getty Images

Llewellyn is a registered trademark of Llewellyn Worldwide Ltd.

Library of Congress Cataloging-in-Publication Data
Names: Carding, Emily, author. | Matthews, Caitlín, author of foreword.
Title: So potent art : the magic of Shakespeare / Emily Carding ; foreword
 by Caitlín Matthews.
Description: Woodbury : Llewellyn Worldwide, Ltd, 2021. | Includes
 bibliographical references and index. | Summary: "*So Potent Art* is a
 study of the esoteric content of Shakespeare's works and the possible
 practical use of his work for modern magical practitioners. It is of
 interest to both lovers of theatre and magic alike, with both academic
 and practical appeal, encouraging a creative approach from which further
 individual work can grow"—Provided by publisher.
Identifiers: LCCN 2021005114 (print) | LCCN 2021005115 (ebook) | ISBN
 9780738756790 (paperback) | ISBN 9780738756943 (ebook)
Subjects: LCSH: Shakespeare, William, 1564–1616—Knowledge and learning. |
 Magic. | Magic in literature. | Renaissance—England.
Classification: LCC PR3004 .C37 2021 (print) | LCC PR3004 (ebook) | DDC
 822.33—dc23
LC record available at https://lccn.loc.gov/2021005114
LC ebook record available at https://lccn.loc.gov/2021005115

Llewellyn Worldwide Ltd. does not participate in, endorse, or have any authority or responsibility concerning private business transactions between our authors and the public.

All mail addressed to the author is forwarded but the publisher cannot, unless specifically instructed by the author, give out an address or phone number.

Any internet references contained in this work are current at publication time, but the publisher cannot guarantee that a specific location will continue to be maintained. Please refer to the publisher's website for links to authors' websites and other sources.

Llewellyn Publications
A Division of Llewellyn Worldwide Ltd.
2143 Wooddale Drive
Woodbury MN 55125-2989

www.llewellyn.com
Printed in the United States of America

*To my endlessly supportive love Stephen, whom
I first terrified at the Globe, and to all who have
walked the pathways of these mysteries.*

Contents

CONTENTS

Foreword

An Unassailable Weaving

WHEN WE GO reaching into the magical world of Shakespeare, we unveil not only the life of the sixteenth and early seventeenth-century theatre, but also the concepts upon which Renaissance magic drew—those ancient mysteries of the natural philosopher who was the wiser before modern science had been invented. These natural philosophers were themselves the successors of medieval magicians, who were in turn the inheritors of the classical mysteries: for each of them, the natural world and the unseen world were of one weaving, not confined to separate boxes as in our own time.

The word *mystery* is used here in its older sense of "a skill or art that belongs to professional practitioners," as when Othello bids Emilia to exercise her mystery as maidservant, and like a good Emilia, Emily Carding evokes Shakespeare's enchanting art for us, both with the skill of a performer and a producer, combining the acting of the rude mechanical Bottom with the high conductive magic of Prospero as she draws us deeper into the magical world of Shakespeare.

The secret art of theatre magic, of enacting and embodying the hidden world, is, of course, an actor's mystery, showing us what we have not yet seen and might not be able to imagine without their help. While we enjoy the play's unfolding of Shakespeare's many stories, we may be less aware of the supporting structures that go into the evocation of this magical world. That Shakespeare was evoking his plays upon the drawing board of the elements, the planets, and the music of the spheres should not surprise us, as he was both heir to the beliefs of the pre-Reformation world where magic was a tangible force and where nature spoke directly to the shepherd, but also to the new learning that was aboard, revealing the classical and ancient understandings of myth. Shakespeare was ancestrally open to the cardinal virtues of faith, hope, and charity, as well as to the world of divination, the alchemical processes, and the revolution of the heavens.

Just as country people were still putting out dishes of cream for the faeries with rustic folk charms and songs, so educated Hermeticists like Elizabeth I's adviser, Dr. John Dee, were invoking angels in good Latin. While Catholics and Puritans were both under threat of fines or worse for their lack of conformity to the Anglican Church, playwrights like Shakespeare were reaching even deeper than the Bible into the book of the ages to bring up the magical tales of Ovid, the ancient *Chronicles of Britain*, and the enchanted tales of times past, weaving them all into one unassailable mantle of magic.

This is what defines what is magical, this fusion and interweaving of one world with the other: the world of everyday disappointment and struggle with the creative world of the spirit that transcends all pain. The richness of this book takes us deeply down into Shakespeare's text, which, if you read it rightly, will also tell you how to move and act; as all actors will tell you, these movements are not the obvious signposts of stage directions like "exit pursued by a bear" or "enter severally," but the implicit movements embedded in any of his plays. For, as you read, you gradually understand that implicit gestures, movements, and speeches transport your body to act and move with the text. All that made up the actor in Shakespeare ensured that we could understand it too.

And so, since magic has to be performed and enacted, the reader is invited to engage with the text, to perform and bring forth the hidden world that is threaded through each play, to reveal the sparkling heavens, the vasty deep, and the glory of the universal globe in ritual, meditation, and sacred rite.

May you proceed peacefully on the way that unfolds before you, for you step with sure guidance, knowing that no ghost will "forebear thee…nor any ill come near thee." I am very glad to have been the beadswoman of Emily Carding's wonderful book, which, like a dear friend, comes in her place to guide you to this so potent art. May it mantle you about and bring you to blessedness!

Caitlín Matthews
OXFORD, 8 JUNE 2020

Introduction

Ye elves of hills, brooks, standing lakes and groves,
And ye that on the sands with printless foot
Do chase the ebbing Neptune and do fly him
When he comes back; you demi-puppets that
By moonshine do the green sour ringlets make,
Whereof the ewe not bites, and you whose pastime
Is to make midnight mushrooms, that rejoice
To hear the solemn curfew; by whose aid,
Weak masters though ye be, I have bedimm'd
The noontide sun, call'd forth the mutinous winds,
And 'twixt the green sea and the azured vault
Set roaring war: to the dread rattling thunder
Have I given fire and rifted Jove's stout oak
With his own bolt; the strong-based promontory
Have I made shake and by the spurs pluck'd up
The pine and cedar: graves at my command
Have waked their sleepers, oped, and let 'em forth
By my so potent art…

—*The Tempest*, ACT 5, SCENE 1

THUS SPEAKS SHAKESPEARE'S beloved mage Prospero in what is commonly thought of as his final play, and it is from this speech we take the title of this book. Many believe that Shakespeare based Prospero on himself at the end of his life, and that the breaking of his staff of power took the place of a broken quill that would write no more, a symbol of magic for the power of his words. But what if the comparison could be taken more literally? It is also thought that Prospero was Shakespeare's tribute to the queen's astrologer and famed occultist John Dee, but what if Shakespeare himself was knowledgeable in the magical arts and wove them into his writing? *So Potent Art* will take you on a journey through Shakespeare's works and unveil the mysteries within.

Enter Shakespeare's World...

Shakespeare's works were borne from a political and spiritual climate in flux. Modern science as we know it began to emerge and separate from its mother philosophies. Knowledge of the power and symbolism of the elements, alchemy, and the planets was still prevalent, as was a system of belief and practice known as Hermeticism, the chief principle of which was the interconnection of all things. There were also Christianized versions of ancient Jewish mysticism known as the Cabala at the forefront of the philosophical wisdom of the time, but these beliefs were giving way to what was to become more modern thinking.

The course of Shakespeare's life and work spanned the shift from the occult and alchemical bias of the Elizabethan age through to the humanist beliefs of the Jacobeans, yet as his contemporaries such as Marlowe and Jonson embraced the new perspective and cast scorn upon magical thinking, Shakespeare's works are steeped in classical romanticism and ancient lore. Dig deeper into the symbolism of his fantastical *Winter's Tale* and you will find echoes not only of the Eleusinian Mysteries of ancient Greece but also the Hermetic text *Asclepius*. Appropriately, there is much Cabalistic wisdom to be found in *The Merchant of Venice*, and whilst the magical content of plays such as *A Midsummer Night's Dream*, *The Tempest*, and *Macbeth* might appear to be obvious, there are many layers of meaning and symbolism to explore and much hidden wisdom to reveal.

This esoteric level of meaning can be found throughout Shakespeare's works alongside more overt references. Tragic events are often foretold by prophecy; herbs are used as both curse and cure; gods and goddesses may be called upon to play their part; and all comedies work through an alchemical process towards their sacred marriage. Of course, Shakespeare didn't only write plays, and we will also be looking at the secrets that may be gleaned from the sonnets and other poetry.

Whilst it is fascinating to explore this content from an academic viewpoint, as previous works by authors such as Frances Yates have done (and whose studies of Shakespeare's last plays in particular are invaluable), in *So Potent Art* we will be taking a further step and finding ways of applying this wisdom in our lives and incorporating it into our practices.

Is This Book for Me?

If you are a lover of Shakespeare's work, or even just drawn to his words and intrigued by the promise of "more things in heaven and earth…than are dreamt of in your philosophy" (*Hamlet*, act I, scene 5), then yes. If you are a magical practitioner who wants to bring poetry and theatre into your practice, then yes. If you are an actor or theatre practitioner who wants to bring a dimension of magic and spirit to your understanding and performance, then yes. And if you are none of these things, but the light of curiosity is lit within your soul and you have read so far and wish to continue reading, then yes, this book is for you. Welcome.

What Is the Magic of Shakespeare?

Oh yeah, but the theatre's magic, isn't it?
You should know. Stand on this stage, say the
right words with the right emphasis at the
right time. Oh, you can make men weep.

—The Doctor, *Doctor Who*, "The Shakespeare Code"

Starting with the broadest and yet most concise definition of magic as a discipline, it is best described as the art of causing change to our outer and/or inner reality in accordance with our will (how appropriate that this should also be Shakespeare's first name). This is meant, of course, as something quite separate from the art of stage magic or illusion, yet since we are "treading the boards" as the subject of this work, the distinction

will be made clear should it become necessary. However, in the context of this work, "magic" may also be taken to mean the esoteric mysteries contained within Shakespeare's work. Some of these references are in plain sight and some are hidden except from those with eyes to see. However, "the magic of Shakespeare" does not only mean those references and secrets to be found within the works. There are many ways in which the works may be taken and adapted for magical intent with a modern or postmodern approach. The act of speaking his words or invoking his archetypal characters with a magical intent and in a repurposed context can be a powerful tool for ritual and self-development. This book's aim is to make Shakespeare's work, and the magic and mysteries contained within it, not only accessible but also useful to the reader.

How Is It Useful?

So Potent Art is ordered into twelve chapters. We begin with an introduction into the world of Shakespeare's lifetime that will provide a foundation to our understanding, looking at the political, philosophical, and spiritual influences that surrounded and informed him. In this chapter we will look at source material that was likely available to Shakespeare at the time, such as Agrippa's *Three Books of Occult Philosophy*, Ovid, *The Chaldean Oracles*, and the *Hermetica*. We will also look at Shakespeare's fellow writers of the time and compare the attitude to magic within their works.

Looking at the lives and works of notable figures such as John Dee, Francis Bacon, Giulio Camillo, Giordano Bruno, and Robert Fludd, we will see how all these influences helped create the landscape of Shakespeare's plays in the form of the sacred architecture of the theatres themselves.

The next three chapters of the book cover different categories of magic and the mysteries that may be found within Shakespeare's works. This begins in the second chapter with an examination of the Hermetic content of the works, noting how mentions of the elements and planets may inform our understanding of character, and ends with an exercise that gives a Shakespearean twist to setting up sacred space! Chapter 3 looks at the Cabalistic imagery within the works and how characters might be seen to relate to the Tree of Life. Chapter 4 looks at another aspect of Renaissance philosophy, namely alchemy, and reveals how many of Shakespeare's plays can be seen to have an alchemical structure or take his characters through alchemical journeys of initiation.

There's a shift of focus as we move into chapter 5 and look at otherworldly beings, starting with ghosts and hauntings, moving into the realm of Fairy in chapter 6, with chapter 7 delving into the world of witches, witchcraft, and embodiments of fate, with surprising revelations about *Macbeth*.

The eighth chapter continues the theme of fate with an exploration of the themes of divination, prophecy, and oracles. The ninth chapter looks at encounters with deity and how Shakespeare wrote powerful invocations to gods, goddesses, and lesser spirits both good and evil, how these powers are called upon for blessings and curses, and how we might use these to enrich our own lives. The tenth chapter looks at how Shakespeare used the rich language of plants in his work and how understanding this language can bring a deeper understanding of the plays, as well as how we can use this knowledge practically.

Each of these chapters is accompanied by practical suggestions, rituals, and exercises for you to try that will enhance your understanding not only of Shakespeare's work but also of yourself.

Chapter 11 returns to the modern day and a more generalised look at the connection between theatre and magic and why it is still relevant. This includes the concept of theatre as magic, the theatre building as a temple, and the actor as a magician, from the common roots in the ritual theatre of ancient Greece to those who consciously combine (or recombine) the disciplines today, and the possible applications and benefits outside the world of theatre.

The final chapter embraces a creative postmodern aesthetic and guides you through the process of creating your own piece of ritual theatre using Shakespeare's words. Not only is this chapter full of creative suggestions, but it also includes an example of a finished piece of ritual theatre created entirely from reordered Shakespeare. We look at the power inherent in the language itself, the significance of iambic pentameter, and how our postmodern world could relate more to Shakespeare's early modern work than we might initially think.

Now Take My Hand...

The creation of this book has been a long journey, with many adventures along the way, some joyous, some challenging. As soon as I got my place at the University of Exeter

Fear Not!

Maybe you've picked up this book because you've seen a couple of productions and you think the concept of Shakespeare and magic is cool but the language is still a bit of a barrier. Don't worry! It's true that this is a deep dive into the mysteries of Shakespeare's works and may seem daunting to beginners, but if you need extra help understanding any of the passages we're looking at or you need more information and background to the plays, then there are some excellent online resources available to help you, including modern "translations." If this would be helpful to you, try https://www.nosweatshakespeare.com/.

A quick online search for "Shakespeare resources" will bring up a whole realm of delights! There are also some wonderful productions available to view online, which is the best way to get to know the plays. Check out https://globeplayer.tv/ for productions from Shakespeare's Globe, and search for "The Show Must Go Online" on YouTube for all of the Shakespeare plays performed on Zoom, the online conferencing software that became a lifeline during the global pandemic.

While we're looking at online resources, since many different versions and edits of Shakespeare's works exist, quotes are taken from opensourceshakespeare.org unless otherwise stated, so all readers should have access to the same source. You'll also find this resource really useful when we get to some of the exercises later.

Paulina inviting Leontes to take Hermione's hand

on the MFA Staging Shakespeare course in 2012, I knew that I wanted my particular focus to be the practical application of the esoteric content of Shakespeare. With two residencies at Shakespeare's Globe and spiritual pilgrimages to Italy led by the original artistic director of Shakespeare's Globe, Sir Mark Rylance (considered possibly the finest Shakespearean actor of his generation), and his spiritual advisor Peter Dawkins, I couldn't have asked for more inspiration.

However, when writing my final thesis on the subject, I was also going through a very painful divorce and losing all stability in my life, including facing the fact I would have to leave the land I had built up such a special connection with in Cornwall. I count it one of my greatest achievements that I was able to finish the thesis at all, but it was not as strong as it could have been and I've always wanted to come back to the idea and develop it further. Whilst the focus of the thesis was on practical ways that actors could bring magical training into their work, much of the applied wisdom remains the same when looking at how magical and spiritual practitioners can use Shakespeare. This work formed the foundation of this book, and the last few years have been spent researching and practicing alongside building up my acting career, touring the world, and being a solo parent.

What started as a thesis is now part theory and part lived experience, always with a practical gain for self-knowledge and illumination. I hope you'll enjoy taking this journey with me.

> It is required
> You do awake your faith. Then all stand still;
> On: those that think it is unlawful business
> I am about, let them depart.

> —Paulina, *The Winter's Tale*, ACT 5, SCENE 3

I stand now as Paulina and invite you to believe in magic. Just as she invites Leontes to take the outstretched hand of the newly reanimated Hermione in the magical closing scene of *The Winter's Tale*, I invite you to join me now in the journey through this book and see what new life can be breathed into our understanding of Shakespeare's works and how that wisdom can enrich every aspect of our lives.

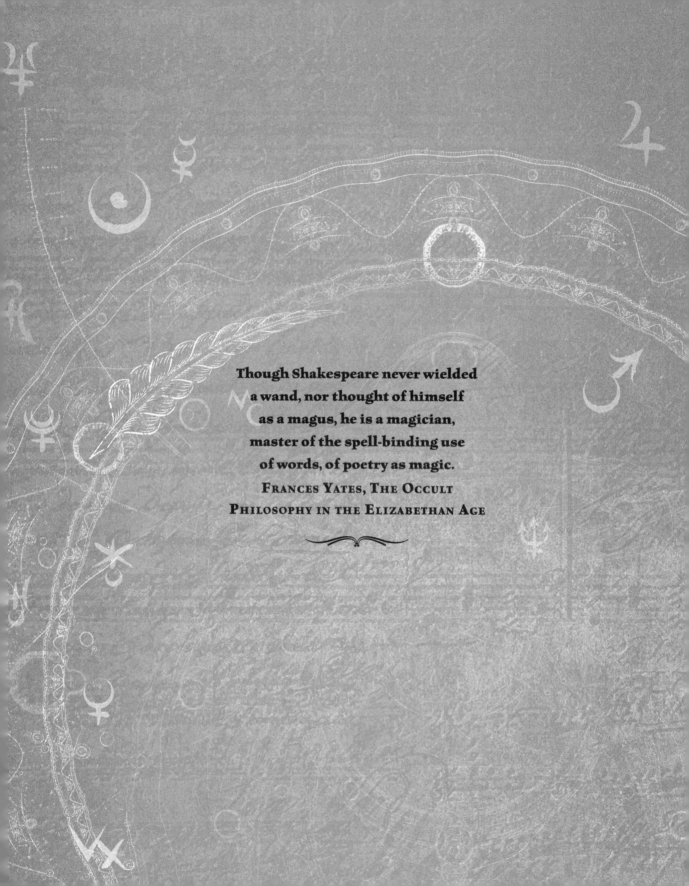

Though Shakespeare never wielded
a wand, nor thought of himself
as a magus, he is a magician,
master of the spell-binding use
of words, of poetry as magic.

FRANCES YATES, THE OCCULT
PHILOSOPHY IN THE ELIZABETHAN AGE

ONE

Shakespeare's Magical World

*S*hakespeare was living and working in a world where the esoteric was widely known and accepted as a part of science, but it was also a time of flux, when it was beginning to be dismissed and challenged by reactionary humanist thought. The occult philosophers of the time were such an influential part of society and so closely connected with the world of the expressive arts that they certainly would have been an influence on Shakespeare's work, as indeed would those who preceded them and helped to build the world as it was.

Origins of Renaissance Occult Philosophy

Esoteric discourse in Shakespeare's time melded together thoughts from various cultures and belief systems. The main three strands that form the foundation of Renaissance philosophy are Neoplatonism, Hermeticism, and a Christianised version of the Jewish mystical tradition of Cabala.

Earth, Air, Fire, and Water

The belief that the world was made of four elements, deriving from ancient Greece and the teachings of Empedocles (490 BCE–430 BCE), was prevalent at this time, and it should be remembered that what is now seen as mystery tradition teaching was then considered science, and it was during the Renaissance that modern science was born out of these ancient philosophies. The four elements in the macrocosm of the outer world are also reflected in the four humours of the microcosm, or inner world, a system first attributed to Hippocrates (460 BCE–370 BCE). These four humours, which formed the basis of medical diagnosis right up to the nineteenth century, were "blood" (air), "yellow bile" (fire), "black bile" (earth), and "phlegm" (water). These were also known as the sanguine (air), choleric (fire), melancholic (earth), and phlegmatic (water) humours. The combination of these four humours at work within the body and mind were believed to explain personality types and illnesses, and thus a cure was attained by rebalancing the humours within an individual.

Hermes Trismegistus

Hermeticism, a system of beliefs and practices based on the works of the philosopher known as Hermes Trismegistus, became extremely popular and influential during the Renaissance period. The collected works are known as the *Hermetica* or Corpus Hermeticum and were thought to be of ancient Egyptian origin, although now they are believed to be of a later period and of Greek origins. The core principles of this philosophical system, still popular amongst modern magical practitioners, are alchemy, astrology, and theurgy, the ultimate goal of which is to achieve perfection of the self by uniting with the gods (a process known as henosis) through prayer, evocation, and invocation. Another text that dealt with theurgy specifically and was an influence on Renaissance philosophy was the *Chaldean Oracles*, similarly mysterious in historical origins to the *Hermetica* but clearly Neoplatonic in thought.

Founders of Renaissance Neoplatonism

Commonly credited with reviving these ancient philosophies and igniting the Renaissance Neoplatonic movement are Marsilio Ficino (1433–1499) and Giovanni Pico della Mirandola (1463–1494). The Italian scholar and Catholic priest Ficino is known for breathing life back into Hermetic philosophy, and the Florentine Pico della Mirandola is famed for his introduction of Christian Cabala (this spelling to differentiate from the traditional Jewish Kabbalah or modern esoteric Qabalah) to the philosophical synthesis. This was around the year 1492, when the Jews were exiled from Spain and the wisdom of their mystical teaching started to spread into new territories. It is thought by some, including scholar Frances Yates, that the philosophical teachings of the mystic Ramon Llull (1232–1316), whose aim was to form a bridge between the three major religions of Islam, Christianity, and Judaism, could be considered a version of Christian Cabala, and indeed there are some common elements, but Ficino and Pico were the first to bring Hermeticism and Cabala together as a united philosophy. This fusion of Hermeticism and Cabala was first named "occult philosophy" by Cornelius Agrippa, author of *Three Books of Occult Philosophy* (first printed in 1531), which is still valued not only as a reference book but for its practical applications today.

Pico and Ficino inspired a number of other pre-Elizabethan Renaissance scholars, including Johannes Reuchlin (1455–1522), a German scholar who was fluent in Latin, Greek, and Hebrew, best known for *De Verbe Mirifico* (1494) and *De Arte Cabalistica* (1517), which is the first work on the Cabala written by a non-Jew. The artist Dürer (1471–1528) was inspired by occult philosophy in his work, and it's thought that his images featuring the melancholic humour contain details from Agrippa's text. Also bridging the gap into the Elizabethan era was the Franciscan monk Francesco Giorgi, a Christian Cabalist, whose works *De Harmonia Mundi* (1525) and *Problemata* (1536) were highly regarded.

Another extremely influential scholar of this time was the Swiss-German scientist and alchemist Paracelsus (1493–1541), who reinvented the system of the four humours and instead considered there to be three humours at work within the human body, inspired by alchemy. These were salt, sulphur, and mercury, representing the body, soul, and spirit in turn, and he considered the balance between these alchemical humours as the key to health and well-being. A pioneer of toxicology and chemical cures for maladies, he also believed in astrology and the influence of stars and planets.

Elizabeth R

The Faerie Queene

In her fair eyes two living lamps did flame,

Kindled above, at the heavenly Maker's light,

And darted fiery beams out of the same,

So passing piersant, and so wondrous bright,

That quite bereaved the rash beholder's sight.

—Edmund Spenser, *The Faerie Queene*, 1590

Elizabeth I ascended to the throne in 1558 and reigned until her death in 1603. The mysterious and seemingly untouchable Virgin Queen was a fitting monarch for the golden age of the Renaissance. Both her appearance and inner power were of such a mythic quality that she inspired great art and poetry, such as Spenser's *Faerie Queene*.

It is fairly well known that Elizabeth I took guidance from a court astrologer, a role filled by the legendary John Dee (more about him later), and it's thought she may have even used magical assistance to conjure the storms that aided the defeat of the Spanish Armada in 1588, something we cannot know for certain. What is certain is that she carefully crafted an image and atmosphere around herself that transcended mortal limits and became an icon of archetypal feminine beauty, intelligence, and strength.

Elizabeth as Goddess

Frances Yates has written extensively on the subject of the mythologizing of Elizabeth as the goddess Astraea and various guises of moon goddess throughout the literature of the time, including Shakespeare. Of course, it is during Elizabeth's reign that Shakespeare established himself as a poet and playwright, with current understanding placing his writing between the years 1590–1614.

It is fascinating to note that with the possible exception of the supposedly negative portrayal of magic in *Macbeth* (although I would suggest that the portrayal of witchcraft in *Macbeth* has far more depth and complexity to it than has perhaps popularly been imagined, and we will look at this in more detail later), Shakespeare's plays become more openly and overtly magical in the less receptive Jacobean era, when his contemporaries were more in line with current political and religious thought. There appears to be a nostalgia for the Elizabethan age and a desire to rekindle a more magical way of thinking, whilst such thought was being brutally persecuted in Europe and becoming increasingly dangerous at home.

John Dee

> Some people are affected more by tragedies, others by comic melodies, and others are affected generally in all cases. Some even react like that barbarian general who, when he heard musical instruments played very skilfully, said he preferred the neighing of his horse. He clearly proved by this that he was a disgrace and was unworthy of appearing to be human (Bruno 1998, 135).

One can't help but wonder whether it was blunt talk like this that cost Giordano Bruno his life at the stake in Rome in 1600. Certainly this key cultural figure appears to have been a very outspoken advocate of occult philosophy at a time when humanist beliefs were on the rise, and his execution at the turn of the century was not only symbolic of a significant shift in society but also a warning to all of the dangers of magical thinking. He spent a great deal of time in England during Shakespeare's working life, and his philosophical thought, together with a progressive approach to science and mathematics, had much in common with his more cautious contemporary John Dee (1527–1608).

Historian Frances Yates has observed that the mystical tradition to which Dee belonged, with his Hermetic beliefs and Vitruvian principles, "is the tradition to which a growing interest in stagecraft would have looked to for advice and assistance" (Yates 1969, 32). As the queen's astrologer and mathematical advisor, Dee is still an iconic figure today and a representative of Elizabethan as opposed to Jacobean culture. His involvement in the development of stagecraft in early modern England is undeniable. Not only was he known as a creator of spectacular and seemingly magical theatrical machines, such as a flying scarab that he created while a fellow at Trinity College, but he is also considered to be responsible for the popularity of Vitruvian principles. It is from these principles that we derive the concepts of microcosm and macrocosm, which are of profound significance in the forming of the early theatres, particularly the Globe, whose very name is evocative of this principle.

Though scarcity of evidence prevents us from knowing to what extent the construction of the early theatres were influenced by such esoteric thought, we will look later in this book at how they were most certainly present in the construction of Shakespeare's

Globe, which stands on London's South Bank today. However, it seems very likely that Dee's experiments and designs of moving statues were in Shakespeare's mind when he wrote the magical closing scene of *The Winter's Tale* and that Dee was an inspiration not only for Shakespeare's magus character of Prospero in *The Tempest*, but also for the less favourable magicians of Marlowe's Dr. *Faustus* and Jonson's *The Alchemist*.

The contrasts between these three plays neatly illustrate the differences between Shakespeare and the most well-known of his contemporary playwrights in terms of attitudes to magic and its practitioners. Ben Jonson used satirical comedy in *The Alchemist* as a "general attack upon the claims of occultists, prophetic poets, or any other enthusiasts to have special insight into the nature of reality" (Mebane 1992, 148), and although Marlowe's Dr. *Faustus* presents the alluring prospect of attaining power, riches, and wisdom through occult means, his ultimate punishment of being dragged to hell shows in the end that the "radical or rebellious impulses in Faustus himself are continually undermined by a series of images and ironies which insist on a conventional Christian orthodoxy" (Mangan 1987, 102). On the other hand, we find in *The Tempest* "a just judge, or a virtuous and reforming monarch, who uses his magico-scientific powers for good" (Yates 1975, 94). At the play's conclusion, his work is done, and in what is both a parallel and a polar opposition to Marlowe's Faustus—who, despairing, asks that his colleagues pray for him—Prospero asks for the audience's "indulgence"—that they should put their hands together in the prayer of applause—to "set him free" so that he may ultimately ascend to heaven.

John Dee

Giordano Bruno

The Jacobean Age

James VI of Scotland became James I of England upon Elizabeth's death in 1603 and reigned until his death in 1625. As the Elizabethan Age of Hermetic philosophy gave way to the Jacobean Age, with its witch-hunts and paranoia about magical practice and occult philosophy, Dee fell out of favour. However, Shakespeare thrived under James's reign, with the monarch's love of theatre prompting him to give patronage to Shakespeare's troupe, who then appropriately renamed themselves "The King's Men." Whilst Marlowe's *Faustus* (written in Elizabethan times) painted magical pursuits as shallow and ultimately dangerous for the immortal soul of the magician, and Jonson, writing in the less-favourable Jacobean era, chose to kick the magus while he was down in his scathing portrayal of Dee, Shakespeare urged us to rescue him from the isolation and disgraced state that Dee had been reduced to. Although Dee did not meet the dramatic end of Giordano Bruno, having wisdom enough to see that the political climate in Italy would be violently unfavourable towards him, he died utterly poverty-stricken and outcast from society. It was a brave political move on Shakespeare's part to portray magic and the magician so favourably in his post-Elizabethan masterpiece *The Tempest* and a bold statement indeed for what is widely considered to be his final noncollaborative work.

Did Dee and Shakespeare Meet?

It seems likely that Dee and Shakespeare would have known each other; after all, why would he choose to make so powerful a statement if they were not at least acquainted? However, since so little is known of the details of Shakespeare's life, it is difficult to say how well. Perhaps Shakespeare might have studied in Dee's library? Frances Yates notes that according to Dee's diaries, clerks and record keepers would often visit Dee's library in order to find rare tomes and papers that were not available elsewhere, which she observes gives "an interesting glimpse of the use of Dee's house as a kind of combined British Museum and Public Record Office" (Yates 1969, 16). Although she doesn't directly link the statement to Shakespeare, Yates also notes of the contents of the library that "A reader who knew no Greek and not much Latin could use Dee's library" (Yates 1969, 12), which brings to mind Ben Jonson's tribute to the author, a line of which famously reads "And though thou hadst small Latin and less Greek…"

Whether or not Shakespeare had access to Dee's extraordinary library at Mortlake, there are certain key texts that were so popular at the time he would almost certainly have been familiar with and whose influence can be seen in his work. The two works most relevant to this discussion are the *Corpus Hermiticum* or *Hermetica* (which also includes the *Asclepius*) and Cornelius Agrippa's *Three Books of Occult Philosophy*.

Prospero's Books

The *Corpus Hermeticum* is a book of ancient Greco-Egyptian philosophy of mysterious origins that teaches principles regarding the seven planets, the four elements, and the nature of divinity in the form of a dialogue between a teacher/father figure and his pupil/son. The mythical Hermes Trismegistus ("thrice-honoured") was the Greek equivalent of the Egyptian god Thoth, and the true name of the presumably mortal author of these works remains unknown. That does not, however, diminish the legacy of the *Hermetica*, the principles of which were known in Shakespeare's time to scholars and laypeople alike.

Cornelius Agrippa, in contrast, was a contemporary of Shakespeare's whose weighty tome has been the primary sourcebook of Western eoteric tradition for the last five hundred years. Unlike the oft-opaque philosophical musings of the *Hermetica*, *Three Books of Occult Philosophy* is highly practical and instructive in all manner of occult and magical practices, including the powers and influences of the planets and how to harness them, magical alphabets, geomancy, necromancy, the elements, the power of music, the power of numbers, divination, and the Kabbalah. Interestingly, Agrippa also has much to say on the simple power of words, a most important principle when considering a magical dimension to theatrical performance:

> Words therefore are the fittest medium betwixt the speaker and the hearer, carrying with them not only the conception of the mind, but also the virtue of the speaker…oftentimes they change not only the hearers, but also other bodies and things that have no life (Agrippa 1993, 211).

Francis Bacon

No overview of major figures of Renaissance philosophy would be complete without mention of Francis Bacon (1561–1626), one of the most significant contributors to knowledge of the age and not only a contemporary of Shakespeare's but also one of the chief alternative candidates for the authorship of his works. Although his main career was within the field of law, firstly as chief counsel to Elizabeth I and then progressing to the lofty heights of the title "Baron Verulam" under James I, he is also credited with being the founder of the empirical method in modern science. Although alchemy and science were still very much hand-in-hand at the time he was working, the extent to which Bacon may or may not have subscribed to magical practices remains a subject for debate. Whilst extremely Christian and reflecting the Neoplatonic philosophies of the time, his writings appear for the most part to be highly sceptical of occult practices and thinking. For example, his view on divination and prophecies, as clearly stated in his essays, was that "they ought all to be despised…almost all of them…have been impostures, and by idle and crafty brains merely contrived and feigned after the event past" (Bacon 2008, 404).

Despite his rational approach and scientific method, albeit all in the service of what he held to be the "true god," there are certainly symbolic depths to his philosophical works that have led many to theorise not only that he was the secret author of Shakespeare's works (it is known that at the very least he wrote poetry and was involved in writing and organising the revels at Gray's Inn), but also that he was a Rosicrucian and perhaps an alchemist. One of the richest pieces of his writing for this mode of thinking is his unfinished utopian fable *New Atlantis,* in which travellers are welcomed to an idyllic island and learn of the spiritual priorities of the inhabitants. He talks of the establishment of an order known as "Salomon's House" that was "dedicated to the study of the Works and Creatures of God" and was established to trade not in material goods "but only for God's first creature, which was Light" (Bacon 1996, 472).

It is no wonder with writings like these that many have theorised Bacon may himself have been a Rosicrucian or more deeply involved in esoteric practices than popular history tells us. Could the reference to Salomon's House (Salomon being an alternative spelling of Solomon) in any way infer familiarity with that most famous of grimoires, the *Key of Solomon,* or is it simply a biblical reference? As to the extent of his influence or involvement in the works of Shakespeare, we can only theorise about that too. An in-depth analysis of this possibility may be found in Peter Dawkins's *The Shakespeare Enigma,* in which the author comes to the conclusion that

> the Shakespeare work is really a group work, led by the group's "Apollo" or
> master artist, in the manner of a Renaissance studio, and that they had an
> extraordinary vision to follow and an unfolding plan to carry out—a plan that

was somehow in harmony with certain celestial events and time-cycles of the world…so that one day, once we are through the dark crucifying materialism that Bacon himself foresaw the possibility of and prayed would not happen, there might be a golden age or heaven on earth, for everyone and everything (Dawkins 2004, 414).

Whether or not he was involved in the authorship of the plays, the investigation of the question has led to the unveiling of some fascinating esoteric depths within the plays and sonnets.

Divine Camillo

Another relevant contemporary of Shakespeare's is Giulio Camillo, whose Hermetic memory system took the form of a small round wooden theatre known as a "memory theatre," where the observer would not sit in the audience but rather stand in the place of the actor. Designed as an aid to remarkable feats of memory, the system involved the visualisation of objects placed within a specific landscape of locations that would represent certain words or notions. There are workable versions of his system that utilise only visualisation, but the physical structure itself was a wonder to behold, built on Hermetic and Cabalistic principles with a seven-fold structure: "The theatre rises in seven grades or steps, which are divided by seven gangways representing the seven planets" (Yates 1992, 141). Camillo was a much-loved public figure, known as "divine Camillo," and though it cannot be proved, one wonders if Shakespeare did not find in his nobility inspiration for his character of the same name in *The Winter's Tale*.

In what is possibly her finest and most popular work, *The Art of Memory*, Frances Yates theorises that not only were the first theatres potentially inspired by Camillo's model, but that his successor in philosophy, Robert Fludd, may well have used the actual Globe stage as the theatre for his memory exercises. In our postmodern times of instant information retrieval on the internet, we marvel at the memory feats achieved by actors in Shakespeare's time. Though we know relatively little about their process, we know there was very little time for rehearsal and that they held a great number of plays in their memory at any given time, often with only a few days to learn their parts. It may be possible that they utilised something like these esoteric memory systems.

The Globe

The Globe Theatre was a magical theatre, a cosmic theatre, a religious theatre, an actor's theatre, designed to give the fullest support to the voices and gestures of the player as they enacted the drama of the life of man within the Theatre of the World (Yates 1969, 189).

Those of us who have stood in the incredible atmosphere of Shakespeare's Globe, the modern reconstruction that has stood on London's South Bank since 1997, have a sense of how extraordinary the "wooden O" that housed many of Shakespeare's plays in his lifetime must have been. The design of these early modern playhouses, the first theatres in England, would seem peculiar to modern theatregoers otherwise: wooden constructions built using green oak, circular, with a large open area in the centre for the "groundlings" (the cheapest tickets for the lowest classes) to stand, with three floors of raised seating surrounding them—the higher the seat, the higher the status (and an extra penny would buy you the luxury of a cushion), all crowned with a thatched roof. There is something truly magical about the Globe that we have today (and we will look at that in much more depth later in the book), but how much magical intent might there have been behind the original construction? There's certainly a powerful energy to be felt at the nearby archaeological remains of its sister theatre, the Rose.

Yates's passion for the theory of Vitruvian thinking behind the construction of the two original Globe theatres (it was rebuilt after burning down in 1613 and its replacement stood until 1644) is almost religious in its fervour, but sadly there is a dearth of archaeological evidence to prove or disprove it either way. We do know that the architect credited with reviving Vitruvian proportion in English theatres, Inigo Jones (1573–1652), also known as Vitruvius Britannicus, was closely associated with Fludd and likely heavily influenced by the work of Dee, but we can only theorise that earlier constructions such as the Globe might have also shown these influences in their design. As the story goes, the original Globe was built by carpenter Peter Street at the behest of London's most famous player of the time, Richard Burbage, using the wood from his first theatre, named simply the Theatre, which he had dismantled due to disputes with the owner of the land it was built on.

Though we may know little of the intricacies and intent behind its design, the name of the theatre itself, the inclusion of the symbolic heavens above and "hell" beneath, and other Hermetic iconography such as the two pillars on the stage (although their original purpose may have been purely practical) does lend itself to the idea of the microcosm reflecting the macrocosm. Certainly Shakespeare himself makes this very clear in Jacques's famous monologue from *As You Like It*, when he says "All the world's a stage" (act 2, scene 7).

Metamorphoses: The Ovidian Influence

TITUS: Lucius, what book is that she tosseth so?

YOUNG LUCIUS: Grandsire, 'tis Ovid's *Metamorphoses*;

  My mother gave it me.

MARCUS: For love of her that's gone,

  Perhaps she cull'd it from among the rest.

TITUS: Soft! See how busily she turns the leaves!

  What would she find? Lavinia, shall I read?

  This is the tragic tale of Philomel,

  And treats of Tereus' treason and his rape:

  And rape, I fear, was root of thine annoy.

—*Titus Andronicus*, ACT 4, SCENE I

In the above quote from *Titus Andronicus*, Shakespeare references his source material for the play in a wonderfully meta moment. It is well known that Ovid, in particular his collection of poetic tales of mythic transformations known as *Metamorphoses*, was a huge influence on many playwrights in the Renaissance, particularly Shakespeare, and many of his magical allusions originate within this classical work. Though it's possible that Shakespeare may have been able to read the poems in the original Latin, it is more likely that he would have used the popular English translation by Arthur Golding that was contemporary to his time. Writers of the time were not referencing the works to be especially clever or knowing—in fact, it was presumed that many of their audience would have been familiar with the work, since Ovid and the ancient myths contained within was an important part of the most basic education at the time, and this would have informed and enriched their enjoyment of the plays. The inclusion of Ovid is more a Renaissance equivalent of a pop-culture reference.

Titus Andronicus:

A Brief Summary

I once played Tamora in a production of Titus where the set was entirely white and all the cast were painted white and wearing entirely white (apart from Aaron the Moor, who was painted red), and by the end we were all extremely red. Because blood. This is a play about the cycle of bloody vengeance, with a Roman general, Titus, and the Queen of the Goths, Tamora, constantly upping the violence against each other, culminating in him baking her two adult sons in a pie and giving it to her to eat. This play also features what is possibly the first black power speech in English literature from Tamora's lover, Aaron, when defending their mixed-race child. The play is an absolute hoot and ends with an enormous body count.

Whilst all of Shakespeare's works are littered with references to Ovid's work and the ancient Greco-Roman myths, some of his works owe a greater debt to them than others. Apart from *Titus Andronicus*, which as shown above not only echoes themes but also makes direct reference to the works, and *Cymbeline*, which similarly has the heroine reading the Ovidian tale of Tereus and Procne, the most obvious examples are Shakespeare's epic poem *Venus and Adonis* and one of his most popular comedies, *A Midsummer Night's Dream*. The latter not only exquisitely parodies the tragic tale of Pyramus and Thisbe but the theme of lovers who are forced into extreme circumstances by the disapproval of their families runs throughout (this theme, of course, also forms the plot of *Romeo and Juliet*), including characters directly comparing their circumstances to Apollo and Daphne—mythological figures featured in *Metamorphoses*:

> The wildest hath not such a heart as you.
> Run when you will, the story shall be changed:
> Apollo flies, and Daphne holds the chase;
> The dove pursues the griffin; the mild hind
> Makes speed to catch the tiger; bootless speed,
> When cowardice pursues and valour flies
>
> —*A Midsummer Night's Dream*, ACT 2, SCENE I

One of the most intriguing (and also blatantly lifted) appearances of Ovid within Shakespeare is the use of Medea's invocation to Hekate from book 7 of *Metamorphoses* as Prospero's farewell to his magical art—the very speech that opens this book and from which it takes its title. We will look at this speech in more detail both in chapter 9 when we work with invocations and in chapter 12 when we look at constructing ritual theatre using Shakespeare's text as raw material.

There is also direct comparison to be made with Ovid's tale of Pygmalion, where a sculptor falls in love with a statue of his own creating and brings her to life with the magical closing scene of *The Winter's Tale*. However, as you will see in the next section, there are far more intriguing and esoteric secrets within this play to be revealed when we look at the inspiration that Shakespeare drew from the books of the *Hermetica* by Hermes Trismegistus.

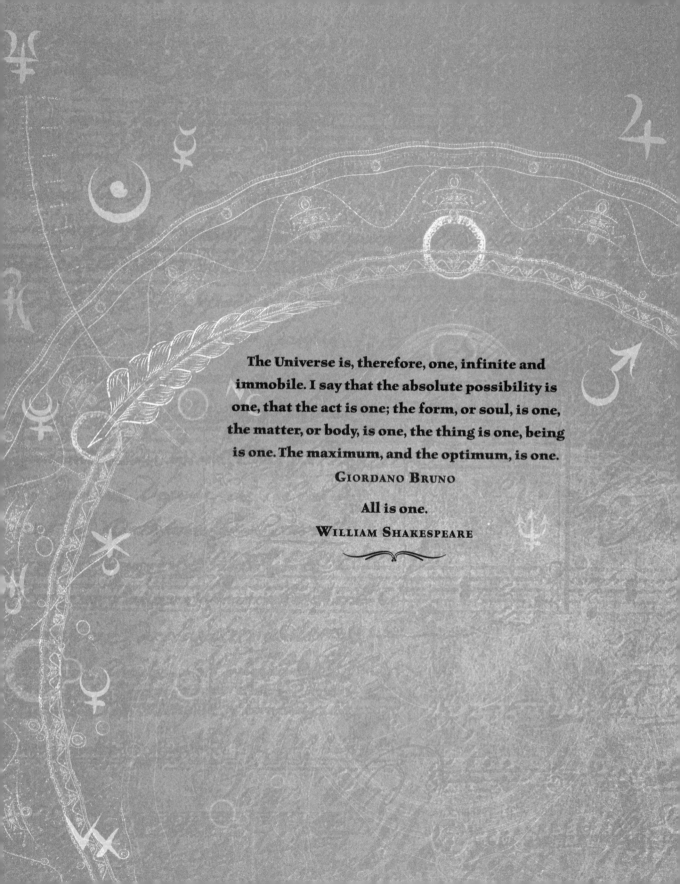

The Universe is, therefore, one, infinite and immobile. I say that the absolute possibility is one, that the act is one; the form, or soul, is one, the matter, or body, is one, the thing is one, being is one. The maximum, and the optimum, is one.

GIORDANO BRUNO

All is one.

WILLIAM SHAKESPEARE

TWO

Hermetic Shakespeare

The Hermetic philosophy, with its three main strands of astrology, alchemy, and theurgy, is ultimately concerned with uniting with the divine and the interconnection of all things. The aim of its practice is the perfection of the soul so that there is no further need to reincarnate on earth. Shakespeare was writing at a time when the language of the planets, elements, and alchemical transformation was readily understood by most people of a standard level of education, and whilst he wrote bawdy jokes for the groundlings (seriously, Shakespeare is filthy), he also wrote deeper meanings behind his characters and stories for those with the eyes to see or ears to hear. These philosophies may not be so well known now amongst the general populace, save for the enduring popularity of a daily horoscope, but the wisdom remains for those who seek it and rewards us with a deeper understanding of the works, ourselves, and the world around us.

King Lear:
A Brief Summary

Lear, the elderly King of Britain, divides his kingdom between his three daughters for their dowries, planning on giving the most generous portion to the one who will swear they love him most. His older daughters, Goneril and Regan, give eloquent but insincere declarations of love, but Cordelia, his youngest and favourite, speaks honestly and plainly. He disowns and banishes Cordelia (and also banishes a loyal follower, Kent, for pointing out that he's being a douche) and splits his kingdom between Regan and Goneril, who treat him (and pretty much everyone else, including each other) appallingly. Meanwhile, the elderly Duke of Gloucester is also having family trouble with his two boys, Edgar and Edmund, the latter of whom was got out of wedlock and plots against his brother to gain his land and influence. He's pretty hot stuff, so Regan and Goneril fight over him, even though they already have husbands. (One of the husbands dies, so…it's okay.) Lear goes mad but finds redemption in the wilds and is eventually reconciled with Cordelia, but…spoiler alert…almost everyone dies. Because, y'know: tragedy.

Astrology

That which is above is from that which is below,

and that which is below is from that which is above.

—*The Emerald Tablet of Hermes Trismegistus*

The above quotation, popularly simplified to "As above, so below," is one of the best-known tenets of Hermetic philosophy that endures as a universal truth to this day and might be said to be the simplest way to sum up occult philosophy and the function of theurgic magic in one sentence, if one were ever required to do such a thing! The most obvious application of this principle is the science or art of astrology, the influence of the planets on human behaviour and characteristics as well as the larger events in the world. We hear varied perspectives on this starry wisdom through the different characters in Shakespeare's plays, and we can perhaps extrapolate something of Shakespeare's own beliefs from the moral and intellectual character of those who respect or mock these principles.

King Lear

An excellent example of this is found in act 1, scene 2 of *King Lear*, where the difference in belief between Gloucester and his bastard son Edmund might be put down to the generation gap and a societal shift away from magical thinking, were it not that Gloucester's conclusions about the astrological climate are entirely accurate to the tragic unfolding of the story:

> GLOUCESTER: These late eclipses in the sun and moon
> portend no good to us. Though the wisdom of nature can
> reason it thus and thus, yet nature finds itself scourg'd by
> the sequent effects. Love cools, friendship falls off, brothers
> divide. In cities, mutinies; in countries, discord; in palaces,
> treason; and the bond crack'd 'twixt son and father. This
> villain of mine comes under the prediction; there's son
> against father: the King falls from bias of nature; there's
> father against child. We have seen the best of our time.

Machinations, hollowness, treachery, and all ruinous disorders follow us disquietly to our graves. Find out this villain, Edmund; it shall lose thee nothing; do it carefully. And the noble and true-hearted Kent banish'd! his offence, honesty! 'Tis strange. (exit)

EDMUND: This is the excellent foppery of the world, that, when we are sick in fortune, often the surfeit of our own behaviour, we make guilty of our disasters the sun, the moon, and the stars; as if we were villains on necessity; fools by heavenly compulsion; knaves, thieves, and treachers by spherical pre-dominance; drunkards, liars, and adulterers by an enforc'd obedience of planetary influence; and all that we are evil in, by a divine thrusting on. An admirable evasion of whore-master man, to lay his goatish disposition to the charge of a star! My father compounded with my mother under the Dragon's Tail, and my nativity was under Ursa Major, so that it follows I am rough and lecherous. Fut! I should have been that I am, had the maidenliest star in the firmament twinkled on my bastardizing.

Though they both come to rather sticky ends (most characters in *King Lear* do, to be fair), Gloucester is an innocent victim of wicked plots and Edmund dies regretting his intensively wicked plotting, so we may deduce that the author is siding with the Hermetic beliefs held by the senior character. This is further emphasised in a brief return to the theme in act 4, scene 3, where the loyal Kent declares, "It is the stars, the stars above us, govern our conditions."

The Stars and Body Parts

Of course, it is not only characters with a tragic destiny who are ruled by the stars, and though we will look at the real depth behind Shakespeare's comedies later in the book, it is worthwhile noting that astrological knowledge was even used humorously. In this scene from act 1, scene 3 of *Twelfth Night*, Sir Toby Belch appears to mock

Andrew Aguecheek for his ignorance whilst boisterously encouraging him to dance and be merry:

> SIR TOBY BELCH: Wherefore are these things hid? Where-
> fore have these gifts a curtain before 'em? Are they like to
> take dust, like Mistress Mall's picture? Why dost thou not go
> to church in a galliard and come home in a coranto? My very
> walk should be a jig; I would not so much as make water but
> in a sink-a-pace. What dost thou mean? Is it a world to hide
> virtues in? I did think, by the excellent constitution of thy
> leg, it was formed under the star of a galliard.
>
> SIR ANDREW AGUECHEEK: Ay, 'tis strong, and it does
> indifferent well in a dun-coloured stock. Shall we set about
> some revels?
>
> SIR TOBY BELCH: What shall we do else? Were we not born
> under Taurus?
>
> SIR ANDREW AGUECHEEK: Taurus! That's sides and heart.
>
> SIR TOBY BELCH: No, sir; it is legs and thighs. Let me see
> thee caper; ha! Higher: ha, ha! Excellent!

However, audiences in Shakespeare's time may well have known that they were both wrong. Agrippa tells us that

> the several signs also of the zodiac take care of their members. So Aries gov-
> erns the head and face, Taurus the neck, Gemini the arms, and shoulders, Leo
> heart, stomach, liver and back, Virgo the bowels, and bottom of the stomach,
> Libra the kidneys, thighs and buttocks, Scorpius the genitals, the privates, and
> womb, Sagittarius the thigh and groins, Capricornus the knees, Aquarius the
> legs and shins, Pisces the feet (Agrippa 1993, 73).

Although this knowledge may seem a minor detail, it can add greatly to our under-standing of the plays to know how Renaissance occult philosophy held that everything was ruled by the planets or signs (which in turn are ruled by the planets), from land masses and great events down to every orifice on the face. For instance, "the right nostril to Mars, the left to Venus" (Agrippa 1993, 72).

Harmony of Stars and the Soul

This heavenly influence also applied beyond the body to the balance of the soul itself:

> But to hasten to the harmony of the soul, we must inquire into it by those mediums by which it passeth to us, i.e. by celestial bodies, and spheres; knowing therefore what are the powers of the soul to which the planets answer, we shall by those things which have been spoken of before, the more easily know their agreements amongst themselves. For the Moon governs the powers of increasing and decreasing; the phantasy and wits depends on Mercury; the concupiscible virtue on Venus; the vital on the Sun; the irascible on Mars; the natural on Jupiter; the receptive on Saturn (Agrippa 1993, 355).

This understanding is inherent to a full appreciation of Shakespeare's work, knowing that when his characters talk of the stars and planets influencing their lives and events, they are not simply being poetic but directly engaging with powers that have very real influence. As we have already discussed, Shakespeare was writing at a time when the old philosophies were being driven out by new thinking, and he continually makes his position clear in his portrayal of elder wisdom and the need to respect it, as with Edmund and Gloucester.

It sometimes feels as though the author is reaching out through his characters to teach us the importance of balance and communion with the planetary powers, as in this extraordinary passage from act 1, scene 3 of *Troilus and Cressida*, Shakespeare's rarely staged take on the Trojan War:

> The heavens themselves, the planets and this centre
> Observe degree, priority and place,
> Insisture, course, proportion, season, form,
> Office and custom, in all line of order;
> And therefore is the glorious planet Sol
> In noble eminence enthroned and sphered
> Amidst the other; whose medicinable eye
> Corrects the ill aspects of planets evil,
> And posts, like the commandment of a king,

Sans cheque to good and bad: but when the planets

In evil mixture to disorder wander,

What plagues and what portents! what mutiny!

What raging of the sea! shaking of earth!

Commotion in the winds! frights, changes, horrors,

Divert and crack, rend and deracinate

The unity and married calm of states

Quite from their fixure! O, when degree is shaked,

Which is the ladder to all high designs,

Then enterprise is sick! How could communities,

Degrees in schools and brotherhoods in cities,

Peaceful commerce from dividable shores,

The primogenitive and due of birth,

Prerogative of age, crowns, sceptres, laurels,

But by degree, stand in authentic place?

Take but degree away, untune that string,

And, hark, what discord follows! each thing meets

In mere oppugnancy: the bounded waters

Should lift their bosoms higher than the shores

And make a sop of all this solid globe.

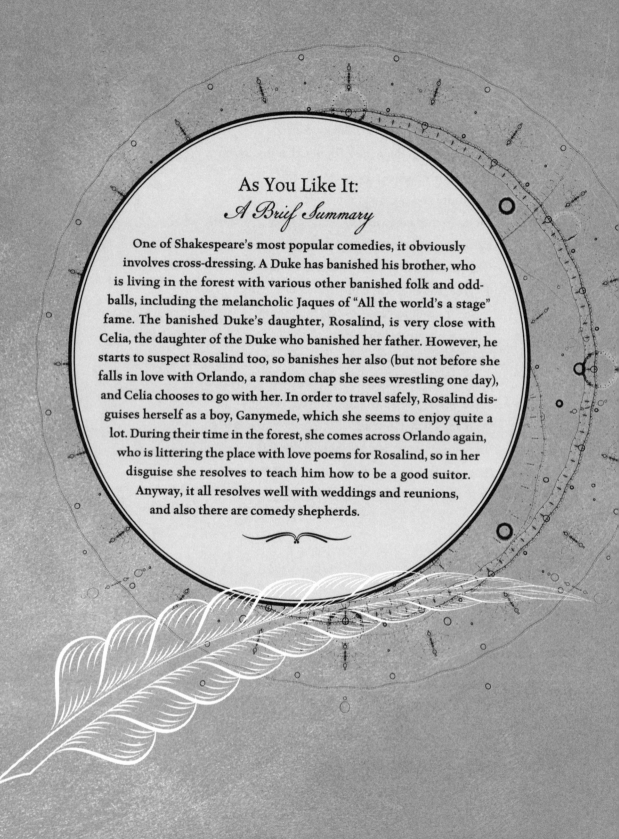

As You Like It:
A Brief Summary

One of Shakespeare's most popular comedies, it obviously involves cross-dressing. A Duke has banished his brother, who is living in the forest with various other banished folk and odd-balls, including the melancholic Jaques of "All the world's a stage" fame. The banished Duke's daughter, Rosalind, is very close with Celia, the daughter of the Duke who banished her father. However, he starts to suspect Rosalind too, so banishes her also (but not before she falls in love with Orlando, a random chap she sees wrestling one day), and Celia chooses to go with her. In order to travel safely, Rosalind disguises herself as a boy, Ganymede, which she seems to enjoy quite a lot. During their time in the forest, she comes across Orlando again, who is littering the place with love poems for Rosalind, so in her disguise she resolves to teach him how to be a good suitor. Anyway, it all resolves well with weddings and reunions, and also there are comedy shepherds.

The Seven Ages of Man

One of Shakespeare's most famous speeches regarding the classical correspondences of the seven planets and the sevenfold structure appears in act 2, scene 7 of *As You Like It*, where Jaques ponders the seven ages of man:

All the world's a stage,
And all the men and women merely players,
They have their exits and entrances,
And one man in his time plays many parts,
His acts being seven ages. At first the infant,
Mewling and puking in the nurse's arms.
Then, the whining schoolboy with his satchel
And shining morning face, creeping like snail
Unwillingly to school. And then the lover,
Sighing like furnace, with a woeful ballad
Made to his mistress' eyebrow. Then a soldier,
Full of strange oaths, and bearded like the pard,
Jealous in honour, sudden, and quick in quarrel,
Seeking the bubble reputation
Even in the cannon's mouth. And then the justice
In fair round belly, with good capon lin'd,
With eyes severe, and beard of formal cut,
Full of wise saws, and modern instances,
And so he plays his part. The sixth age shifts
Into the lean and slipper'd pantaloon,
With spectacles on nose, and pouch on side,
His youthful hose well sav'd, a world too wide,
For his shrunk shank, and his big manly voice,
Turning again towards childish treble, pipes
And whistles in his sound. Last scene of all,
That ends this strange eventful history,
Is second childishness and mere oblivion,
Sans teeth, sans eyes, sans taste, sans everything.

This speech mostly fits the classical structure but with one significant difference. At first examination, the age ruled by the sun appears to be absent. The infant is the moon, the schoolboy Mercury, the lover Venus, the soldier Mars, the justice Jupiter, and old age Saturn. The sun rules the age of virility, which should appear between the lover and soldier, but instead we appear to have two ages of Saturn. It is possible that Shakespeare is teaching an esoteric lesson here, in that when we die and lose our attachment to our physical world, we rejoin the spiritual source, represented by the sun. If we wished to take this theory on board, we might also take the repeated use of the words *sans* ("without") as a pun of the missing planetary body, the sun. It's also interesting to note that the speech appears in scene 7 of the second act. Of course, we cannot know the author's intention for certain, but this sequence seems to make sense, especially when we understand the initiatory journey contained in many of the plays, which we will look at as we continue to delve deeper throughout this book.

Ruling Planets of Characters

But then there was a star danced,

and under that was I born.

—Beatrice, *Much Ado About Nothing*, ACT 2, SCENE 1

Especially useful for actors or directors but of interest to anyone wishing to deepen their understanding of Shakespeare's characters is working out what planet or sign the character most embodies. Sometimes the clue is in the character's name or they will simply declare that they are born under a particular planet, but if we do not have these clues to go on, we can theorise ourselves about which planet's qualities best fit. Hermeticism is primarily concerned with the seven classical planets, and there are remnants of this sacred structure of seven in our society even now, including the days of the week. Let's take a look at each planet in the order of the day of the week over which they rule and find examples of characters which may be ruled by them.

Sol/ The Sun

The sun is associated primarily with royalty, leadership, and all the qualities that make a good leader, as well as with wealth and success, so the most obvious connection to make is with Shakespeare's kings. Since every virtuous quality also has its shadowy vice, this also means the villainous kings might also be considered to be ruled by the sun, as the negative qualities associated with our star are arrogance, tyranny, insatiable ambition, and pride.

In act 2, scene 4 of *Henry IV, Part 1*, the young prince Hal (later to become Henry V) takes a break from his debauched Falstaff-led behaviours in Eastcheap to introduce himself to the audience and explain his motivations:

> I know you all, and will awhile uphold
> The unyoked humour of your idleness:
> Yet herein will I imitate the sun,
> Who doth permit the base contagious clouds
> To smother up his beauty from the world,
> That, when he please again to be himself,
> Being wanted, he may be more wonder'd at,
> By breaking through the foul and ugly mists
> Of vapours that did seem to strangle him.
> If all the year were playing holidays,
> To sport would be as tedious as to work;
> But when they seldom come, they wish'd for come,
> And nothing pleaseth but rare accidents.
> So, when this loose behavior I throw off
> And pay the debt I never promised,
> By how much better than my word I am,
> By so much shall I falsify men's hopes;
> And like bright metal on a sullen ground,
> My reformation, glittering o'er my fault,
> Shall show more goodly and attract more eyes
> Than that which hath no foil to set it off.
> I'll so offend, to make offence a skill;
> Redeeming time when men think least I will.

Henry IV, Parts I & II:
A Brief Summary

As the title suggests, the focus of these plays is the reign
of Henry IV and his handling of rebellious forces from the
north, following his usurping of the throne from Richard II in
the play of the same name. However, the real star is the young Prince
Hal, who is destined to become Henry V, and his journey from (apparently intentionally) misbehaving youth to worthy king. Whilst he has
his true, rather austere and guilt-ridden father figure in Henry IV, he also
has an alternate father figure in the rotund drunkard Falstaff, a marvel-
lously comic character who was a favourite of the queen, as well as various other notorious inhabitants of Eastcheap's inns and brothels. Prince
Hal also has a foil in the valiant but impulsive Hotspur, his equivalent
on the side of the northern rebels. Hal proves himself by defeating
Hotspur at the end of part one and then ultimately shedding his
former ways upon the death of his father and his rejection
of Falstaff at the end of part two, though we do see some
glimpses of the old Hal in moments of *Henry V*.

Falstaff also refers to Hal as "the sun of England," using a son/sun pun which Shakespeare appears to be fond of when referring to royal lineage.

Perhaps the most famous example of this is in the opening speech of *Richard* III (for a brief synopsis of *Richard* III, see page 122), when Richard (still Duke of Gloucester at this point) refers to his brother Edward IV as "this sun of York," which both refers to the "glorious summer" that Edward has won with his victories after the "winter of our discontent" and the fact that Edward is a son of the house of York. It is also possibly a reference to the Yorkist banners that were carried into battle, on which the white rose appeared like a sun.

Duncan, as rightful king, is also a "sun," hence Lady Macbeth's exclamation of "O, never shall sun that morrow see!" (act 1, scene 5) when plotting his murder with her ambitious husband, and even his blood is described as being golden when she says she will "gild the faces of the grooms" (act 2, scene 2) with it to imply their guilt. Macbeth then usurps the solar status but encapsulates all the negative qualities of the sun, the corrupt microcosm seemingly causing the macrocosm to become tainted, with nature turning in on itself until order is finally restored with his downfall. *Macbeth* is a wonderful example of the ancient principle of the king and the land as one.

King Lear also reflects this principle, which is a variation of "As above, so below" and originates in Arthurian mythology. *Lear* is a story taken from Geoffrey Monmouth's *History of the Kings of Britain*, which also features King Arthur and this very phrase, so Shakespeare would have been familiar with this concept. Lear, however, as a fading monarch besieged by ill judgement, is better represented by the more negative aspects of Jupiter's energies or as one afflicted by old age under Saturn.

As one who has had the power of the sun and yet fallen, Richard II associates himself with Apollo's son, Phaeton, as he gives in to Bolingbroke: "Down, down I come; like glistering Phaethon" (act 3, scene 3).

It is not only monarchs that are represented by the sun; it is often used as a romantic description for lovers. Shakespeare gives Romeo free reign with the cliché in the classic lines "But, soft! what light from yonder window breaks? It is the east, and Juliet is the sun" (act 2, scene 2), but he turns this ideal on its head in Sonnet 130, "My mistress' eyes are nothing like the sun"!

It should also be noted that the god Apollo, frequently mentioned in Shakespeare's works, particularly in connection with oracles and Delphi, is associated with the sun.

The Moon

Mystery, illusion, and dreams are the province of the moon, as well as cycles of expansion and contraction, magic and the subconscious. The moon rules over the phlegmatic humour. Although the traditional association is feminine, it is not exclusively female characters who claim connection to this energy. We can link Lady Macbeth with the moon (and also the witches) for her ability to show different faces, her connection to mysterious forces, and, in the darkest aspect, the nightmare she finds herself inhabiting due to her diseased subconscious. In act 3, scene 1 of A *Midsummer Night's Dream*, we read:

> The moon methinks looks with a watery eye;
>
> And when she weeps, weeps every little flower,
>
> Lamenting some enforced chastity.

Titania (and her mortal counterpart Hippolyta) is strongly linked to lunar powers, and we will look at her and the significance of her connection with the moon in depth in a later chapter.

Falstaff claims kinship with the moon as ruler of thieves, declaring "we that take purses go by the moon and the seven stars, and not by Phoebus, he, "that wandering knight so fair" (*Henry* IV, *Part* I, act 1, scene 2), but he also is a jovial character with some of the shadow side of Venus through his overindugence.

In *Richard* III, Queen Elizabeth declares herself as a grieving widow to be ruled by the moon in act 2, scene 2:

> Give me no help in lamentation;
>
> I am not barren to bring forth complaints
>
> All springs reduce their currents to mine eyes,
>
> That I, being govern'd by the watery moon,
>
> May send forth plenteous tears to drown the world!
>
> Oh for my husband, for my dear lord Edward!

Paulina links Leontes with the dark side of lunar qualities when she notes "I dare be sworn, these dangerous unsafe lunes i' the king, beshrew them!" (*The Winter's Tale*, act 2, scene 2), another case of an unwell subconscious and giving in to one's own self-generated illusions.

Diana is the goddess of the moon most mentioned in Shakespeare's works, as is Hecate, who is often mentioned in her darker aspect. Additionally, as a votaress of Diana, Thaisa in *Pericles* would certainly be ruled by the moon.

Mars

Mars is the planet of action, power, and conflict and rules over the choleric humour. Those who are quick to anger and make hasty decisions are said to be born under Mars, but so are those who show great courage in adversity. Since the classical planets are named for gods of the same qualities, mentions of either the planet or the god help us in Shakespeare's works.

In act 1, scene 1 of *All's Well That Ends Well*, Helena engages in witty banter with Parolles in which she definitely emerges victorious:

> HELENA: Monsieur Parolles, you were born under
>   a charitable star.
> PAROLLES: Under Mars, I.
> HELENA: I especially think, under Mars.
> PAROLLES: Why under Mars?
> HELENA: The wars have so kept you under that you must
>   needs be born under Mars.
> PAROLLES: When he was predominant.
> HELENA: When he was retrograde, I think, rather.
> PAROLLES: Why think you so?
> HELENA: You go so much backward when you fight.
> PAROLLES: That's for advantage.
> HELENA: So is running away, when fear proposes the safety;
>   but the composition that your valour and fear makes in you
>   is a virtue of a good wing, and I like the wear well.

The jest that the planet must have been in retrograde—i.e., appearing to move backwards as he runs away from danger—uses such specifically astrological language that it shows Shakespeare not only was educated in astrology, but that he expected his audience to be also.

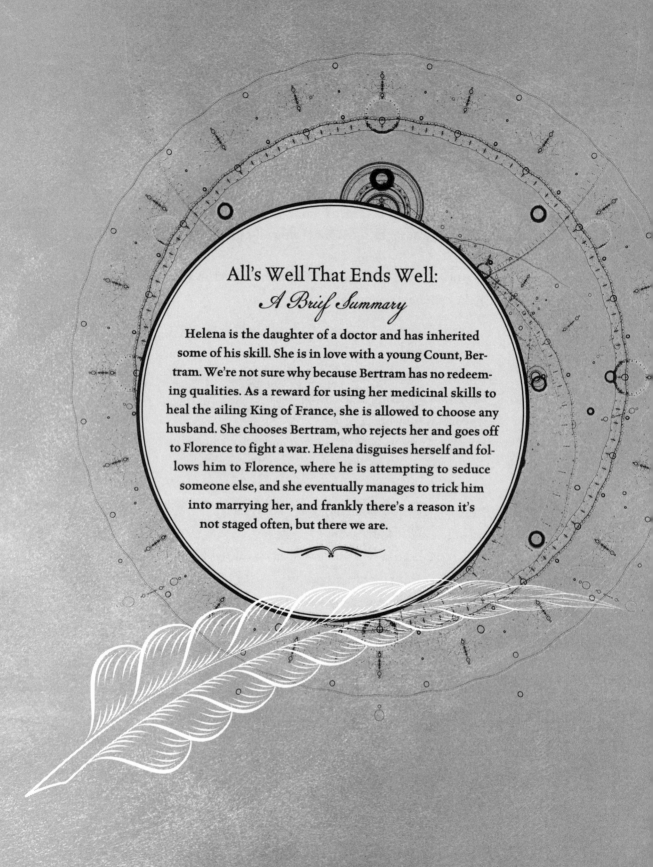

All's Well That Ends Well:
A Brief Summary

Helena is the daughter of a doctor and has inherited some of his skill. She is in love with a young Count, Bertram. We're not sure why because Bertram has no redeeming qualities. As a reward for using her medicinal skills to heal the ailing King of France, she is allowed to choose any husband. She chooses Bertram, who rejects her and goes off to Florence to fight a war. Helena disguises herself and follows him to Florence, where he is attempting to seduce someone else, and she eventually manages to trick him into marrying her, and frankly there's a reason it's not staged often, but there we are.

A character who can be defined by the characteristics of Mars in their most idealised form is Antony, who—much like the god for whom the planet is named—is much influenced by his Venus, Cleopatra. *Antony and Cleopatra* opens with Antony's close friend Philo directly comparing him to the god for whom the planet is named and bemoaning how his attentions have been diverted from leadership to love:

> PHILO: Nay, but this dotage of our general's
> O'erflows the measure: those his goodly eyes,
> That o'er the files and musters of the war
> Have glow'd like plated Mars, now bend, now turn,
> The office and devotion of their view
> Upon a tawny front.

His love interest is notoriously changeable. In one of her less favourable moods, she describes him as "painted one way like a gorgon, the other way's a Mars" (*Antony and Cleopatra*, act 2, scene 5).

Coriolanus, in the play of the same name, is a similarly martial character, even called "thou Mars" by Aufidius, and Hotspur is called "Mars in swathling clothes" by the king in *Henry IV, Part 1*. Hotspur not only has the soldier's prowess that might be expected for one ruled by this planet but also the hasty temperament and rage that might be counted among the more negative aspects of Mars. In a less conventional sense, we can also associate these qualities with our two lead characters in *Taming of the Shrew*, which we will look at in a bit more detail later, when we look at the elements and humours.

Mercury

Mercury is the planet of communication and its shadow, deception. It also rules travel, works of the mind, magic, science, healing, and thievery. One such thief who proudly declares himself to be "littered under Mercury" is Autolycus of *The Winter's Tale*, who is a talented con artist, using a gift with words and disguise to outwit the poor shepherd characters and yet is a very likable character. Autolycus is an Ovidian inspiration, a name taken from a character in Greek mythology who was reputed to be the son of Hermes and thus gifted with remarkable skills of trickery.

Sometimes we are not directly told which planet a character is ruled by, but there may be a clue in the name. Shakespeare took the name "Marcuccio" from his source material for *Romeo and Juliet* and transformed him into Mercutio, quick-witted best friend to Romeo and no longer rival, as he was in the original tale. Instead he pits Mercutio and Tybalt against each other, which is an example of the multilayered meanings Shakespeare used in his plays, as Mercutio is an esoteric pun on the name George Silver (Mercury = Quicksilver), a famous sword teacher of the time, and Tybalt is more obviously the name of rival swordsman Thibault.

As the messenger god, Mercury acts as psychopomp—one who can travel and guide between realms—so Mercutio belongs to both Montague and Capulet camps and even facilitates Romeo's presence at the Capulet gathering where he first meets Juliet. Taking on a similarly liminal role is Lucio in *Measure for Measure*, who strolls with ease between both courtly life and the brothels but whose cutting remarks about the Duke eventually become his undoing.

This ability to pass between worlds of different status is something that is shared by Shakespeare's fools, who also come under Mercury's rule, and of course they also live by their gift with words. Feste even conveys a blessing of Mercury onto Olivia when she stands up for him against the dour Malvolio: "Now Mercury endue thee with leasing, for thou speakest well of fools!" (*Twelfth Night*, act 1, scene 5).

Benedick and especially Beatrice are famed for their quick wits, and it may well be that Mercury was the star that danced as Beatrice was born.

Many of Shakespeare's adventurous heroines have not only the quick wit but also such talent for disguise that even those closest to them, or at least the men who profess to love them, cannot recognise them in male attire. Androgyny and gender fluidity are certainly ruled by Mercury, and thus we can count Portia (*Merchant of Venice*) and her sharp mind, Rosalind (*As You Like It*), Viola (*Twelfth Night,*) and Julia (*Two Gentlemen of Verona*) amongst characters who channel the influence of this planet, although there are other planetary influences also at work, as we shall discuss later. It also goes without saying that all messengers in Shakespeare are also governed by Mercury.

Jupiter

Jupiter shares many qualities with that of the sun, including honour, leadership, good judgement, and wealth. This is the planet of expansion, optimism, good fortune, and joy, although, again like the sun, the shadow of this planet's influence presents in tyranny, ill luck, and overconsumption. Jupiter is connected to the sanguine humour.

The god Jupiter himself appears in *Cymbeline's* act 5, scene 4 (for a synopsis of *Cymbeline*, see page 130) in response to the demands of the ancestral spirits of Posthumus Leonatus, whom he declares is under his protection due to being born under the planet Jupiter:

> JUPITER: No more, you petty spirits of region low,
> Offend our hearing; hush! How dare you ghosts
> Accuse the thunderer, whose bolt, you know,
> Sky-planted batters all rebelling coasts?
> Poor shadows of Elysium, hence, and rest
> Upon your never-withering banks of flowers:
> Be not with mortal accidents opprest;
> No care of yours it is; you know 'tis ours.
> Whom best I love I cross; to make my gift,
> The more delay'd, delighted. Be content;
> Your low-laid son our godhead will uplift:
> His comforts thrive, his trials well are spent.
> Our Jovial star reign'd at his birth, and in
> Our temple was he married. Rise, and fade.
> He shall be lord of lady Imogen,
> And happier much by his affliction made.
> This tablet lay upon his breast, wherein
> Our pleasure his full fortune doth confine:
> and so, away: no further with your din
> Express impatience, lest you stir up mine.
> Mount, eagle, to my palace crystalline.

In *Merry Wives of Windsor*, Falstaff calls upon Jupiter to aid him in his amorous pursuits in act 5, scene 5:

> The Windsor bell hath struck twelve; the minute
> draws on. Now, the hot-blooded gods assist me!
> Remember, Jove, thou wast a bull for thy Europa; love

set on thy horns. O powerful love! that, in some
respects, makes a beast a man, in some other, a man
a beast. You were also, Jupiter, a swan for the love
of Leda. O omnipotent Love! how near the god drew
to the complexion of a goose! A fault done first in
the form of a beast. O Jove, a beastly fault! And
then another fault in the semblance of a fowl; think
on 't, Jove; a foul fault! When gods have hot
backs, what shall poor men do? For me, I am here a
Windsor stag; and the fattest, I think, i' the
forest. Send me a cool rut-time, Jove, or who can
blame me to piss my tallow?

Falstaff's jovial nature and bodily expansiveness does indeed mark him out for that planet, albeit not entirely favourably.

A more respectable example of a Jupiter-ruled character might be the Duke in *Measure for Measure*, who strives to restore balance and fair judgement in his dukedom and to increase the fortune of those who have been unfairly treated.

Venus

Venus is the planet of beauty, fertility, sensuality, and, of course, love. Since divine love is the transformational power and wisdom behind many of Shakespeare's plays, this planet is well represented in the canon.

One of the most beautiful and Venusian descriptions of any character in the works is from act 2, scene 2 of *Antony and Cleopatra*:

The barge she sat in, like a burnish'd throne,
Burn'd on the water: the poop was beaten gold;
Purple the sails, and so perfumed that
The winds were love-sick with them; the oars were silver,
Which to the tune of flutes kept stroke, and made
The water which they beat to follow faster,
As amorous of their strokes. For her own person,

> It beggar'd all description: she did lie
>
> In her pavilion—cloth-of-gold of tissue—
>
> O'er-picturing that Venus where we see
>
> The fancy outwork nature: on each side her
>
> Stood pretty dimpled boys, like smiling Cupids,
>
> With divers-colour'd fans, whose wind did seem
>
> To glow the delicate cheeks which they did cool,
>
> And what they undid did.

Twelfth Night opens with the words "If music be the food of love, play on," uttered by Duke Orsino, who might be considered to be under the planet Venus. Although we have already discussed Viola as one of the cross-dressing heroines who might be associated with Mercury, her deep capacity for love also shows her to be under the influence of Venus. We should also consider Antonio from the same play to be ruled by this planet, but alas, his love for Sebastian, whom he rescued from the shipwreck, goes unrequited.

Arguably the most famous work in the English language on the theme of love must be *Romeo and Juliet*, and both titular characters may be considered to be ruled by this planet:

> O, she doth teach the torches to burn bright!
>
> It seems she hangs upon the cheek of night
>
> Like a rich jewel in an Ethiope's ear;
>
> Beauty too rich for use, for earth too dear!
>
> So shows a snowy dove trooping with crows,
>
> As yonder lady o'er her fellows shows.
>
> The measure done, I'll watch her place of stand,
>
> And, touching hers, make blessed my rude hand.
>
> Did my heart love till now? forswear it, sight!
>
> For I ne'er saw true beauty till this night.
>
> (ACT 1, SCENE 5)

Whilst Romeo might not directly mention Venus in his description of Juliet, he uses imagery connected to the planet and the goddess, such as doves and how brightly she shines in the night.

In *Othello* we might consider Desdemona's devotion to Othello and defiance of her family and society as being the influence of Venus, as is her physical beauty. Sadly, it is the shadow side of this planet's power, jealousy, that brings her tragic end.

Saturn

The planetary energies of Saturn relate to age, wisdom, and death. Saturn also rules over agriculture, discipline, time and the melancholic humour.

In Shakespeare's work we do encounter one character named for this planet, Saturninus, emperor of Rome in the famously bloody *Titus Andronicus*. However, he does not really reflect the qualities of Saturn that we might expect, being more of a choleric disposition. A character from the same play who consciously channels the darker aspects of this planetary power is Aaron the Moor in act 2, scene 3:

> Madam, though Venus govern your desires,
> Saturn is dominator over mine:
> What signifies my deadly-standing eye,
> My silence and my cloudy melancholy,
> My fleece of woolly hair that now uncurls
> Even as an adder when she doth unroll
> To do some fatal execution?
> No, madam, these are no venereal signs:
> Vengeance is in my heart, death in my hand,
> Blood and revenge are hammering in my head.

A similarly villainous character of the "very melancholy disposition" (act 2, scene 1) is Don John in *Much Ado About Nothing*. When talking to Conrade in act 1, scene 3, he seems to be accusing him of only saying he's born under Saturn in order to fit with Don John's own way of being:

> I wonder that thou, being, as thou sayest thou art,
> born under Saturn, goest about to apply a moral
> medicine to a mortifying mischief. I cannot hide
> what I am: I must be sad when I have cause and smile
> at no man's jests, eat when I have stomach and wait
> for no man's leisure, sleep when I am drowsy and

tend on no man's business, laugh when I am merry and

claw no man in his humour.

More gentle and benevolent characters also carry this planet's energy, including Jaques of *As You Like It*, whose "seven ages of man" speech shows great understanding of time's effect on our lives and as result seems consumed with melancholy. We might also consider the ever-mourning Olivia of *Twelfth Night* to be ruled by this planet, especially since she is known for constantly wearing a veil, which is one of the planet's associated objects.

Saturn has a strong presence in *The Winter's Tale*, not only because of its theme of death, resurrection, and restoration, but also that Time itself appears briefly as a chorus:

> TIME: I, that please some, try all, both joy and terror
> Of good and bad, that makes and unfolds error,
> Now take upon me, in the name of Time,
> To use my wings. Impute it not a crime
> To me or my swift passage, that I slide
> O'er sixteen years and leave the growth untried
> Of that wide gap, since it is in my power
> To o'erthrow law and in one self-born hour
> To plant and o'erwhelm custom. Let me pass
> The same I am, ere ancient'st order was
> Or what is now received: I witness to
> The times that brought them in; so shall I do
> To the freshest things now reigning and make stale
> The glistering of this present, as my tale
> Now seems to it. Your patience this allowing,
> I turn my glass and give my scene such growing
> As you had slept between...
>
> (ACT 4, SCENE I)

The agricultural life of the Bohemians we encounter may be considered to be ruled by Saturn, but the joy it brings them is more in the realms of Jupiter or Venus.

Much has been written about Hamlet's melancholy and hence Saturnine connection, yet Hamlet endures as a complex and contradictory character, seemingly mocking the principle of the humours for being over-simplistic when he says to Rosencrantz and Guildenstern that he is "but mad north-by-northwest. When the wind is southerly, I know a hawk from a handsaw" (act 2, scene 2), referring to the directions of the winds that corresponded to the different humours. A more complex picture may be formed when we also take into account any elemental descriptions of characters.

Elements and Humours

Does not our life consist of the four elements?

—*Twelfth Night*, ACT 2, SCENE 3

One of the most essential understandings behind the Hermetic and Platonic beliefs which inform alchemy and all Renaissance occult practice is the principle of the four elements (five including aether/spirit) and their microcosmic equivalents, the humours. Most people know the basics of earth, air, fire, and water. Each element is accorded two qualities, the latter of which it shares with the next element in the sequence, giving them a sense of cyclic movement.

> For Fire is hot and dry, Earth dry and cold, the Water cold and moist, the Air moist and hot. And so after this manner the elements, according to two contrary qualities, are contrary one to the other, as Fire to Water and Earth to Air (Agrippa 1993, 8).

When functioning within the human body, these four elements with their two qualities are known as the "humours," and these humours translate into behaviour as four corresponding temperaments.

Fire (hot and dry) = yellow bile = choleric

Earth (dry and cold) = black bile = melancholic

Water (cold and moist) = phlegm = phlegmatic

Air (moist and hot) = blood = sanguine

A Note for Actors

Actors looking for a way to increase the spiritual and energetic dimension of their performance may wish to spend time invoking the planet and/or elements that seem to resonate most strongly with their character/s. When I have the luxury of time in rehearsal, I will always consider what the planetary and elemental makeup of the character is and how I might best embody that both in my internal mental and emotional process and in my physicality. Naturally, there may be a cycling through the elements during the course of a play, and then on a more detailed level, even through the course of a speech. This is a handy thing to bear in mind when working on a monologue as a stand-alone piece or for an audition!

Look to chapter 9 for more information and suggestions regarding invocation. Magical practitioners considering incorporating Shakespeare into their work may wish to call upon the archetypes that some of these characters represent. Suggestions contained within the practical exercises for this chapter and following chapters may be expanded upon according to magical understanding and skill level.

Agrippa goes on to explain that the elements can also be split into passive/heavy (earth and water) and active/light (air and fire), and that each element is also assigned three qualities. Earth has "darkness, thickness, and quietness," and fire has "brightness, thinness, and motion," which sets earth and fire as opposites, with water and air both inheriting two qualities from one element and one from the other, so water has darkness, thickness, and motion whilst air has thinness, motion, and darkness.

> The Fire is to the Air, so Air to the Water, and Water to the Earth; and again,
> as the Earth is to the Water, so the Water to the Air, and the Air to the Fire
> (Agrippa 1993, 8).

This complex yet harmonious system of opposing and complementary forces gives a sense of constant transmutation and movement from one state to another. This is sometimes reflected in Shakespeare's works where he uses the elements as metaphors for human behaviour:

> The sun's a thief, and with his great attraction
> Robs the vast sea: the moon's an arrant thief,
> And her pale fire she snatches from the sun:
> The sea's a thief, whose liquid surge resolves
> The moon into salt tears: the earth's a thief,
> That feeds and breeds by a composture stolen
> From general excrement...
> (*Timon of Athens*, ACT 4, SCENE 3)

Characters will often compare their plights or emotional and mental states to the workings of the macrocosm, again reflecting the philosophy of "As above, so below":

> When heaven doth weep, doth not the earth o'erflow?
> If the winds rage, doth not the sea wax mad,
> Threatening the welkin with his big-swoln face?
> And wilt thou have a reason for this coil?
> I am the sea; hark, how her sighs do blow!
> She is the weeping welkin, I the earth:
> Then must my sea be moved with her sighs;

Then must my earth with her continual tears

Become a deluge, overflow'd and drown'd;

For why my bowels cannot hide her woes,

But like a drunkard must I vomit them.

(*Titus Andronicus*, ACT 3, SCENE 1)

Shakespeare often has characters either identify themselves or others with certain elements. Whereas to be born under a certain planet would naturally be a lifelong influence, and since the planets also rule certain elements that would dictate tendencies of character and temperament, one of the aims of Hermeticism is to achieve balance between the elements, and this balance is often shifting through the different experiences and ages of characters' lives. Whilst some characters may be strongly identified with a single element or humour, Shakespeare often gives us combinations of elements in order to provide a more in-depth expression.

Cleopatra, in her final moments, famously describes herself in act 5, scene 2 as "fire and air; my other elements I give to baser life" as she leaves her mortal body behind to join her love in spirit. In a much more amusing moment, the same elemental combination is assigned to Lewis the Dauphin's horse in act 3, scene 7 of *Henry V*:

...It is a beast for

Perseus: he is pure air and fire; and the dull

elements of earth and water never appear in him, but

only in Patient stillness while his rider mounts

him: he is indeed a horse; and all other jades you

may call beasts.

At the peak of Hamlet's erratic behaviour, after accidentally slaying his mother's elderly counsellor, Polonius, she describes him in act 4, scene 1 as "Mad as the sea and wind when both contend which is the mightier." This powerful description ties in with the landscape of the play, once again compared the outer landscape to the inner realm of the mind. When Hamlet first encounters the ghost of his father, the event which initiates the events of the play and Hamlet's descent into seeming madness, Horatio is rightly concerned that the spirit might be his doom and also directly compares the element of water when it is agitated, as in a stormy sea, to madness:

The Taming of the Shrew woodcut engraving, 1838

What if it tempt you toward the flood, my lord,

Or to the dreadful summit of the cliff

That beetles o'er his base into the sea,

And there assume some other, horrible form

Which might deprive your sovereignty of reason

And draw you into madness? Think of it.

The very place puts toys of desperation,

Without more motive, into every brain

That looks so many fadoms to the sea

And hears it roar beneath.

(ACT I, SCENE 4)

The element of water also relates to the pure emotion of love, and in *All's Well That Ends Well*, Helena describes her unrequited love as water she willingly pours into something that cannot contain it:

I know I love in vain, strive against hope;

Yet in this captious and intenible sieve

I still pour in the waters of my love

And lack not to lose still: thus, Indian-like,

Religious in mine error, I adore

The sun, that looks upon his worshipper,

But knows of him no more.

(ACT I, SCENE 3)

Though Shakespeare has a good number of fiery couples, there can be none of a more choleric disposition than Kate and Petruchio in *The Taming of the Shrew*. Petruchio uses this as an excuse for some of his ill treatment of Kate, and it may be interpreted that this reasoning is genuine, if extreme:

I tell thee, Kate, 'twas burnt and dried away,

And I expressly am forbid to touch it;

For it engenders choler, planteth anger;

And better 'twere that both of us did fast,

Since, of ourselves, ourselves are choleric,

Than feed it with such over-roasted flesh.

Be patient; to-morrow 't shall be mended.

And for this night we'll fast for company.

Come, I will bring thee to thy bridal chamber.

(ACT 4, SCENE 1)

In *Henry IV, Part 1*, Prince Hal, in a string of jestful insults, calls Falstaff "this sanguine coward, this bed-presser, this horseback-breaker, this huge hill of flesh" (act 2, scene 4). It might be more accurate to describe Hal himself in his earlier guise as sanguine and Falstaff as phlegmatic, a humour not often mentioned by name in the works, perhaps because characters of this disposition do not usually support interesting tales. If we take this as the case, then the undoubtedly melancholy disposition of Henry IV and the choleric temperament of Hotspur give this play a somewhat unique balance of the humours within its main characters.

You may wish to expand these ideas by looking at the overall elemental and planetary composition of the play as opposed to isolated characters. The Hermetic application of the Jewish mystical system known as the Cabala, which we will explore in the next chapter, gives us a kind of map that ties these aspects together and gives us an insightful lens through which we can view the plays. We can then start to realise their potential as initiatory gateways with profound transformations and messages of divine moral guidance as well as contemplations on the secrets within nature and the universe.

Exercise: Creating Sacred Space

As we go on to explore various practical explorations of the ideas discussed within each chapter, it is a good idea to get a strong foundation in place. Those amongst you who are experienced in any magical tradition will no doubt be familiar with the practice of creating sacred space before ritual work in order to aid focus, contain positive energies, and prevent unwanted energies from entering. Practices for creating sacred space may vary from the simple yet potent to the extremely complex and specific, depending on the nature of the work to be performed. For our purposes a simple blessing and calling in of the elements and directions will suffice.

Those who have experience working within the Celtic mysteries and Fairy tradition will no doubt be familiar with the principle of calling in the seven directions of east, south, west, north, above, below, and within. When I have taught theatre workshops I have also used this exercise to connect the group, aid in focus, and bring positive energies into the space and practitioners—I highly recommend it for rehearsals! Here is a Shakespeare-specific version for you to try, which you may wish to utilise before the other exercises in this book or to bring in inspiring energies for any creative activity, either in a group or solo. When working with a group, it is helpful to have one person leading the activity and the rest follow the actions and repeat each phrase as it is spoken.

TIMING: Any. Use before and after group or solo magical work and at the opening and closing of rehearsals.

PREPARATION: None required, other than to discover where the directions are in relation to your space. You may wish to take a ritual bath before working, depending on your intent.

CALLING IN THE DIRECTIONS (OR CREATING "SHAKE-READ" SPACE): If in a group, stand in a circle. Begin by facing the east with a strong upright posture and arms extended upwards in a V formation, palms outward. If working in a group, replace I/me/my with we/us/our.

> *I call to the east and the element of air! Grant me the logic and*
> *clear-headedness of Portia, the intellect and wisdom of Prospero,*
> *and the quick wit of Mercutio to aid me in my work this day!*
> *The grey-eyed morn smiles on the frowning night,*
> *Chequering the eastern clouds with streaks of light.*
> *Hail and welcome!*

Lower hands, turn in a clockwise direction to the South, raise hands once more, and say:

> *I call to the south and the element of fire! Grant me the courage of*
> *Henry V, the passion of Cleopatra, and the will of Beatrice to aid*
> *me in my work this day!*
> *O for a Muse of fire that would ascend the brightest heaven of invention.*
> *Hail and welcome!*

Lower hands, turn in a clockwise direction to the west, raise hands once more, and say:

>I call to the west and the element of water!
>
>Grant me the intuition of Miranda, the true heart of Viola, and
>
>>the compassion of Rosalind to aid me in my work this day!
>
>The diamonds of a most praised water
>
>>do appear to make the world twice rich.
>
>Hail and welcome!

Lower hands, turn in a clockwise direction to the north, raise hands once more, and say:

>I call to the north and the element of earth!
>
>Grant me the stability of Horatio, the steadfastness of Paulina,
>
>>and the joy of Falstaff to aid me in my work this day!
>
>Earth's increase, foison plenty, barns and garners never empty.
>
>Hail and welcome!

Turning clockwise again to face the centre, now raise your right hand so that the palm faces upwards and direct your energy to the above:

>I call to the above and the celestial realm!
>
>Grant me the blessings of Diana and Apollo, all the divine inspiration
>
>>of the planetary heavens, to aid me in my work this day!
>
>Good morrow to the sun. Hail, thou fair heaven!
>
>Now, by the burning tapers of the sky, be witness to me,
>
>>O thou blessed moon.
>
>Hail and welcome!

Now bend down and touch the earth with the palm of your right hand.

> *I call to the below, the realm of the ancestors and Fairy beings!*
>
> *Grant me the wisdom and guidance of those who have walked this path before me, and of Titania and Oberon, queen and king of the hidden realm, to aid me in my work this day!*
>
> *Hand in hand, with fairy grace, will we sing, and bless this place.*
>
> *Hail and welcome!*

Now face the centre and focus inwards. Join hands in a group or, if performing alone, fold your hands onto your heart and say:

> *I call to the within, to the spear-shaker within each of us, to the author of the works and the authors of all works to come, grant us the awakening of our higher selves that we may find clarity, connection and creativity to aid us in our work this day!*
>
> *They sparkle still the right Promethean fire; they are the books, the arts, the academes, that show, contain, and nourish all the world.*
>
> *Hail and welcome!*

When closing perform in reverse order, turning anticlockwise, and change "grant me/us" to "I/we give thanks for." End with "hail and farewell" after each direction.

It may well be call'd Jove's tree,
when it drops forth such fruit.

AS YOU LIKE IT

ACT **3**, SCENE **2**

THREE

The Tree of Life

The Christianised version of Jewish mysticism known as the Cabala was a very significant aspect of Renaissance occult philosophy, and it is one that provides us with a useful tool for mapping how Shakespeare's plays can act as transformative initiatory gateways. The Tree of Life gives us a model for spiritual progress from the mundane, physical world to unity with the divine, or for the descent of divine energy into the world. This is through a progression of ten spheres or sephiroth, all of which have a set of correspondences including the seven planets, and these are connected by twenty-two paths that all have their own wisdom lessons.

The Sephiroth (Spheres)

A full study of the sephiroth and paths of the tree would require more space than we have to spare here, and many excellent books and online resources are available on the subject

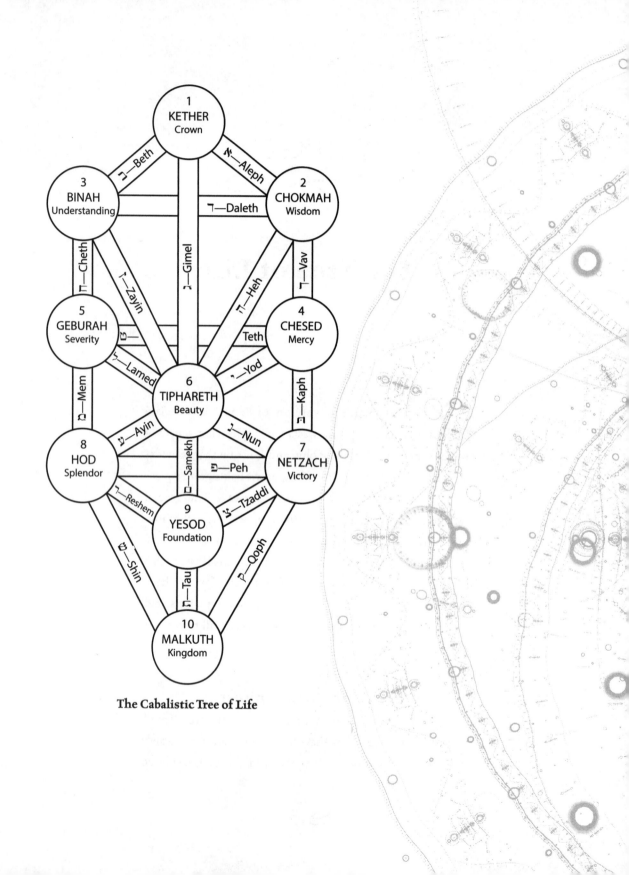

The Cabalistic Tree of Life

for those who wish to inquire further. For our purposes, we will take a quick look at the sephiroth in order and their basic correspondences, including the planets, so that we can connect this learning with the aspects of Hermetic philosophy we have already covered.

1. KETHER (CROWN): Kether is the ultimate unknowable source of Spirit in its purest form. It does not represent any of the seven planets as it is the source from which they are manifested, but it is more closely connected to the big bang or "first swirlings" of the universe. Its colour is white, and it corresponds to the top of the head in the human body.

2. CHOKMAH (WISDOM): Chokmah is the first breaking away from source into manifestation and is traditionally seen as a masculine expression of Spirit. It represents the fixed stars beyond our own solar system, its colour is grey, and it corresponds to the left side of the face.

3. BINAH (UNDERSTANDING): Binah corresponds to Saturn, as Saturn in the ancient world up to a couple of centuries ago was the limit of the known universe. Binah is seen as a feminine emanation of the source and the connecting point between our understanding and infinity. Its colour is black, and it corresponds to the right side of the face. The three sephiroth at the top of the tree are known as the supernal triad.

4. CHESED (MERCY): Chesed corresponds to Jupiter and the highest vibration of the element of water. It is directly below Chokmah and is the highest that form can travel before crossing the abyss, where all becomes pure energy. Its colour is blue, and it rules the left arm and hand in the body.

5. GEBURAH (SEVERITY): Geburah represents Mars. An alternative name for this sphere is Din, meaning "justice," and it encapsulates the power of will and energy. Its colour is red, and it connects to the right arm and hand.

6. TIPHARETH (BEAUTY): Tiphareth is at the heart of the Tree of Life and thus represents the heart of our solar system, the sun, and also the heart in the human body. It is interesting to note that this understanding

preceded science's discovery of the sun, rather than the earth, being at the centre. It is a knowable reflection of the ultimate divine of Kether, and its colour is gold or yellow. These three sephiroth together are known as the ethical triad.

7. **NETZACH (VICTORY):** Netzach resonates with the planet Venus and similarly expresses the power of love. It corresponds to the left leg and hip, and its colour is green.

8. **HOD (SPLENDOUR):** Hod corresponds to Mercury, the right hip and leg, and the colour orange.

9. **YESOD (FOUNDATION):** Yesod relates to the moon, and just as the moon reflects the light of the sun, Yesod is a reflection of Tiphereth. This sephiroth rules the astral realm, illusion, and dreams, and it is a mirror that too many get caught in on their way up the tree, presenting a crossroads where the path forward must be chosen. Its colour is silver, and in the human body it is the genitalia. The lower triad of the tree is known as the astral triad.

10. **MALKUTH (KINGDOM):** Malkuth is connected to the four elements that comprise our physical existence on earth. It is the ultimate physical manifestation of the divine and the starting point or gateway for all who progress up the tree. Its colour is brown, and it is represented in the body by the feet.

11. **DAATH (KNOWLEDGE):** Yes, I know I said ten sephiroth, and here's number eleven! Its number is eleven, but it is not counted amongst the sephiroth. Daath is an invisible sphere that lies on the path between Kether and Tiphareth on the middle pillar and acts as an interface between the supernal triad and the rest of the tree. It is known as "the sephira that isn't," it has no colour as it is invisible, and it is represented in the body by the throat.

The Pillars

This basic knowledge of the sephiroth plus the three pillars are enough to add insight into this dimension of Shakespeare's works. The three pillars are simply how the sephiroth are connected vertically down the tree, so the pillar of Severity is black, female, contains Binah, Geburah, and Hod, and runs down the left side; the pillar of Mercy is white, male, runs down the right side, and contains Chokmah, Chesed, and Netzach. The central pillar is known as the pillar of Harmony and is grey, androgynous, and contains Kether, Tiphereth, Yesod, Malkuth, and would contain Daath if it existed, but it doesn't. Or does it? It's a mystery.

The Quality of Mercy

Whilst Shakespeare's use of Cabalistic imagery may not be as obvious as the astrological or elemental content, it is nevertheless undeniably present. It is entirely appropriate that one of the clearest examples of Shakespeare demonstrating his knowledge of Jewish mysticism is in Portia's famous "quality of mercy" speech in the trial scene of *The Merchant of Venice*.

We have already looked at how Shakespeare's witty, learned, cross-dressing heroines could be considered to be ruled by Mercury. However, we must also consider that Portia represents the sun within *The Merchant of Venice* and is therefore the central sphere of Tiphareth. She is undoubtedly the heart of the play, and her beauty is highly praised by her suitors, including her golden hair or "sunny locks" (act 2, scene 1). Her betrothed, Bassanio, even suggests she could take the place of the sun if it were absent: "We should hold day with the Antipodes, if you would walk in absence of the sun" (act 5, scene 1). In addition, during the trial scene (act 4, scene 1) in which this speech takes place, she is disguised as a young male lawyer, Balthazar, thus uniting male and female and becoming androgynous, as befits the central pillar of Harmony on which Tiphareth is located. With this in mind, let us proceed with a Cabalistic analysis of the speech:

> The quality of mercy is not strain'd,
>
> It droppeth as the gentle rain from heaven
>
> Upon the place beneath…

Mercy refers to Chesed, which we know represents Jupiter and also water in its most divine form. The pillar of Mercy is also known as the pillar of water. The "rain from

The Merchant of Venice:
A Brief Summary

The titular merchant, a Christian called Antonio, borrows money from Jewish moneylender Shylock (the only job Jews were allowed to do at the time) in order to help his friend Bassanio woo the wealthy, beautiful, and intelligent heiress Portia, who is definitely too good for him. Shylock, hurt by many years of racism from the Christians, grudgingly agrees, provided that Antonio signs a contract that a pound of his flesh will be paid if he is unable to pay back the loan. Antonio loses his fortune and Portia saves the day with cross-dressing and the extraordinary "quality of mercy" speech, as well as pointing out that though the contract specifies flesh, it does not include blood. Everyone is happy except for Shylock, who is cruelly forced to convert to Christianity. This would have been considered an act of mercy and a contribution to the greater good in Shakespeare's time, and yet we have seen enough of Shylock to know that pride in his religion and culture are all he has left. He is a broken man. (It's possible that Shakespeare's highlighting of this cruelty could have been meant to evoke empathy for the many Catholics being forced to convert to Protestantism during his lifetime.) This play also includes the famously moving "hath not a Jew eyes" speech. Christians and Jews are equally fairly awful to each other throughout, but the Christians are awful from a position of privilege.

heaven" symbolises divine energy passing down directly from the divine source to Chokmah and the pillar of Mercy; also, dew from Kether passes through the invisible Daath down to the rest of the tree. Since Tiphereth is located directly below Kether, she is also referring to herself as a source of Mercy and messenger of the divine.

> …it is twice blest;
> It blesseth him that gives and him that takes…

Other than its obvious surface meaning, the power of Mercy moves both up and down the tree, benefiting both the source and the mundane world and both active and receptive forces. Again, as Tiphareth Portia is located centrally, both giving and receiving energy in all directions.

> …Tis mightiest in the mightiest: it becomes
> The throned monarch better than his crown…

The crown is a reference to Kether, the ultimate source of pure spirit. Portia is implying that knowledge of the divine is futile without acting with mercy.

> …His sceptre shows the force of temporal power,
> The attribute to awe and majesty,
> Wherein doth sit the dread and fear of kings…

Monarchs are often pictured holding the sceptre in their right hand as a symbol of their power and will. The right hand is obviously ruled by Geburah, as previously discussed. This is indeed where the strength of the monarch would appear to lie and that which inspires awe.

> …But mercy is above this sceptred sway…

Mercy/Chesed is indeed higher in sequence up the tree than Geburah.

> …It is enthroned in the hearts of kings,
> It is an attribute to God himself…

Here she seems to be referring to the balancing power of Tiphareth again, which is indeed in the heart and the first direct reflection of Kether and what most experience as "God himself."

An 1838 woodcut engraving of a court of justice
from act 4, scene 1 of *The Merchant of Venice*

…And earthly power doth then show likest God's

When mercy seasons justice…

When we consider Geburah's alternative name of Din, or "justice," this seems a direct call for balance between the two pillars as the path to the divine.

…Therefore, Jew,

Though justice be thy plea, consider this,

That, in the course of justice, none of us

Should see salvation: we do pray for mercy;

And that same prayer doth teach us all to render

The deeds of mercy.

Portia finishes by stating that in order to truly cross the abyss into the supernal triad, we cannot allow ourselves to get stuck in the sephira of Geburah and the principles of Severity that it represents, but that we must pass through Chesed/Mercy, and that the ideal state in life is the true balance between the pillars that may be found in Tiphareth.

Sweet Harmony

Of course, this is not an isolated example, and the whole play can be seen to be a journey from imbalance to harmony. All characters have lessons they have to learn, and all begin from the unbalanced state of melancholy. The very first lines of the play, setting the scene and mood, come from the titular merchant Antonio:

In sooth, I know not why I am so sad:

It wearies me; you say it wearies you;

But how I caught it, found it, or came by it,

What stuff 'tis made of, whereof it is born,

I am to learn;

And such a want-wit sadness makes of me,

That I have much ado to know myself.

One of the fundamentals of magical practice, to "know thyself" is the phrase famously written across the entrance to the temple of Apollo at Delphi. Indeed, all of the main characters are on a mission to know themselves, whether they are aware of it or not. It is no coincidence that the first words from our heroine, Portia, echo this sentiment, when in the opening of the second scene she bemoans to her servant Nerissa, "By my troth, Nerissa, my little body is aweary of this great world." She is unhappy that according to her father's will, she must leave her choice of husband to a peculiar rite that he has devised. She has no interest in any of her suitors thus far but is committed to marry whomever chooses the correct casket in a choice between gold, silver, or lead. This seems like a fairly obvious alchemical reference, and we've already discussed how Portia is compared to the sun, representing Tiphareth, and hence the colour gold. However, her father clearly knew her well enough to see that she would want someone who didn't go for the obvious choice and would see beyond appearances. She knows this and is able to guide Bassanio, the first suitor she has taken an interest in (Bassanio for the base metal lead, perhaps?) to make the wise choice of the lead casket, which contains her picture. Thus, faith in the universe and the path set down by elder wisdom is rewarded with love.

Mapping Plays onto the Tree

Once one is familiar with the Tree of Life, the sephiroth, the planets, and the elements, it is a useful exercise to map out which character fits where on the tree and what their purpose is on the overall journey that it represents. For example, we already have Portia placed at Tiphereth, so where might Bassanio be in relation to her? And where do we place Shylock, who perhaps faces the greatest spiritual challenges of the play?

Author, scholar, and spiritual teacher Peter Dawkins has written several books on the esoteric content of the individual plays and still teaches workshops on the subject, with the Tree of Life and the alchemical journey through the play being key aspects of his works. In his analysis of *The Merchant of Venice*, he places Portia at the centre, with her father (whose influence is felt but whom we never meet since he is deceased) at the unknowable Kether, and Bassanio just below her in Yesod. Shylock, being Saturnian in nature, is placed at Binah, with Antonio appropriately placed opposite at Chokmah.

Mapping any of the plays onto the tree in this way (including the paths for the more adept student of the mysteries) can yield much insight, whether or not the resonances were all intended by Shakespeare. Whilst the assignation of some of the lesser characters may sustain some interrogation, there is much to ponder in this work, with the need for Severity to be balanced with Mercy by the central heart of Tiphereth brought into clarity through this image.

Music of the Spheres

Once balance is restored through the course of the play, we are rewarded with this rich vision of the cosmic harmony:

> How sweet the moonlight sleeps upon this bank!
> Here will we sit and let the sounds of music
> Creep in our ears: soft stillness and the night
> Become the touches of sweet harmony.
> Sit, Jessica. Look how the floor of heaven
> Is thick inlaid with patines of bright gold:
> There's not the smallest orb which thou behold'st
> But in his motion like an angel sings,
> Still quiring to the young-eyed cherubins;
> Such harmony is in immortal souls;
> But whilst this muddy vesture of decay
> Doth grossly close it in, we cannot hear it.
> [Enter Musicians]
> Come, ho! and wake Diana with a hymn!
> With sweetest touches pierce your mistress' ear,
> And draw her home with music.
> (ACT 5, SCENE 1)

Music is a powerful tool of transformation. It can alter moods according to its nature and create a powerful atmosphere. If you've ever watched clips from emotive moments of well-known movies with the music track silenced, you'll know what a profound difference it makes to the emotional impact of a scene. The transportive effect of early modern theatre on its audience was much more reliant on words and music than our large-scale modern theatre. Although there was some investment in lavish costumes

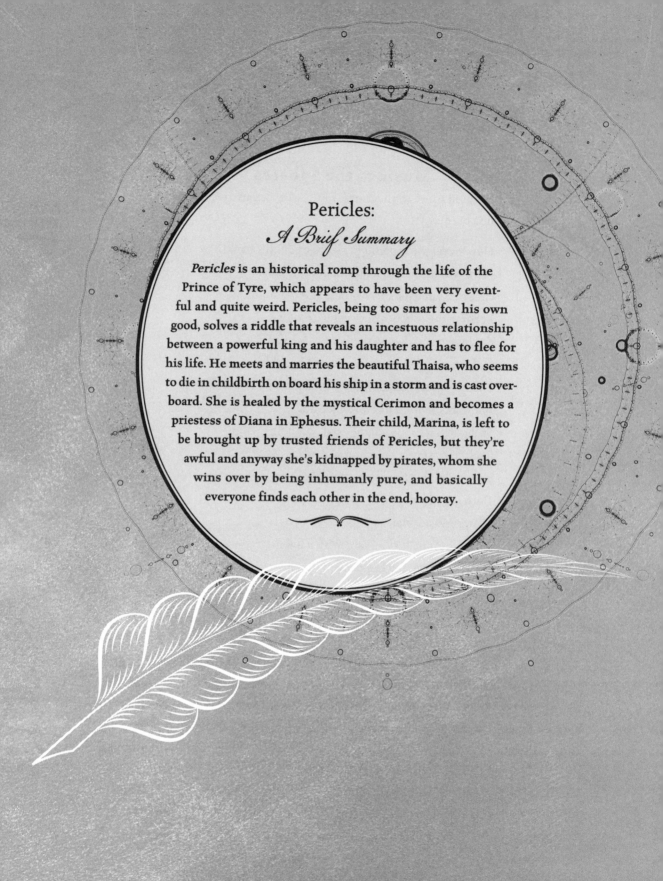

Pericles:
A Brief Summary

Pericles is an historical romp through the life of the Prince of Tyre, which appears to have been very eventful and quite weird. Pericles, being too smart for his own good, solves a riddle that reveals an incestuous relationship between a powerful king and his daughter and has to flee for his life. He meets and marries the beautiful Thaisa, who seems to die in childbirth on board his ship in a storm and is cast overboard. She is healed by the mystical Cerimon and becomes a priestess of Diana in Ephesus. Their child, Marina, is left to be brought up by trusted friends of Pericles, but they're awful and anyway she's kidnapped by pirates, whom she wins over by being inhumanly pure, and basically everyone finds each other in the end, hooray.

when required, in order to indicate characters of high stature, with only daylight or candles to illuminate the stage and players, along with minimal props and set, it was not considered the visual spectacle that it is today (though this started to change towards the end of Shakespeare's life with the growing fashion for extravagant Jacobean masques). Audiences would talk about going to *hear* a play rather than see a play, and we know that Shakespeare made good use of music in his plays from how often his characters call upon musicians or mention music and harmony in his works. However, there is more to it than creating mood and emphasising the emotion of the moment.

As is referenced in Lorenzo's famous speech at the end of *The Merchant of Venice*, the planets were believed to each emit songs or notes of their own, based upon mathematical proportions observed by Pythagoras. When these were harmonious, events were fortuitous; when out of harmony, ill fortune was portended.

Though it may seem as though this is no more than philosophical theory, especially since sound cannot travel through space due to the lack of air, recent years have brought the discovery that there is more truth to this than previously thought. In 1977 the space probes Voyager and Voyager II recorded electromagnetic vibrations of planets, stars, and space itself, which NASA was able to translate into an otherworldly celestial harmony (these recordings are readily available on YouTube—search for NASA Voyager Recordings).

Shakespeare shows his understanding of the power of music by using it to highlight magical occurrences in his plays or making the music itself part of that magical occurrence. Paulina calls upon music to awake the statue of Hermione in the climax of *The Winter's Tale*, Ariel creates unearthly music in order to dictate movements of characters according to Prospero's will in *The Tempest*, and the pure Marina sings her father back into harmony, restoring his sanity, prompting a vision of Diana herself accompanied by "the music of the spheres" in act 5, scene 1 of *Pericles*.

Exercise: Finding Your Voice

One of the things that both magical and theatrical training have in common is the use of voice, but in both disciplines it seems to be something of a dying art, with more actors being used to radio mics and magicians often learning from books rather than training in person, or even conducting rituals through virtual forums online. Our voice is what carries our words, our music, our magic. The power of our true note carries our energy signature—and thus our will—into the world. It is the most powerful tool at our disposal and hence the first tool you should add to your kit when looking to bring Shakespeare's wisdom into your art.

Your voice does not come from the throat but from your solar plexus energy centre, which is in the same location as your diaphragm (just below your rib cage, your centre). A useful exercise to help get throat tension out of the way is to yawn before doing any vocal work, then try to keep that same sense of openness at the back of your throat that came with that yawn.

Lying with your back flat on the floor and your knees bent, you can locate the diaphragm by lightly panting and holding your hand over your centre just below your ribs. Now relax and introduce a light "ha" sound to the pant and feel the muscle working.

Take some deep breaths in and release slowly three times. Now take a deep breath in and release slowly on a hissing sound, allowing the breath to exit from the bottom of the lungs and keeping the rib cage expanded for as long as possible until you're out of breath. This may take some practice, but it's worth persevering with. Now try the same thing but instead of hissing, release a humming sound. Play with pitch until you find somewhere that feels natural and comfortable to hold a note and that you can feel vibrating and resonating in your body. Keep taking deep breaths and repeating as often as you wish, working on resonating your hum and strengthening it. When you feel ready, on your next deep breath, release the note into any vowel sound and release it into the room. Imagine your voice soaring up to the sky and entirely filling your body and the space around you.

If you can make this part of a regular practice, you can try all the different vowel sounds and experiment with elongating words and resonating them, as well as allowing melodies to come through. This is your soul expressing itself in a pure form. Imagine a golden light that builds in your centre and that extends out with your voice. This is your signature note and resonance. Remember to empower your voice in this way for all your magical work.

You are an alchemist;
make gold of that.
TIMON OF ATHENS
ACT 5, SCENE 1

FOUR

Alchemy and Magic

$\mathcal{M}$uch has been written by scholars and academics over the centuries of the alchemical nature of Shakespeare's plays, but how much of it is genuinely present and intentional, and how much is fairy gold that might turn to leaves under scrutiny? We have already seen the extensive references to the elements and planets, and we know that Shakespeare was aware of at least the basics of the alchemical process from his direct references to transmuting base substances to gold. However, since Shakespeare was not writing from a perspective of openly mocking alchemy, its process, or its practitioners, as his contemporary Ben Jonson was in *The Alchemist*, the unfavourable political atmosphere of the Jacobean period meant that great care was needed to keep certain aspects of magical content hidden. This leaves an amount open to subjective interpretation, of course, but this art is no less potent for it. After all, who is the true initiate of the process of any play? Is it the characters within or the audience who experiences it? If the audience, then surely the effect is valid regardless of the original intent or the accuracy of the content in relation to ancient processes? From what we have looked at already, we know that Shakespeare was incorporating a mix of Hermetic and mythological content, so in order to decode what underlying alchemical structure there might be in the plays on a larger scale—that is, what is reflected in the play as a whole rather than in individual characters—we must break down the alchemical process into clear, simple steps and see if any of the plays (or repeating themes within the plays) reflect this.

Solve et Coagula

The alchemical process is not so easy to simplify, of course, and there are many different approaches and interpretations. The ultimate aim of esoteric alchemy, in line with Hermetic philosophy, is the perfection of self in parallel with the pursuit of the fabled philosopher's stone, which would enable any ill to be healed and any base metal to be transmuted to gold. The alchemical process is one of transformation, both inner and outer, involving a breaking down, purifying, and reassembling of the self/substance in its purest form. The mysteries of this process are veiled with symbolism and obscure language in medieval and Renaissance texts, which are further confused by individual alchemists using their own codes and applying their own methods to achieve the ultimate aim, not wishing their secrets to be stolen by others or too easily attained by the uninitiated. The emblems used in illustrating the alchemical process are a language that it is very possible Shakespeare understood and used himself, full of strange beasts and fantastical occurrences, which explains, for example, lions, bears, and coastlines where you might not usually expect to see them.

In more recent centuries, the study of alchemy has become more transparent, and the modern understanding of psychology has also been applied. The essential four stages of the process are:

☞ Nigredo/blackening, in which the earthly self is burnt and dissolved away.

☞ Albedo/whitening, in which the lunar, feminine aspect of the soul is awakened.

☞ Citrinitas/yellowing, in which the solar, masculine aspect
of the soul is awakened.

☞ Rubedo/reddening, in which the male and female are joined
as one to form the androgyne, and the golden child
or philosopher's stone is born.

Within each of these four processes are repeated cycles of breaking down and purification, which have been variously documented as anything up to seventy-five key
stages! For our purposes, and in keeping with the sacred Hermetic structure of seven,
we may compare events in Shakespeare's plays to seven key stages in the alchemical
process based on the sequence as illustrated in the Azoth of the Philosophers (see next
page): calcination, dissolution, separation, conjunction, fermentation, distillation, and
coagulation. This number and correlation to the number of the "wandering stars" makes
sense since alchemists (there are some still working in practical alchemy today) work
with base metals—lead (Saturn), tin (Jupiter), iron (Mars), copper (Venus), and quicksilver (Mercury)—in order to translate them to silver (moon) and gold (sun). Therefore,
these seven stages also can be related to the qualities of the seven planets.

The number seven also connects to the four elements of earth, water, fire, and air plus
the three essentials of alchemy: salt, sulfur, and mercury. The interplay of these three
archetypes, also known as Corpus, Spiritus, and Anima respectively (Body, Spirit, and
Soul), is fundamental to the understanding of alchemy on both physical and a spiritual/
psychological level. Alchemists believe that these three forces are at work within all
substances as much as within the human consciousness, again an expression of the overriding philosophy of "All is one" or "As above, so below."

Calcination (Saturn/Lead/Fire)

I am thy father's spirit,

Doom'd for a certain term to walk the night,

And for the day confin'd to fast in fires,

Till the foul crimes done in my days of nature

Are burnt and purg'd away.

—*Hamlet,* ACT 1, SCENE 5

The Azoth of the Philosophers © Dennis
William Hauck, 2013. Based on
Le Azoth des Philosophes, 1659.

Calcination is the first stage in the purification of a subject whereby the gross and unnecessary matter is burnt away, leaving only what is essential and true. This process relates to physical death, or seeming death, or more accurately a process by which the ego and false self that is built up by ego is purged.

Symbols relating to this first stage in the nigredo or blackening process are skulls, black crows/ravens, bonfires, red lions fighting other creatures, a solar king figure burning, and yellow lions fighting green serpents. Lions and serpents of varying colours are significant reoccurring symbols, as are the solar king and the lunar queen. The latter represent the male and female polarity of the personality or, at its most basic level, thoughts and feelings respectively. The red/yellow lion represents fiery sulphur, and the green serpent stands for unrefined mercury that must be purified.

Dissolution (Jupiter/Tin/Water)

Captain: Assure yourself, after our ship did split,

When you and those poor number saved with you

Hung on our driving boat, I saw your brother,

Most provident in peril, bind himself,

Courage and hope both teaching him the practise,

To a strong mast that lived upon the sea;

Where, like Arion on the dolphin's back,

I saw him hold acquaintance with the waves

So long as I could see.

Viola: For saying so, there's gold.

—*Twelfth Night*, ACT 1, SCENE 2

In dissolution the remains of the calcination process are dissolved in water or acid. Here we see the conscious mind losing itself in the waters of the subconscious, uncovering through dreams and visions aspects that may have been buried and allowing trauma to be released.

In this stage the green snake becomes the more evolved form of the green lion as the mercury begins to be purified; the black bird watches itself become white. Imagery related to kings and queens swimming in water, dark dragons, and demons or beasts guarding treasure all relate to this stage.

Separation (Mars/Iron/Air)

Some say the lark makes sweet division;

This doth not so, for she divideth us.

—*Romeo and Juliet*, ACT 3, SCENE 5

In this part of the process, the unnecessary substances that have been separated from the essential parts in the previous stages are discarded, and the parts that are to continue being purified are saved through a process of filtration. At this stage the revealed aspects of self are seen as being in conflict with each other or at least under challenging circumstances, so symbolism related to this stage includes apocalyptic imagery, weapons being wielded, heaven and earth being separated, and king and queen being forcibly separated, often by an aggressive caduceus-wielding Hermes! Birds taking flight are also associated with this stage: the original black bird is seen to split into two white birds as we enter the albedo or whitening stage of the overall process.

Conjunction (Venus/Copper/Earth)

I might ask you for your commission;

but—I do take thee,

Orlando, for my husband. There's

a girl goes before the priest;

and, certainly, a woman's thought

runs before her actions.

—*As You Like It*, ACT 4, SCENE I

This stage of the process involves the joining together of the purified components that have been retained from the overall process thus far. This is represented by intercourse, the rejoining of heaven and earth, and the marriage of the rational mind as Sun King and intuitive feeling as Moon Queen. This joining of male and female is also represented by

Janus or other two-faced figures, and also hermaphrodites. It is also sometimes shown as a rainbow or a bird descending into flames.

Fermentation (Mercury/Quicksilver/Sulphur-Spiritus)

For if the sun breed maggots in a dead dog,

being a god kissing carrion.

—*Hamlet,* ACT 2, SCENE 2

Fermentation is a two-stage process towards elevating the newly rejoined components to their higher spiritual selves, which begins with putrefaction. This part of the process is shown by more images of skulls, crows perching on corpses or rotting earth, and general images of death and decay. This is followed by the rebirth of the fermentation stage, which shows shoots and new life emerging from the darkness. Sometimes winged versions of the king and queen are shown to indicate their shedding of physical form and ascension to spirit. This brings about the yellowing or citrinitas stage in which a yellow ferment emerges from the putrid mixture. This was heralded by the multicoloured oily film known as "the peacock's tail."

Distillation (Moon/Silver/Mercury-Anima)

To his good friends thus wide I'll ope my arms

And, like the kind life-rend'ring pelican,

Repast them with my blood.

—*Hamlet,* ACT 4, SCENE 5

In distillation the fermented matter is boiled and condensed in order to release any volatile gases and leave it in a purer form, closer to its final solidity. This stage is represented by a unicorn, doves, a five-petaled rose, or the rosy cross (that is, a cross with the five-petaled rose at the centre). Sometimes distillation is represented by a pelican, a bird that was thought to nourish its young with its own blood, but also the name of a crucial piece of alchemical equipment. Psychologically at this stage, the last remnants of ego are stripped away so that the true potential of the unborn self can be revealed.

Coagulation (Sun/Gold/Salt-Corpus)

That done, our day of marriage shall be yours;

One feast, one house, one mutual happiness

—*Two Gentlemen of Verona*, ACT 5, SCENE 4

The final stage is the creation of the philosopher's stone or "lapidem," represented by an androgynous youth emerging from a grave or simply an egg-shaped stone. This is the rubedo/reddening stage and is sometimes shown as red birds rising from a purple moon. Other images associated with this stage are the phoenix, eagle, golden scales, lions and serpents harmoniously joined, and the king and queen appearing in their heavenly forms as Sol and Luna. Of course, this stage is also represented by pure gold, which is produced by this stage in successful metallurgical alchemy. This is the perfected form of the self, an enlightened and unified soul, spirit, and mind that carries within the full understanding that we are all one.

The Alchemical Process at Work in the Plays

Are you a god? would you create me new?

Transform me then, and to your power I'll yield.

—*Comedy of Errors*, ACT 3, SCENE 2

Once these key stages and symbols of the alchemical process are understood, we can quickly see how they may be applied to Shakespeare's plays, with some focusing on certain stages more than others but with the comedies in particular following the whole process. For example, many of these stages can be seen in *Hamlet* (for a synopsis, see page 116), with its iconography particularly dwelling on the putrefaction stage and the themes of death and melancholy encapsulating the spirit of Saturn. Many of the other stages can also be found, however. The ghost of Hamlet senior describing purgatory might well be also describing calcination, and the dead king is an appropriate symbol for the first stage of the process. Hamlet, as mercurial as he is saturnine, trying to separate the newly married Gertrude and Claudius, resembles the image for separation. The drowning of Ophelia could be related to dissolution, and so on. The stages are there but darkly twisted and out of sequence, with the state of Denmark being so rotten that the rebirth can only be found through the death of all corrupt characters and the son figure of Hamlet being replaced by another son, Fortinbras, with only the seemingly uncorrupted Horatio remaining.

Similar patterns are found throughout the tragedies, where peace is ultimately found through the sacrifice of the tragic heroes or villains who come to know and face themselves during the course of the plays. In the comedies we find that the individual may be redeemed through the alchemical process, yet in the tragedies the land is healed through sacrifice. In the late romances we find that both land and individual are united and redeemed, in keeping with the principle that the king and the land are one. Whilst we will look in more detail at the most obviously alchemical and initiatory *The Tempest* and the less well-known depths of *The Winter's Tale* in a moment, it is first rewarding to look at the innately alchemical structure of Shakespeare's comedies, which all too often may be dismissed as simply being frivolous fun. We will take *Twelfth Night* as an example, which should give you the necessary tools in order to interpret the inherent alchemical language and structure of the other plays at your leisure. However, even a surface read shows that the themes of separation, transformation, challenges, and reconciliation are the core of all the comedies.

The Alchemical Journey in Twelfth Night

A spirit I am indeed;

But am in that dimension grossly clad

Which from the womb I did participate.

—*Twelfth Night*, ACT 5, SCENE 1

When considering the events of a play, it is valuable to take into account those events that are described as already having taken part before the play itself begins, for they are also part of the process. In *Twelfth Night* we learn that twins Viola and Sebastian lost their father when they were thirteen years old, and we also know that Olivia is in mourning for her brother after already having lost her father at an early age. Thus the calcination process has already begun with physical deaths, and with the play opening with Orsino's melancholy brought on by Olivia's mourning state and refusal to entertain

Twelfth Night:
A Brief Summary

Shipwreck! Twins! Confusion! A dash of melancholy. *Twelfth Night* is one of Shakespeare's most beloved plays, following the adventures of Viola, an intrepid cross-dressing heroine who finds herself on a strange shore and separated from her twin, Sebastian, whom she presumes drowned after their ship is wrecked. She takes employment with the local count, Orsino, under the name Cesario, undertaking to woo the reluctant Countess Olivia on his behalf, who is in a long period of mourning for her own brother and father. Olivia falls for Cesario, Viola falls for Orsino, and Orsino is very confused about his feelings for Cesario. There is also a very entertaining subplot with Olivia's debauched relative, Sir Toby Belch; his sidekick, Sir Andrew Aguecheek; and Olivia's maid, Maria, plotting to humiliate Olivia's proud steward, Malvolio. A fake letter! Yellow stockings! A madhouse! Yes, it escalates quickly. In any case, Sebastian is fine, he marries Olivia, the twins are joyfully reunited, Viola reveals that Orsino need no longer be confused about his sexuality, and mostly people are happy—except for the rather unfairly treated Malvolio, who swears vengeance, and the sea captain, Antonio, who is responsible for rescuing Sebastian and has unrequited love for him. Oh, and Sir Andrew, who is callously cast aside by Sir Toby. Perhaps he and Antonio find each other later; that would be nice.

his romantic advances, there is no doubt of Saturn's influence. We then enter the dissolution and separation stage as Viola and Sebastian are shipwrecked and separated, each believing the other to be drowned.

Viola then takes on the guise of the androgyne or hermaphrodite by disguising herself as a boy, instantly falling under the influence of Venus as she falls in love with Orsino and Olivia falls for her male disguise, Cesario. Meanwhile, Sebastian is rescued by Antonio, who falls for him. This causes a quickening and a shift into the conjunction phase. The fermentation phase may be represented by the extreme drinking of Toby Belch and company, as well as in the sorrow caused by the apparent unrequited nature of Viola's love for Orsino, as this short extract clearly contains imagery and colour symbolism relating to this stage of the alchemical process:

> ORSINO: And what's her history?
>
> VIOLA: A blank, my lord. She never told her love,
>
> But let concealment, like a worm i' the bud,
>
> Feed on her damask cheek: she pined in thought,
>
> And with a green and yellow melancholy
>
> She sat like patience on a monument,
>
> Smiling at grief. Was not this love indeed?
>
> (ACT 2, SCENE 4)

The distillation process occurs as confusion and conflict reach their peak, with all characters put under stress until their true identities and feelings are revealed, resulting in the coagulation of multiple marriages in the final scene.

Symbols, themes, and plot points to look for:

> TWINS/CLOSE FRIENDS THAT SEPARATE AND REJOIN: Twins are the most obvious symbol of one being that is divided, especially when they are indistinguishable, as in both *Twelfth Night* and *The Comedy of Errors*. However, the same applies to close friends who describe themselves as inseparable and then are forced apart by conflict. For example, in *Two Gentlemen of Verona*, the self is split into the constant Valentine, who represents the immortal spirit, and the shifting Proteus, who must be put through challenges in order to once again rejoin his higher self. We also

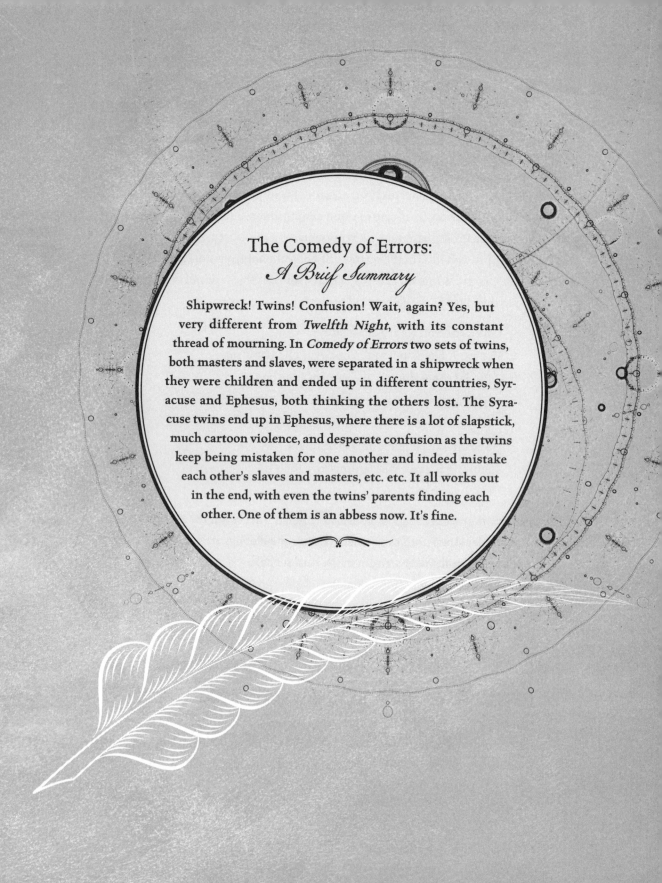

The Comedy of Errors:
A Brief Summary

Shipwreck! Twins! Confusion! Wait, again? Yes, but very different from *Twelfth Night*, with its constant thread of mourning. In *Comedy of Errors* two sets of twins, both masters and slaves, were separated in a shipwreck when they were children and ended up in different countries, Syracuse and Ephesus, both thinking the others lost. The Syracuse twins end up in Ephesus, where there is a lot of slapstick, much cartoon violence, and desperate confusion as the twins keep being mistaken for one another and indeed mistake each other's slaves and masters, etc. etc. It all works out in the end, with even the twins' parents finding each other. One of them is an abbess now. It's fine.

see this kind of friendship between Helena and Hermia in A *Midsummer Night's Dream*, made clear by Helena's description in act 3, scene 2:

> We, Hermia, like two artificial gods,
>
> Have with our needles created both one flower,
>
> Both on one sampler, sitting on one cushion,
>
> Both warbling of one song, both in one key,
>
> As if our hands, our sides, voices and minds,
>
> Had been incorporate. So we grow together,
>
> Like to a double cherry, seeming parted,
>
> But yet an union in partition;
>
> Two lovely berries moulded on one stem;
>
> So, with two seeming bodies, but one heart…

ANDROGYNOUS YOUTH/HERMAPHRODITE/CROSS-DRESSING/ DISGUISE: The androgyne or hermaphrodite is a key symbol in the alchemical process as male and female sides of the personality come into balance, represented by such cross-dressing heroines as Viola, Rosalind, Julia, Portia, and Imogen.

KINGS AND QUEENS BEING SEPARATED AND REUNITED: Similarly to twins/siblings/friends being separated and reunited, the Sun King and Lunar Queen are symbols that may be represented by characters in Shakespeare's plays, most obviously in A *Midsummer Night's Dream* where the conflict between Oberon and Titania, who has one of the names of the moon goddess Diana (much more about her in a later chapter), has caused nature to be out of balance. In *Pericles* Thaisa is thought drowned at sea but is miraculously brought to life and becomes a priestess of Diana, until she is reunited years later with her royal husband and her pure daughter, Marina, during the coagulation stage of the play. In this instance, the reuniting of king and queen with their child, Marina, represents the discovery of the philosopher's stone.

KINGS/QUEENS AND THEIR CHILDREN BEING SEPARATED BY DEATH OR PRESUMED DEATH: Another recurring theme of separation and reunification, the kings and queens represent the old self and their children the new, purified self. In comedies and romances, this tends to be an illusory death; in tragedies the death is literal and the alchemical operation is failed or incomplete. Those who are separated are not reunited, and healing can only be brought about through sacrifice. Examples of successful reunions include Pericles, Thaisa, and Marina in *Pericles*; Alonso and Ferdinand in *The Tempest*; Cymbeline and Imogen in *Cymbeline*; Leontes, Hermione, and Perdita in *The Winter's Tale*. Tragic examples include Hamlets senior and junior in *Hamlet* and Lear and Cordelia in *King Lear*.

EXTREME ENCOUNTERS WITH THE ELEMENTS: An unexpected coastline in a country known to be landlocked (as in *The Winter's Tale*), characters being lost at sea or presumed dead, and extreme storms or fires—all of these may mark the alchemical process at work within the play.

LIONS, SERPENTS, RAVENS, DOVES, BEARS AND OTHER UNUSUAL ANIMAL REFERENCES: Lions and serpents, especially when mentioned together or in close succession, are symbols of the alchemical process at work, as are ravens and doves, or at least they can be read this way. It's difficult to be certain in all cases that the imagery is intentionally alchemical, but viewing it through the lens of esoteric learning can lend a deeper dimension to the text. Sometimes a lion may well just be a lion, but if it seems to be related to a key stage in the process that the characters are currently experiencing, it may be interpreted as an alchemical symbol. In *As You Like It*, we have a clear example of an alchemical process being described when Orlando's brother Oliver, with whom he has been in conflict, describes in act 4, scene 3 how they came to be reconciled:

> OLIVER: Lo, what befell! He threw his eye aside,
> And mark what object did present itself.
> Under an oak, whose boughs were moss'd with age,
> And high top bald with dry antiquity,
> A wretched ragged man, o'ergrown with hair,
> Lay sleeping on his back. About his neck

A green and gilded snake had wreath'd itself,

Who with her head nimble in threats approach'd

The opening of his mouth; but suddenly,

Seeing Orlando, it unlink'd itself,

And with indented glides did slip away

Into a bush; under which bush's shade

A lioness, with udders all drawn dry,

Lay couching, head on ground, with catlike watch,

When that the sleeping man should stir; for 'tis

The royal disposition of that beast

To prey on nothing that doth seem as dead.

This seen, Orlando did approach the man,

And found it was his brother, his elder brother.

CELIA: O, I have heard him speak of that same brother;

And he did render him the most unnatural

That liv'd amongst men.

OLIVER: And well he might so do,

For well I know he was unnatural.

ROSALIND: But, to Orlando: did he leave him there,

Food to the suck'd and hungry lioness?

OLIVER: Twice did he turn his back, and purpos'd so;

But kindness, nobler ever than revenge,

And nature, stronger than his just occasion,

Made him give battle to the lioness,

Who quickly fell before him; in which hurtling

From miserable slumber I awak'd.

The imagery here takes us through fermentation into coagulation, with the colours green and gold emphasised, the image of Oliver appearing possibly already dead under the tree with the serpent wrapped around him, and the lioness whose udders are dry. These forces are overcome by Orlando, which brings about an awakening of higher consciousness and a reconciliation of the two brothers, as if the old "unnatural" version of Oliver had indeed been eaten away.

91

When a number of specifically alchemical symbols are mentioned in close succession, the author draws our attention to the stage of the alchemical process the character is experiencing, such as this moment of dissolution for Juliet. The key symbols of a dragon guarding a cave and a bird being both black and white at once are described here in *Romeo and Juliet's* act 3, scene 2:

> O serpent heart, hid with a flowering face!
>
> Did ever dragon keep so fair a cave?
>
> Beautiful tyrant! fiend angelical!
>
> Dove-feather'd raven! wolvish-ravening lamb!

Perhaps one of the most famous characters in all of Shakespeare's works is the bear of "exit, pursued by a bear" fame. In *The Winter's Tale*, the unfortunate Antigonus is chased and then consumed by a bear as he arrives by boat and leaves King Leontes' newly born rejected heir, Perdita, under a tree with a small chest of gold, which has a number of parallels with the symbolic language of the later nigredo stage of dissolution.

In some cases, particularly in the history plays, references to unexpected beasts may be more heraldic than alchemical, but experience, discernment, and judgement can lead to wise interpretation of which is the case.

The Late Plays

If this be magic, let it be an art lawful as eating.

—*The Winter's Tale*, ACT 5, SCENE 3

The most overtly Hermetic of Shakespeare's plays appear towards the end of his life, where he even shows magicians in a favourable light, giving us the wise Cerimon in *Pericles*, Paulina in *The Winter's Tale*, and, of course, Prospero in *The Tempest*. These late plays, which must include *Cymbeline* and its extraordinary direct appearance of the god Jupiter and themes that seem to encompass an initiatory journey, are exceptionally bold statements to make during the reign of the devout James I. It seems that Shakespeare was nostalgic for the reign of Elizabeth I, and he was not alone in hoping that James I's son and heir, Henry, would revive the golden age when he took the throne. Sadly, he died of typhoid fever in 1612 at the age of only eighteen, and Shakespeare's last play that we know of is dated to 1613.

Within these late plays we find a multilayered tapestry of magic and initiatory systems, as if Shakespeare was wishing to convey secrets learned through years of study and experience to his audiences, adding details that diverge in significantly magical ways from his source material. Although when the first folio was published in 1623 these plays were categorised alongside the comedies and tragedies, they defy the standard structure of those categories and nowadays are referred to as the romances.

Pericles

In act 3 of *Pericles*, Thaisa's coffin is washed up on the shore in Ephesus after a terrible storm in which she was thought to have died in childbirth. Her apparently dead body is discovered by Cerimon, a highly respected physician of the town, who is in no way ambiguous about his practice of the Hermetic arts:

> Virtue and cunning were endowments greater
>
> Than nobleness and riches: careless heirs
>
> May the two latter darken and expend;
>
> But immortality attends the former.
>
> Making a man a god. 'Tis known, I ever
>
> Have studied physic, through which secret art,
>
> By turning o'er authorities, I have,
>
> Together with my practise, made familiar
>
> To me and to my aid the blest infusions
>
> That dwell in vegetives, in metals, stones;
>
> And I can speak of the disturbances
>
> That nature works, and of her cures; which doth give me
>
> A more content in course of true delight
>
> Than to be thirsty after tottering honour,
>
> Or tie my treasure up in silken bags,
>
> To please the fool and death.
>
> (ACT 3, SCENE 2)

He then uses music to bring Thaisa back to life (or, at the very least, awareness). His learning appears to be based on principles that may be found in Agrippa or Paracelsus.

The Winter's Tale:
A Brief Summary

King Leontes of Sicilia suspects his pregnant wife, Hermione, of sleeping with his oldest friend, Polixenes, King of Bohemia. He tries to get the loyal Camillo to poison Polixenes, but Camillo warns him that Leontes has lost the plot, and they both flee to Bohemia. Leontes puts Hermione, who has just given birth to their daughter, on public trial, but when an oracle from Delphi reveals that she is true, Leontes totally flips and orders their newly born daughter banished. Their young son, Mamillius, dies of grief, and Hermione collapses. Paulina, a woman of the court and friend to Hermione who is afraid of no one, chides the king, telling him that Hermione has died, and he suddenly realises that he's been an absolute ass and goes into mourning. Paulina's husband takes the child to the shore of Bohemia, naming her Perdita. He gets eaten by a bear and she gets found by shepherds, who take her in. Anyway, sixteen years pass. Perdita falls for Polixenes' son, Florizel, and there's some larks with shepherds in Bohemia, everyone works through a lot of issues, they all end up back in Sicilia, and Paulina brings them all to a statue of Hermione, whom she brings to life. Everything is almost perfect, but Mamillius is gone forever.

As a modern audience we are sceptical that this is a legitimate case of revivification, but even if she were comatose, as opposed to actually deceased, it is a potent display of arcane ability. Thaisa's first words upon awakening are to the goddess Diana, to whom she then devotes herself in the temple. If we were left in any doubt as to Shakespeare's intention of showing Hermeticism in a positive light, then Cerimon ends the scene with "and Aesculapius guide us," a reference to the god of healing who guides his work and potentially also the book of *Asclepius*. This is one of many parallels between this scene and Hermione's resurrection in *The Winter's Tale*.

The Winter's Tale

In Shakespeare's source for the story of *The Winter's Tale*, Robert Greene's *Pandosto*, the queen dies after being accused of adultery and the king kills himself from remorse when he realises his error, so the fantastical animation of Hermione's statue and the reconciliation of king and queen once lessons are learnt are entirely Shakespeare's creations. We know, or at least strongly suspect, that Hermione must have only appeared dead at the time and has been kept in a secret location all these years by Paulina, especially since reference is made to the fact that she has aged, which Paulina explains away as "so much the more our carver's excellence; which lets go by some sixteen years and makes her as she lived now" (act 5, scene 3). However, if we, or Leontes, do not "awake our faith" as Paulina asks us to, the magic may not move our souls the way it is intended. We must be active, willing participants in the process. This particular rite appears to be inspired by a passage from the Hermetic book of *Asclepius*, in which the ancient Egyptian practice of the ensoulment of statues is mentioned. This connection seems even stronger when we consider the name Hermione has resonance with the divine name "Heimarmene," a goddess of Fate mentioned in the teachings of Asclepius:

> What we call Heimarmene, Asclepius, is the necessity in all events, which are always bound to one another by links that form a chain. She is the maker of everything then, or else the supreme god, or the ordering of all things in heaven and earth made steadfast by divine laws (Copenhaver 2002, 91).

Whether or not Paulina wields genuine magical powers that might be considered beyond usual human ken is ambiguous, but her use of music to alter consciousness, her wisdom in keeping Leontes and Hermione separate until the correct time, and her sage counsel to Leontes throughout show that she understands the alchemical nature of transformation and how to harness it. The multilayered mythological and magical nature of *The Winter's Tale* is undeniable. The alchemical journey is clear:

CALCINATION: Leontes, king of Sicilia, accuses his loyal queen, Hermione, of sleeping with his closest friend, Polixenes, king of Bohemia, and of carrying Polixenes' child. This conflict originates in a character fault within Leontes (named for the lion that he represents in this process) that must be purged, though he imagines the queen to be at fault, and she seemingly dies. Their young son also dies…

DISSOLUTION: …but their baby daughter is taken by water to Bohemia by Paulina's husband, Antigonus, who is eaten by a bear.

SEPARATION: Sixteen years pass, with Leontes thinking Hermione dead and his baby daughter lost, who grows into a young woman, Perdita, raised by shepherds in Bohemia. (Incidentally, this same period of time passes at around the same point in *Pericles* as we see baby Marina, whose mother Thaisa also seemed to die, grow from baby to young woman.)

CONJUNCTION: The shepherds hold a celebration in which Perdita and Florizel, the king of Bohemia's son who has disguised himself as a shepherd, are betrothed.

DISTILLATION: Polixenes is furious that his son would choose a lowly shepherdess against his will and forbids the union. Florizel and Perdita flee across the water to Sicilia, with Perdita disguised as a boy.

FERMENTATION: A mournful yet reformed Leontes plus Polixines, Florizel, and Perdita are taken by Paulina to visit the memorial statue of the supposedly deceased Hermione.

COAGULATION: The queen is miraculously restored to life, reunited with her daughter, the king redeemed, the couples joined.

The Mysteries of Eleusis

However, our magician figure Paulina plays a key role in another level of mystery within this play. She has no fear of standing up to Leontes and is a psychopomp in that she goes between the court and the outer world, seemingly wielding her own authority wherever she goes. She is the protectress of Hermione over many years. In the greater initiatory rite represented by this play, she stands for the goddess Hekate and her role within the Eleusinian mysteries, the ancient initiatory tradition of death and resurrection based upon the myth of Persephone. *The Winter's Tale* becomes a far less mysterious title when we realise that it is essentially a retelling of this myth that tells how winter came to be, with Hermione as Demeter and Perdita (meaning "lost" in Latin) as Persephone. If there was any doubt to the intention of this connection, Shakespeare confirms it with Perdita's mention of her mythological equivalent in her first scene ("Proserpina" is the Roman name for Persephone, and "Dis" or "Pater Dis" is an alternative name for Hades/Pluto):

> O Proserpina,
>
> For the flowers now, that frighted thou let'st fall
>
> From Dis's waggon!
>
> (ACT 4, SCENE 4)

There are now many versions of this myth, but the earliest that we know of may be found in the Homeric hymn to Demeter from around the seventh century BCE. Briefly, the story goes as follows:

The god of the underworld, Hades, becomes enamoured of the youthful daughter of the goddess Demeter, Kore (Persephone), and kidnaps her, stealing her away to his realm of the dead and making her his queen. The grain goddess Demeter is devastated and wanders the land searching for her precious daughter, during which time nothing can grow because of her all-encompassing grief. After ten days, Demeter speaks with the torch-bearing Hekate, who heard the cries of Kore as she was taken but did not see who it was. Hekate accompanies Demeter to ask guidance from the solar deity Helios, who reveals that it was Hades who took her. The messenger god Hermes is able to bring Kore back to Demeter, now with the new name Persephone, befitting her role as queen of the underworld. However, because Persephone ate of the food of the underworld, four pomegranate seeds (the number of seeds varies in different versions), she must return to that realm for a third of every year, a month for every seed consumed. Hekate then takes the psychopomp role and becomes Persephone's guide and companion, protecting her on her journey to Hades and back every year. When Persephone is in the darkness of the underworld, Demeter grieves and we have winter, with the growth of life returning with her daughter in the spring.

The parallels are clear, even though there are obvious differences in the story, but the name of the play plus the certain details that Shakespeare adds make it clear that this is one of the esoteric layers of meaning that he has intended. Here are the relevant points:

Hermione is Demeter, lost in grief at the death of her son Mamillius and with fear of what will happen to her newborn daughter. Paulina (Hekate) is her close friend and advisor. Hermione appears to die of heartbreak and Sicilia descends into grieving. Perdita ("lost") is cast away to a distant shore. When we next see her, she is a young woman who has been raised by shepherds. Not only does this emphasise the connection with growth and crops, but also with the god Hermes/Mercury, who ruled over shepherds, and whose representative, Autolychus, we first meet in this setting. Her connection to the spring and divinity is further emphasised by her taking on the role of the spring goddess Flora in the shepherds' festival celebrations. Autolychus (Mercury) is instrumental in her return to Sicilia. Paulina holds a ceremony in which Hermione appears to be miraculously restored to life and is reunited with her daughter, bringing joy and restoration.

From what we know of the Eleusinian initiatory rites, they involved a death and resurrection experience, bringing about a deep transformation of awareness of the nature of life and death, with initiates no longer fearing death after experiencing the immortal nature of their soul. We know that a version of these rites also took place in Sicily, where the play is set, and that there was an important temple dedicated to Demeter, Persephone, and Hekate at Selinunte in Sicily.

As a final fascination, in what we can only put down to magical synchronicity since it seems unlikely that Shakespeare could have been aware, a Roman tomb inscription from the fourth century tells us of a priestess called Paulina who was an "initiate of Ceres and the Eleusinian Mysteries, initiate of Hecate at Aegina, tauroboliata, hierophant" (D'Este 2009, 28).

We'll be returning to *The Winter's Tale* in later chapters, where we will look at how aspects of the play can be applied in ritual. An exercise inspired by this play is included at the end of this chapter.

The Tempest

But this rough magic I here abjure…

—*The Tempest*, ACT 5, SCENE 1

The last of our Shakespearian magicians and one of the most famous practitioners of the art in all literature is, of course, Prospero of *The Tempest*. Reputed to be the final non-collaborative play in the canon (it seems likely that *Henry VIII*, co-written with John Fletcher, came after), it is also the most obvious portrayal of benevolent Hermetic magical practice and is the key to unlocking much of the content of his earlier plays. It also makes a profound political statement about the treatment of Dee and other magical practitioners of the time, as well as showing Shakespeare's hopes for the future.

Firstly, let us apply the Hermetic systems we have learned so far to the play and see how its plot and characters fit within them.

The Four (Five) Elements in the Tempest

Starting with the simplest building blocks, we can apply the four elements to the main characters quite easily. Miranda, all compassion, empathy, and deep feeling, embodies the element of water. Prospero's logic, book learning, and clarity marks him as the element of air. Caliban is literally referred to by Prospero as "thou earth," and his connection to the natural ways and secrets of the island show this to be an accurate placing. The element of fire may be seen both in its positive aspect in the desire of the young Ferdinand or in its negative aspect in the cruelty and severity of Antonio. One might be tempted to place Ariel as air (as an "airy spirit") or fire, but Ariel might be better fitted to the invisible fifth element, the quintessence. Ariel represents the Mercurius, the hermaphroditic spiritual fire and essential active principle of the alchemical process, so let us look at that process at work within the play next.

The Alchemical Journey of the Tempest

The Tempest is the most obviously alchemical of Shakespeare's plays. As John S. Mebane observes,

> Shakespeare may well have been aware of the alchemical meaning of the term *tempest*: it is a boiling process which removes impurities from base metal and facilitates its transmutation into gold (Mebane 1992:181).

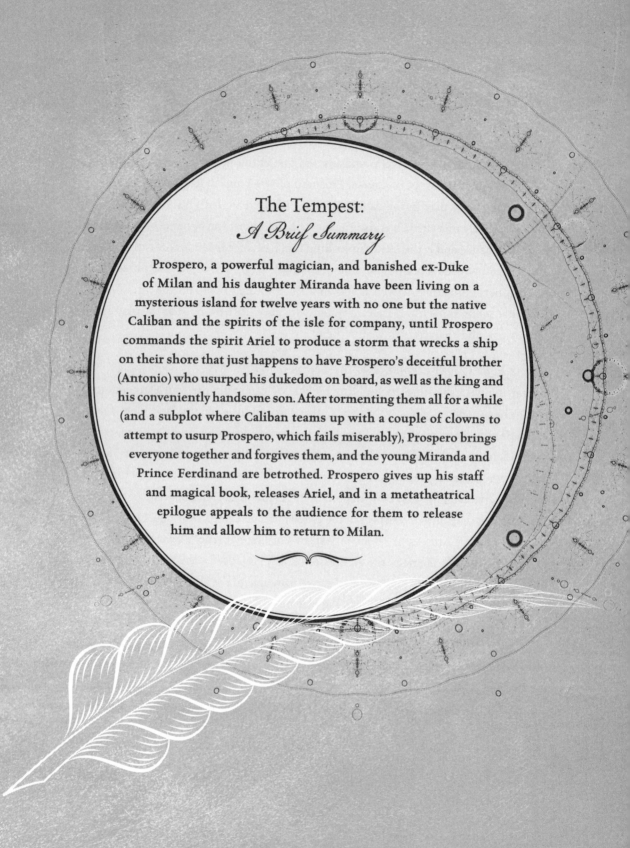

The Tempest:
A Brief Summary

Prospero, a powerful magician, and banished ex-Duke of Milan and his daughter Miranda have been living on a mysterious island for twelve years with no one but the native Caliban and the spirits of the isle for company, until Prospero commands the spirit Ariel to produce a storm that wrecks a ship on their shore that just happens to have Prospero's deceitful brother (Antonio) who usurped his dukedom on board, as well as the king and his conveniently handsome son. After tormenting them all for a while (and a subplot where Caliban teams up with a couple of clowns to attempt to usurp Prospero, which fails miserably), Prospero brings everyone together and forgives them, and the young Miranda and Prince Ferdinand are betrothed. Prospero gives up his staff and magical book, releases Ariel, and in a metatheatrical epilogue appeals to the audience for them to release him and allow him to return to Milan.

Whilst Prospero is the guiding will of the alchemist throughout this process, it is facilitated by the conjured spirit Ariel, whose name means "Lion of God" in Hebrew. Since we've already seen how crucial the symbol of the lion is within alchemy, the resonance of the name is clear. In his excellent in-depth study *Prospero's Island*, Noel Cobb proposes that

> Ariel is none other than the Mercurius hailed by the alchemists as both the
> prima materia of the Work and the highest transformation of it into the lapis…
> He is the beginning, the middle and the end of the Work (Cobb 1984, 55).

Once the work is complete, Prospero releases Ariel to the elements; once we have achieved unity, there is no longer need for possession and control.

CALCINATION: We begin the play with Ariel in a fiery form, creating the
titular tempest and driving all the crew and passengers aboard out of
their wits:

> I boarded the king's ship; now on the beak,
> Now in the waist, the deck, in every cabin,
> I flamed amazement: sometime I'ld divide,
> And burn in many places; on the topmast,
> The yards and bowsprit, would I flame distinctly,
> Then meet and join. Jove's lightnings, the precursors
> O' the dreadful thunder-claps, more momentary
> And sight-outrunning were not; the fire and cracks
> Of sulphurous roaring the most mighty Neptune
> Seem to besiege and make his bold waves tremble,
> Yea, his dread trident shake.

(ACT 1, SCENE 2)

From this description, given retrospectively in the second scene, we see that fire and burning came before the air and water elements of the storm, as befits the sequence of the alchemical process. The fire splits the ship, and all are plunged into the water.

DISSOLUTION: As in the shipwreck of *Twelfth Night*, the first three stages
in the sequence come swift on the heels of each other. The passengers
and crew, which include the king of Naples, Alonso, and his son

Ferdinand, are plunged into the water once the fire has divided the ship. Curiously, they emerge dry, not soaked. This might hint that the waters in fact represent quicksilver/mercury, Ariel as Mercurius in liquid form, from which they would emerge dry.

SEPARATION: The crew and passengers find themselves unharmed and in different locations upon the island, including the king and prince, who each presume the other to have drowned. In continuation of the Mars-ruled severity of this process, Alonso, Antonio, and Sebastian, the "three men of sin" as Ariel refers to them, are exposed to great terrors and discordant sounds created by Ariel under Prospero's command, including Ariel appearing as a harpy and reminding them of their wrongs against Prospero. King Alonso is deeply moved and transformed by this process.

CONJUNCTION: Miranda and Ferdinand meet, and after being put through many trials by Prospero, they are blessed as a couple by conjured versions of the goddesses Ceres, Juno, and Iris. However, the ceremony cannot be completed as there is still work to be done to deal with the corrupt Caliban, Stephano, and Trinculo, who plot against his life.

FERMENTATION: Act 4, scene 1 then takes on a melancholic and meditative feel with one of the most beautiful and moving speeches of any of the plays. When we read it within its full context, we see the fragility and mortality of Prospero, and indeed all life, revealed:

> Our revels now are ended. These our actors,
> As I foretold you, were all spirits and
> Are melted into air, into thin air:
> And, like the baseless fabric of this vision,
> The cloud-capp'd towers, the gorgeous palaces,
> The solemn temples, the great globe itself,
> Ye all which it inherit, shall dissolve
> And, like this insubstantial pageant faded,
> Leave not a rack behind. We are such stuff

As dreams are made on, and our little life

Is rounded with a sleep.

From this the scene shifts to the more literal fermentation of the drunken plotters Caliban, Stephano, and Trinculo.

DISTILLATION: Those that have chiefly wronged Prospero have been kept confined for some time in magical imprisonment, left with only their grief and realisations of their sins. Even the spirit Ariel recognises that this has been sufficient time for them to have been purified and urges Prospero to act with his conscience to release them and progress to the final stage in act 5, scene 1:

> ARIEL: They cannot budge till your release. The king,
>
>   His brother and yours, abide all three distracted
>
>   And the remainder mourning over them,
>
>   Brimful of sorrow and dismay; but chiefly
>
>   Him that you term'd, sir, 'The good old lord Gonzalo;'
>
>   His tears run down his beard, like winter's drops
>
>   From eaves of reeds. Your charm so strongly works 'em
>
>   That if you now beheld them, your affections
>
>   Would become tender.
>
> PROSPERO: Dost thou think so, spirit?
>
> ARIEL: Mine would, sir, were I human.
>
> PROSPERO: And mine shall.

The description of the tears "like winter's drops" particularly brings to mind the physical process of distillation.

COAGULATION: The king is reunited with his son, and his son is to be joined in marriage with Miranda, whose purity represents the attainment of the philosopher's stone. Prospero regains his dukedom, and we, the audience, are left to decide his fate. Curiously, Antonio seems to be unmoved by the whole journey, but we see that it was Prospero who truly needed to be redeemed and who emerges as the ultimate philosopher king, as was aspired to in Plato's *Republic*.

Astrology in the Tempest

> I find my zenith doth depend upon
> A most auspicious star, whose influence
> If now I court not but omit, my fortunes
> Will ever after droop.

The above quote from act 1, scene 2 highlights that Prospero is not as all-powerful as he may sometimes seem; his powers depend on divine providence and timing. Indeed, *The Tempest* shows Shakespeare at his most time conscious, being very clear how much time passes in every instance, from the twelve years that Ariel has spent trapped in the tree, the equal length of time it has been since Prospero freed him upon his and Miranda's arrival on the island, down to how many hours pass between the events of the play. His plan must be enacted within this strict span of time in order to come to fruition. This fits with the magical workings found in Agrippa's *Three Books*, which Prospero is almost certainly working from. The name of the spirit Ariel is also to be found there and is described as "the name of an angel, and is the same as the Lion of God; sometimes also it is the name of an evil demon" (Agrippa 1993, 553). Perhaps Ariel's moral compass depends upon who commands him, but we know that there are tasks he will not perform as it was refusal to perform the dark will of Sycorax for which she punished the spirit by binding him in the tree.

The period of twelve years is not circumstantial. Twelve is a significant number within occult traditions as detailed also in Agrippa:

> The number twelve is divine, and that whereby the celestials are measured; it is also the number of the signs in the zodiac over which there are twelve angels as chiefs…In twelve years also Jupiter perfects his course (Agrippa 1993, 292).

So it would appear that the star upon which Prospero is dependant for his operation is the movement of the planet Jupiter, which was regarded as "auspicious" indeed.

Music as Magic in the Tempest

Songs, music, and sound play a crucial part in the magic as it is worked by Prospero through Ariel. It is the means by which Ariel chiefly manipulates his charges but also is an innate quality of the isle, hence Caliban's poetic description in act 3, scene 2:

Be not afeard; the isle is full of noises,

Sounds and sweet airs, that give delight and hurt not.

Sometimes a thousand twangling instruments

Will hum about mine ears, and sometime voices

That, if I then had waked after long sleep,

Will make me sleep again: and then, in dreaming,

The clouds methought would open and show riches

Ready to drop upon me that, when I waked,

I cried to dream again.

Just as music brings Thaisa back to life and Pericles back to sanity, so the songs of Ariel can distract, provoke, drive insane, or evoke deep, cathartic remorse and grief. The innate ability of music to alter states of human consciousness is a parallel within both magic and theatre. Agrippa mentions music frequently throughout the *Three Books*, remarking that:

> Musical harmony also is not destitute of the gifts of the stars; for it is a most powerful imaginer of all things, which whilst it follows opportunely the celestial bodies, doth wonderfully allure the celestial influence, and doth change the affections, intentions, gestures, motions, actions and dispositions of all the hearers, and doth quietly allure them to its own properties, as to gladness, lamentation, to boldness or rest (Agrippa 1993, 333).

The Tempest on the Tree of Life

There are no fixed and certain answers as to where we might place the various elements of any play upon the Qabalistic Tree of Life, but here are my own thoughts based upon my own current level of understanding. You may reflect upon these and surmise your own as you wish, according to your own insights.

From the tenth sephira ascending:

MALKUTH (KINGDOM): In Malkuth, or the Kingdom, I place Caliban. He is accompanied there by the base fools Stephano and Trinculo, but whilst he mistakes them for gods for a while, he is the true ruler of the earth element and the inheritor of the earthly natural wisdom of the isle. He is incapable of ascending beyond this sphere, but he does not aspire to. Noel Cobb compares Caliban to "a kind of demi-god of the forests. Although he doesn't actually possess magical powers of transformation, intuition and enchantment, he resembles, at least in one respect, the archetypal Celtic Wizard-Shaman, Merlin, in his manifestation as 'The Ward of the Wood'" (Cobb 1984, 121). Caliban is the dark shadow of Prospero that he must integrate, which he does at the end of the play when he admits, "This thing of darkness I acknowledge mine" (act 5, scene 1). It is then fitting that Caliban be placed in line directly beneath Prospero (whom I have placed at the heart of the tree, in Tiphareth).

YESOD (FOUNDATION): The foundation of the play is the island itself, which is a character in its own right. It reflects and obeys Prospero once he has gleaned its secrets from Caliban, and, as is fitting for a sphere ruled by the moon, is a place of illusion and the subconscious, where the land reflects the inner landscape of self. We may also place Sycorax in this sephira, "one so strong that could control the moon" (act 5, scene 1). (More on Sycorax later when we talk about witches!)

HOD (SPLENDOUR): Hod, being ruled by Mercury, must be the sephira of Ariel, the alchemical Mercurius and spiritual servant of Prospero.

NETZACH (VICTORY): Venus rules this sphere, so here we place the young lovers Miranda and Ferdinand.

TIPHARETH (BEAUTY): Prospero is placed here at the heart of the tree, representing the sun, around which all the action revolves and reflecting the divine light of Kether.

GEBURAH (SEVERITY): In Geburah, sphere of Mars, are placed the opposing, aggressive forces of Antonio, Sebastian, and initially Alonso. Alonso, King of Naples, enabled and encouraged Antonio's ousting of Prospero from Milan. However, through the course of the play he is transformed, and by the end he may be placed with Gonzalo in Chesed.

CHESED (MERCY): In the sephira of Jupiter we may place the merciful and compassionate Gonzalo, who demonstrates patience, kindness, empathy, and wisdom throughout the play. It is due to the kindness of Gonzalo that Prospero was able to take his books from Milan to the island and thus enable the entire plot.

BINAH (UNDERSTANDING): Heading the pillar of severity is Naples itself, which along with its king is brought into harmony through the course of the play.

CHOKMAH (WISDOM): Opposite from Naples, heading the pillar of Mercy, is Milan, the wisdom to which Prospero is able to return to balance.

KETHER (CROWN): Since Kether is an unknowable divine source, we have a choice of either leaving it unknowable and placing nothing here; naming it as the spiritual source from which ultimately Prospero draws his power; naming it as Miranda's mother, whom we hear nothing about other than she is "a piece of virtue" (act 1, scene 2); or a wildcard option: the audience. Prospero breaks the fourth wall utterly in the epilogue when he directly appeals to the audience to set him free. Is the imagination of the audience the source of his power all along?

DAATH (KNOWLEDGE): In the mysterious eleventh invisible sephira we place Prospero's books. But what are they? Most likely Agrippa's *Three Books of Occult Philosophy*, but additionally, possibly, the works of John Dee.

Dee = Prospero = Shakespeare

There have naturally been many comparisons made between Prospero and Elizabeth's favoured astrologer, navigator, mathematician, and magician, John Dee, with good reason. It seems very likely that Dee's fall from grace and eventual death in poverty in 1608/9 would have been an influence on the writing of Shakespeare's final play in 1610–11. It has also been said that Prospero represents Shakespeare himself and that the breaking of Prospero's staff and drowning of his book is symbolic of Shakespeare putting down his quill and writing no more. This also rings true, and if so, it seems likely that Shakespeare related to Dee on a profound level. Frances Yates observed that Prospero's magic was unlike that of our other magicians of the late plays, Cerimon and Paulina, noting that out of the kinds of magic featured in Agrippa's *Three Books*,

> Prospero would seem to use mainly the Cabalistic conjuring magic, rather than the healing magic of Cerimon, or the profound natural magic which pervades *The Winter's Tale* (Yates 1975, 94).

—which certainly would connect him to the methods that Dee was known for, but might the others not also have some connection? After all, they were written at a time when Shakespeare may have been trying to show the beneficent nature of magic to fight the tide that was most certainly turning against the old occult practices. Cerimon's Paracelsian healing fits with Dee's philosophy of interconnectness, but most pertinently, Paulina and her theatrics have a direct connection.

In his early career, Dee was involved in design for theatre and created such wonders that he was accused of conspiring with devils to achieve impossible effects. In 1547 he famously created a huge beetle, large enough for a man to ride, which was then brought to life and flown out across the audience. To this day it is uncertain how this effect was achieved, but he maintained it was purely mathematics:

> Dee believed such artificial marvels showed that, with mathematics, man could achieve miracles to rival God (Wooley 2001, 14).

This apparent miraculous achievement—the animating of the inanimate with a hidden rational explanation—is very reminiscent of Paulina's "resurrection" of Hermione. But are these methods truly any less magical if the intended effect of wonder and transformation is the same?

Magic = Art = Theatre

Both magic and theatre are forms of art, and they are both branches of the same tree, with its roots in the enaction of the mysteries of ancient Greece. Magic and theatre's most profound effect is within the self, the purpose being initiation and connection with the divine. Shakespeare understood this, and in the last words of his last play, he gives us the key by which we may unlock this mystery: the process requires us, as Paulina requested, to awaken our faith. We must believe in the magic and be active participants or we will not be transported and transformed.

Exercise: Animating the Statue

This exercise is inspired by the final act of *The Winter's Tale* and the animating of Paulina's statue of Hermione. Whether we choose to interpret this scene literally as an act of magic or whether Paulina has been visiting Hermione in a secret location for sixteen years until this moment, it is still an intensely magical scene and one that finds its roots in the Hermetic tradition and the book of *Asclepius*. Beyond the spectacle of Hermione returning to life, what we are truly moved by in this scene is the redemption of Leontes. He has served his time in penance and learned the lessons of the past and, by a seeming miracle, what was lost to him is then returned.

The aim of this exercise is to face those events from our own pasts from which we seek redemption (actions we have committed that we carry through our lives as a burden of guilt) and to earn forgiveness through a positive act or actions in the world.

TIMING: Although this ritual can be performed at any time that is convenient, be sure that you are undistracted from the demands of daily life. It would be most powerful during a waning moon, particularly when Mercury is in retrograde motion—these timings are readily available on the internet or a good astrological almanac.

MATERIALS REQUIRED: Any natural biodegradable materials you are happy to make a small doll/statue/sculpture from; for example, wood, clay, papier-mâché, or cardboard.

A white candle or tealight in an appropriate holder.

Something on which to play music, either live or recorded. If recorded, choose a piece of music that brings to mind what you are seeking redemption for. Music played by yourself on an instrument may be similarly chosen or improvised in the moment as you choose.

INCENSE (OPTIONAL): For preference, rosemary (for remembrance). If you have access to fresh rosemary, you may wish to use it in the creation of your statue. Our sense of smell is directly connected to access of memory and is a powerful tool in ceremonies of this kind.

PREPARATION: Choose a time and place you know you will not be
disturbed to create your statue. Take the time to envision how you wish
to represent the wrong for which you wish to be forgiven. Is it a person?
An object? An abstract symbol? If abstract, try to find a way to personify
it so that it has a means by which it may communicate with you. As you
create your statue, invest it with love and your intent to heal the wounds
of the past. You may wish to sing to it as you create it. Think of a simple
and evocative name for your statue.

Once you are happy that your statue is complete, place it somewhere prominent in
your home so you will see it every day, and leave it for one full month. Leave it little
offerings and talk or sing to it daily. Once this month is passed, you are ready to perform
the ritual.

Ritual of Redemption

Before the ritual take a bath or shower to purify yourself and be sure you are wearing
clean and comfortable clothing and that you will not be disturbed. Be sure that you
have everything that you need before you start, that your statue is placed in a safe and
prominent position, and that you have somewhere comfortable where you will be able
to sit upright.

Light your candle and address the statue with the following words:

> O *royal piece,*
>
> *There's magic in thy majesty* (blow your breath into the statue)
>
> *Would you not deem it breathed and that those veins*
>
> *Did verily bear blood?* (blow your breath into the statue
>   a second time)
>
> *If you can behold it,*
>
> *I'll make the statue move indeed, descend*
>
> *And take you by the hand* (blow your breath into the statue a
>   third time)
>
> (with arms outstretched) *It is required*
>
> *You do awake your faith. Then all stand still;*
>
> *On: those that think it is unlawful business*

I am about, let them depart.

(play or sing music)

(with one hand extended towards statue)

'Tis time; descend; be stone no more; approach

Strike all that look upon with marvel. Come,

I'll fill your grave up: stir, nay, come away,

Bequeath to death your numbness, for from him

Dear life redeems you.

Take in as much detail you can about the statue in front of you. Sit in a comfortable, upright position with your arms and legs uncrossed, hands with palms upright, resting gently in a receptive posture. Chant the following until you are ready to visualise the statue in full detail with your eyes closed:

'Tis time; descend; be stone no more; approach

'Tis time; descend; be stone no more; approach

'Tis time; descend; be stone no more; approach…

When you are ready, close your eyes. A white fog surrounds you; you feel safe and calm. As the fog clears, you see your statue in front of you, the same size as you, in human form. Reach out your hand towards the statue and call it by name. In your own words, ask for forgiveness from the statue and what action it would ask you to perform in order to earn this forgiveness. Wait for the vision of your statue to give you an answer. You may receive this clearly as words or visuals or simply as an impression of what must be done. Thank your statue and promise to perform the act requested. If satisfied, the statue will take your hand. If not, you must return to this state after the requested act is performed and the statue will take your hand or request further action—repeat until the statue in your vision takes your hand. The white fog returns and you may open your eyes. Kiss your statue and return it to its place of reverence. Blow out the candle.

End. Close your space and ground yourself.

You now have a task or tasks to perform in the real world. Keep your statue in its place so that you see it every day as a reminder of this task until it is complete. Once it is complete, you may thank your statue and release it to the world by burying it in an appropriate space.

Now it is the time of night,
That the graves all gaping wide,
Every one lets forth his sprite,
In the church-way paths to glide…
A MIDSUMMER NIGHT'S DREAM
ACT 5, SCENE 1

FIVE

Ghosts

*W*hen the daytime-dwelling human folk are sleeping, it's then time for the other world of ghosts, fairies, and witches to take the proverbial (and literal) stage. The division between these three is often quite blurred in folklore, and whilst Shakespeare's work seems for the most part to keep a clear distinction, we shall see that there is some overlap in certain cases. Let us begin with one of the most famous plays in all literature, which, though it is known as a great tragedy and a study of human nature, melancholy, and existential angst, is also, arguably, a ghost story.

Hamlet: A Ghost Story

What is a ghost? Stephen said with tingling energy.

One who has faded into impalpability through death,

through absence, through change of manners.

—James Joyce, *Ulysses*

There is something tangible and dynamic about the ghost of Hamlet's father. He appears less the piteous shade and more the call to action who demands attention—and revenge. Unlike other ghosts within Shakespeare's canon, who we will discuss later, the ghost of Hamlet senior is seen by a number of people who are not directly connected to his story. In the very first scene, he appears to those who are keeping watch in the night-time hours as a very physical manifestation walking the battlements of Elsinore. He is clearly and instantly recognisable as the recently deceased King of Denmark by the guards Marcellus and Barnardo and, most significantly, the scholar and sceptic Horatio, Hamlet's closest friend. The fact that Horatio sees the ghost in the very first scene and then, as the play goes on, is established as the most grounded, level-headed, and trustworthy character in the play tells us that we are to believe the ghost to be real and in no way simply a projection of Hamlet junior's clearly unstable psyche (at least to begin with).

However, that still does not answer whether the ghost has good or ill intent. This question, along with other more famous conundrums, is for Hamlet to agonise over later. Marcellus and Barnardo designate Horatio as the best person to question the ghost since he is a scholar. This mention of his studious nature is not only important to establish him as a man of learning but also, for an early modern audience, would have placed him firmly in the humanist Protestant camp as opposed to the Catholic and more esoteric beliefs of the medieval and earlier Renaissance period. In fact, it is specified that both Horatio and Hamlet are students at Wittenberg University, where Martin Luther himself taught theology, and it was known that Lutheran philosophy embraced doubt and questioning within religious faith. However, as a man of learning faced with the irrational reality of a ghost risen from the Catholic purgatory, he also knows the proper way to question it. Within the papal tradition it was said that a ghost would appear three times silently and on its fourth appearance, if properly questioned, it would state the reason for its walking abroad. There was a tradition of questioning known as *discretio spirituum* where a ghost is forced to submit to a rigorous cross-examination centred on six key questions: Quis? Quid? Quare? Cui? Qualiter? Unde? In another, simplified version of this judicial ritual, there are three questions: Nomen? Causas? Remedium? (Greenblatt 2013, 103)

In modern English these questions translate to Who? What? Why? Which? How? Where? or the simplified Name? Cause? Remedy?

Horatio instantly identifies the unquiet spirit as the king and questions it before it vanishes as the first signs of dawn arrive. However, it does not answer, perhaps because it is not yet its traditional fourth appearance and that honour is reserved for the son of the deceased, young Hamlet himself.

> MARCELLUS: It faded on the crowing of the cock.
>
> Some say that ever 'gainst that season comes
>
> Wherein our Saviour's birth is celebrated,
>
> The bird of dawning singeth all night long:
>
> And then, they say, no spirit dares stir abroad;
>
> The nights are wholesome; then no planets strike,
>
> No fairy takes, nor witch hath power to charm,
>
> So hallow'd and so gracious is the time.
>
> (ACT I, SCENE 5)

Here again we have the mention of ghosts, fairies, and witches in one thought (plus a bonus mention of planetary influences). Horatio chooses to tell Hamlet of this sighting, not least because of what it might mean for the kingdom—"This bodes some strange eruption to our state" (act I, scene I)—as well as on a personal level for the recently bereaved prince. Hamlet is suddenly spurred out of melancholic reflection and into action at this news, with a string of questions for his friend as to the demeanour and appearance of the ghost—again, traditional questions that would inform of its nature and purpose—and resolves to watch with them that night in case it appears for the all-important fourth time. Of course it does and will speak with Hamlet alone after the proper questioning. Before the requisite plot point of demanding revenge, as is traditional for a ghost of this type and in keeping with the source material (a number of earlier versions of the tale exist, and spirits calling for revenge is handed down from the classical tradition), the spirit of Hamlet's father confirms his identity and describes his

Hamlet:
A Brief Summary

Something is rotten in the state of Denmark. The old King Hamlet has been dead less than two months and already the queen has married his slimy brother, Claudius. What's worse is that the old king isn't done yet; it turns out that he was murdered by Claudius and is haunting the battlements, calling for revenge from his son Hamlet, who really isn't that sort of prince. Prince Hamlet is more of an intellectual, a perpetual student and philosophiser with a possible tinge of Oedipal complex. At any rate, he does seem to have a problem with women, as he treats his young love, Ophelia, quite appallingly. Plus he accidentally kills her father, the queen's advisor Polonius; Ophelia goes mad and drowns herself, and her brother Laertes is, to understate matters slightly, not best pleased. Many excellent soliloquies, quotes you won't even realise you knew from this play, and even random pirates halfway through. Oh, and pretty much everyone except Hamlet's best friend Horatio and the invading Fortinbras dies at the end, obviously.

unfortunate otherworldly circumstances at length, making it as clear as possible that he is visiting from Catholic purgatory, a concept that in Shakespeare's time had recently been abolished:

> I am thy father's spirit,
>
> Doom'd for a certain term to walk the night,
>
> And for the day confin'd to fast in fires,
>
> Till the foul crimes done in my days of nature
>
> Are burnt and purg'd away. But that I am forbid
>
> To tell the secrets of my prison house,
>
> I could a tale unfold whose lightest word
>
> Would harrow up thy soul, freeze thy young blood,
>
> Make thy two eyes, like stars, start from their spheres,
>
> Thy knotted and combined locks to part,
>
> And each particular hair to stand on end
>
> Like quills upon the fretful porcupine.
>
> But this eternal blazon must not be
>
> To ears of flesh and blood. List, list, O, list!
>
> If thou didst ever thy dear father love…
>
> (ACT I, SCENE 5)

If that description was not enough for his audience to understand the nature of this particular spirit's otherworldly prison, as Hamlet returns to Horatio after the sighting, he exclaims that there is offence done and swears it in the name of St. Patrick, who was the keeper of the gates of purgatory. Thus, with the ghost of King Hamlet, Shakespeare gives us a creation that is truly liminal. Not only does he manifest from between worlds just as night turns to dawn, an all-too-brief sojourn from his holding place between earthly existence and heaven, but he symbolises the end of one era of belief and the dawning of another and gives cause to his son, our protagonist, to spend much of the rest of the play questioning everything he's been taught in the modern humanist school of philosophy.

Hamlet facing his father's ghost

A *Very Modern Ghost*

Hamlet's questioning of the nature of the ghost and what his true nature might be is at the very centre of the play, and it's also one of the things that makes *Hamlet* so unique in terms of its portrayal of the supernatural. Without the ghost's appearance, it's likely that not much would have happened at all, but it's not only the call to revenge that is crucial here in terms of plot. Indeed, this is the only aspect of the ghost's appearance that is in any way traditional and familiar to the Elizabethan audience. The ghosts of the classical tradition were the clear roots and inspiration for Elizabethan and Jacobean vengeful murdered ghosts, especially those found in the writings of Seneca, which was widely available in English translation during Shakespeare's time. Most ghostly appearances in plays were still echoing this old formula: appearing to a solitary individual, describing the classical Pagan underworld, and calling loudly for revenge (often with much wailing). This became an almost comical cliché, however, which Shakespeare very cleverly avoids in his most famous of tragedies.

The ghost's clear description of purgatory and his final request of "remember me" almost superseding the call for vengeance causes a deep theological problem for Hamlet and his audience. They have been told that purgatory is no longer a real place. It is the lies of the old Catholic Church. Purgatory is cancelled. This also means that a ghost cannot be the spirit of one who is trapped between worlds but must be either a heavenly messenger, a devil from hell come to cause mischief, or a hallucination brought on by an overly melancholic disposition. These are all possibilities that Hamlet discusses with the audience repeatedly. He would have us believe that were it not for these doubts as to the nature of the ghost, he would have avenged his father more swiftly, even as he also accuses himself of cowardice.

> For it cannot be but that I am pigeon liver'd and lack gall to
>   make oppression bitter, or ere now I should have fatted all
>   the region kites with this slave's offal…
> …the spirit that I have seen may be the devil, and the devil
>   hath power to assume a pleasing shape, yea, and perhaps
>   out of my weakness and my melancholy, as he is very
>   potent in such spirits, abuses me to damn me…
>
> (ACT 2, SCENE 2)

Both Hamlet and his audience are caught between the old world and the new, between the folkloric belief of the time in which ghosts (and fairies and witches, for that matter) were still considered to be very real and the contrasting beliefs of the dawning age of science shadowed by the new dominant religion. By having King Hamlet's ghost come from purgatory rather than the classical tradition of Hades, Shakespeare gave his audience a very modern hero visited by a very modern ghost, and as a result his dilemma would have seemed much more real and relatable to them. Whilst the existence of purgatory was denied, belief in hell as a destination that the soul could be doomed to eternity in was very real. Whilst we can enjoy the poetry, philosophy, and tragedy of *Hamlet* in our own rational age, the performance loses something of an edge if that belief is taken away. Hamlet is seen as vacillating, but he is facing the prospect of his own soul being damned for eternity if he is wrong. To take away the supernatural and religious reality of the original intent of the play and to present it in a completely psychological context is to lose something of its power and our primal connection to the themes. However, Shakespeare was also ahead of his time in this, and though he sets up the situation in order to show as much evidence as possible that the ghost and otherworldly phenomenon are real, he also gives his characters and audience cause to question whether this is always the case or whether they may sometimes be the manifestation of an unbalanced mind.

To be certain that the ghost was honest in his accusation of Claudius as his murderer (his own brother and ergo Hamlet's uncle), Hamlet stages "The Mousetrap," a play replicating the circumstances of his father's death to which Claudius's reactions confirm his guilt. Hamlet has no more excuses, at least in otherworldly terms. He is committed to vengeance as sworn "by heaven" after the first sighting. It's at this point that he seems to start to lose control of his mind for real after his initial supposedly performative "antic disposition," and it's also at this point that we meet the ghost again, in very different circumstances.

The Ghost in His Mother's Closet

The next time we meet the spectral Hamlet senior is during what is known as "the closet scene," where Hamlet confronts his mother in her private chambers after passing up an opportunity to dispatch Claudius as he is praying. Mistaking the concealed Polonius for the king, Hamlet commits his first murder and then forces his mother to confront her guilt over such swift remarriage to Claudius after the death of her first husband. It is almost as though his description—"see what a grace was seated on this brow; Hyperion's curls, the front of Jove himself" (act 3, scene 4)—acts as a conjuration of his father's ghost, but the marked difference with this appearance is that only Hamlet can see and hear him. Queen Gertrude is baffled by her son's apparent conversation with the air and thinks him mad. Are we to believe that the ghost has chosen not to reveal himself to Gertrude as he does not want to unsettle her further, or are we to consider the possibility that at this point the ghost is indeed "the very coinage" of his brain? "The transposition of furies and ghosts from external forces to internal mental states is a significant clue to Shakespeare's representation of the paranormal" (Bate 2018).

It is tempting to come to the conclusion, as Jonathan Bate does, that because we're given the possibility that the later sighting of the ghost is a psychological projection, that means the ghost's earlier appearances are also conjurations of a feverish mind and indeed leap to the final overarching theory that Shakespeare himself did not believe in magic or the supernatural. However, this discounts not only the multiple witnesses to the ghost's appearance in the play's opening scenes, but also the common folkloric knowledge that ghosts could choose to appear or not appear to whomever they choose. It seems more likely that the author enjoyed using the juxtaposition of medieval and modern philosophies to engage his audience in active thought and discussion about the subject. Unlike other playwrights of his time, there is usually some evidence of truth behind paranormal encounters that lends them believability and gravitas in their own right, whilst at the same time reflecting the inner mental landscape of his protagonists.

Coward Conscience: Ghosts and Suppressed Guilt

Thus conscience does make cowards of us all…

—*Hamlet*

O, coward conscience, how dost thou afflict me!

—*Richard* III

Having spent a good part of the last five years inhabiting both the roles of Hamlet and Richard III, it has been fascinating for me to note their linguistic overlap, in particular their use of "coward" and "conscience" in relation to each other. Another kinship

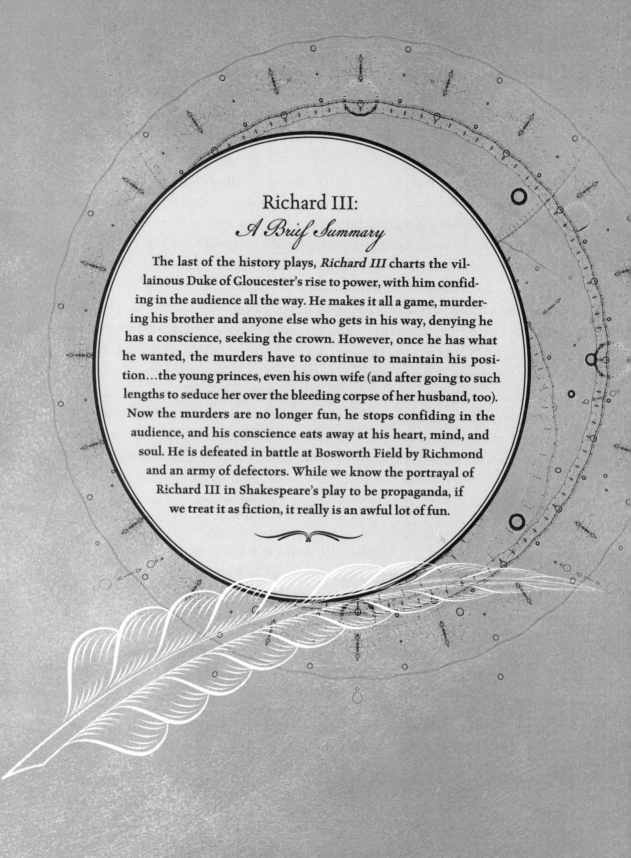

Richard III:
A Brief Summary

The last of the history plays, *Richard III* charts the villainous Duke of Gloucester's rise to power, with him confiding in the audience all the way. He makes it all a game, murdering his brother and anyone else who gets in his way, denying he has a conscience, seeking the crown. However, once he has what he wanted, the murders have to continue to maintain his position…the young princes, even his own wife (and after going to such lengths to seduce her over the bleeding corpse of her husband, too). Now the murders are no longer fun, he stops confiding in the audience, and his conscience eats away at his heart, mind, and soul. He is defeated in battle at Bosworth Field by Richmond and an army of defectors. While we know the portrayal of Richard III in Shakespeare's play to be propaganda, if we treat it as fiction, it really is an awful lot of fun.

between these characters is the significant influence that ghosts have upon them, but whilst Hamlet's ghost is a major plot point, the influence of ghosts on Richard's character is a purely internal one unless we believe they have the power to bless and to curse.

Richard III

Richard III is the first of Shakespeare's plays (as we currently understand the chronology) to feature ghosts. Unlike *Hamlet*, where the ghost appears in the very first scenes and is the initial spur for action, in *Richard* III they appear as the action reaches its climax. Richard has already proved himself a villain and is "in so far in blood that sin will pluck on sin." In order to gain and hold on to the coveted crown, he's already bumped off his brother, the Duke of Clarence, as well as Lord Hastings, Rivers, Grey, Vaughn, the two young princes, Lady Anne, Lord Buckingham, and (in the preceding *Henry* VI, *Part* III) Henry VI and Henry's son, the young Prince Edward. It's quite the body count. And they all come back to haunt him in his dreams as he sleeps in his tent the night before the Battle of Bosworth. This might be easily dismissed as simply the subconscious manifestations of a guilty conscience except for the fact that they simultaneously visit his enemy. Richmond, the supposedly far more wholesome rival to the crown whom Richard must face on the morrow, is also sleeping in his tent and also visited by each of Richard's victims in turn. In Shakespeare's time, most stage directions were to be derived from the dialogue—what we see in modern editions is all added by an editor—so it is fascinating to see how Shakespeare moulds this scene.

CURSES AND BLESSINGS BEFORE THE BATTLE

The ghosts appear one after the other in the order of their deaths, each systematically taking their turn to curse Richard, then bless Richmond. At this point we can derive simply from reading it that the stage must be split into the two camps so that action can quickly shift from one to the other. Each ghost bids Richard "despair and die" and Richmond to live and flourish. Buckingham's ghost is the last to speak:

> (To Richard) The first was I that helped thee to the crown;
> The last was I that felt thy tyranny.
> O, in the battle think on Buckingham,
> And die in terror of thy guiltiness.
> Dream on, dream on, of bloody deeds and death.

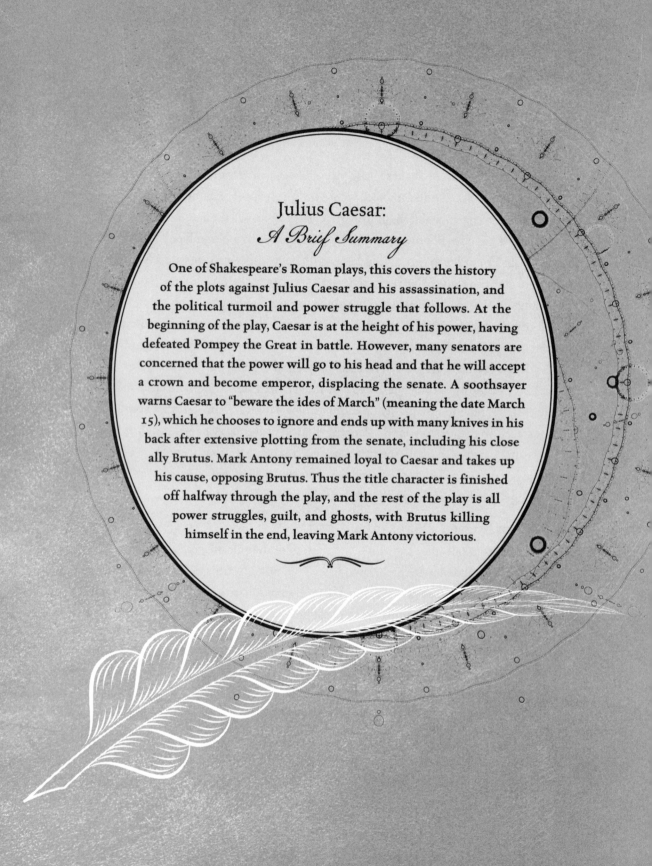

Julius Caesar:
A Brief Summary

One of Shakespeare's Roman plays, this covers the history of the plots against Julius Caesar and his assassination, and the political turmoil and power struggle that follows. At the beginning of the play, Caesar is at the height of his power, having defeated Pompey the Great in battle. However, many senators are concerned that the power will go to his head and that he will accept a crown and become emperor, displacing the senate. A soothsayer warns Caesar to "beware the ides of March" (meaning the date March 15), which he chooses to ignore and ends up with many knives in his back after extensive plotting from the senate, including his close ally Brutus. Mark Antony remained loyal to Caesar and takes up his cause, opposing Brutus. Thus the title character is finished off halfway through the play, and the rest of the play is all power struggles, guilt, and ghosts, with Brutus killing himself in the end, leaving Mark Antony victorious.

Fainting, despair, despairing yield thy breath.

(To Richmond) I died for hope ere I could lend thee aid;

But cheer thy heart, and be thou not dismayed.

God and good angels fight on Richmond's side,

And Richard fall in height of all his pride

(*Richard* III, ACT 5, SCENE 3)

Though it is mentioned in Holinshed's *Chronicles*, Shakespeare's source for the play, that Richard dreams of devils the night before battle, there is no mention of ghosts, so we know that this is entirely the author's dramatic invention. There are multiple layers of reality at work. When Richard awakes he is initially so full of horror that he is shouting as though he's in his last moments of life on the battlefield. This could be seen as simply a vivid nightmare except that it proves to be accurately prophetic. Although he is relieved when he realises that he is still in his tent as he utters "Soft, I did but dream," when Ratcliffe comes to his tent to help him into his armour, he admits that "shadows tonight have struck more terror to the soul of Richard that can the substance of ten thousand soldiers, armed in proof and led by shallow Richmond" (act 5, scene 3). This is a rare admittance of vulnerability for a character who previously has protested so much his lack of conscience that he has proclaimed "tear falling pity dwells not in this eye" (act 4, scene 2). He believes the spirits that appeared in his dream to be a manifestation of the conscience that he has been suppressing in order to become the villain he promised us he would become and is now himself horrified by, and this experience transforms him. Of course, he can never know that Richmond also sees the souls of his murdered victims, nor can Richmond know that they also visited Richard. Each character believes they have merely dreamt, yet we the audience are given the greater perspective and insight. For some reason, Shakespeare wants us to believe that the spirits of the dead can influence the lives of his characters and, perhaps by extension, our own.

Caesar and Banquo

There's less ambiguity about the appearances of ghosts in both *Julius Caesar* and *Macbeth*, though of course they are still open to a range of interpretation on the modern stage according to the aims of the production. The appearance of Caesar's ghost to Brutus is taken almost word for word from Shakespeare's source material (Plutarch's *Life of Brutus*). In both works the ghost does not specify that he is the spirit of the assassinated Caesar (it is only specified in the stage directions of *Julius Caesar*), but Brutus's "evil spirit." The ghost appears only to Brutus, and as all around him are sleeping, we cannot be sure if others would have been able to perceive its presence. Brutus remains calm in this first encounter, as though he accepts it as his fate that his actions should have otherworldly consequence or that this visitation may perhaps be a manifestation of a guilty conscience. In act 5, scene 3 of *Julius Caesar*, upon discovery of Cassius's body, Brutus exclaims:

> O Julius Caesar, thou art mighty yet.
> Thy spirit walks abroad, and turns our swords
> In our own proper entrails.

There is certainly a belief that the spirit has power beyond simply an extension of their internal guilt.

Interestingly, the ghost of Caesar is not the only spirit in the play, though it is the only personal encounter that we see. In the opening act of the play there are signs of boding, including spirits, that are described fearfully by Cassius in act 1, scene 3:

> But if you would consider the true cause
> Why all these fires, why all these gliding ghosts,
> Why birds and beasts from quality and kind,
> Why old men fool and children calculate,
> Why all these things change from their ordinance
> Their natures and preformèd faculties
> To monstrous quality—why, you shall find
> That heaven hath infused them with these spirits
> To make them instruments of fear and warning
> Unto some monstrous state.

When we include mentions of these unspecified ghosts and spirits, there is more ghostly presence in *Julius Caesar* than any other of Shakespeare's plays!

Macbeth is one of Shakespeare's most popular plays and is well known for its supernatural soliciting. The witches and their predictions dominate the play, even when they are not directly featured in the action (and we will come to them in detail in the next chapter), but there is only one scene featuring a ghost. The freshly murdered Banquo makes a dramatic appearance at Macbeth's coronation feast, as he promised he would when living. More than any other of Shakespeare's ghosts, this really does seem to be a vision borne of a diseased mind and guilty conscience. The newly crowned Macbeth is surrounded by his dinner guests and closely observed by Lady Macbeth as he crumbles with fear at a ghastly spectral sight that is visible only to him. Banquo's ghost doesn't even speak, and his actions are only detailed by the descriptions given by Macbeth himself, so that it's equally possible to stage the scene without an actor portraying the ghost at all and only show Macbeth's reactions. A vivid and gory picture of the ghost is painted by the words Shakespeare gives to Macbeth in act 3, scene 4:

> Thy bones are marrowless, thy blood is cold,
>
> Thou hast no speculation in those eyes
>
> Which thou dost glare with!

Macbeth's conscience had already caused him to have hallucinations of a dagger leading him to Duncan's chamber. Since the ghost's appearance is immediately preceded by Macbeth saying to the assembled guests that he had hoped Banquo would be present (a poor attempt to cover up the fact he hired two murderers to hunt down Banquo and his son, Fleance) and Lady Macbeth also makes the comparison with the "air drawn dagger," it seems most likely that the intent here is to show the extent to which a guilty conscience can haunt a murderer. Though much of *Macbeth* can be seen to be drawn from Holinshed's *Chronicles*, the ghost is entirely Shakespeare's invention.

The Odd One Out

Our final apparitions follow none of these conventions and appear in one of Shakespeare's most surreal plays, *Cymbeline*. In act 5, scene 4 we see our heroine Imogen's husband, Posthumus Leonatus, welcome imprisonment and imminent death as rightful justice. He believes Imogen dead under his orders (when he mistakenly thought her unfaithful) and is ready to relinquish his own life in return. As he sleeps in his cell, a whole family of ghosts appears. More specifically, his own family that he has never known, as his brothers and father died in battle and his mother in childbirth. These ancestral spirits are of a type encountered nowhere else in Shakespeare's works. Although they died violent deaths, they were certainly not murdered by Posthumus. Although this haunting is slightly similar to the visitation of Richmond by Richard's victims, as they are bringing helpful energies while he sleeps, they do not address him directly but instead are petitioning Jupiter to intervene on his behalf.

Banquo's ghost doesn't even speak…

FIRST BROTHER: Like hardiment Posthumus hath

> To Cymbeline perform'd:
>
> Then, Jupiter, thou king of gods,
>
> Why hast thou thus adjourn'd
>
> The graces for his merits due,
>
> Being all to dolours turn'd?

SICILIUS LEONATUS: Thy crystal window ope; look out;

> No longer exercise
>
> Upon a valiant race thy harsh
>
> And potent injuries.

MOTHER: Since, Jupiter, our son is good,

> Take off his miseries.

SICILIUS LEONATUS: Peep through thy marble mansion; help;

> Or we poor ghosts will cry
>
> To the shining synod of the rest
>
> Against thy deity.

Here Shakespeare is giving us ancestral guardian spirits acting as intermediaries between their living mortal son and the all-powerful Jupiter (whose appearance we have already looked at in chapter 2). All of this is witnessed by Posthumus in a dream, yet both the audience and Posthumus are given evidence that it was a true spiritual encounter as he discovers a mysterious written oracle about his future, which even names him so as to banish doubts, in his cell as he awakes.

Although this scene is sometimes dismissed as being silly and clumsily written (indeed, it has been theorised that it might not have been written by the same author as the rest of the play but in an apprenticeship or collaboration), it makes a powerful magical statement about how we are supported by the spirits of our ancestors and how they may still act in our interests in an otherworldly capacity.

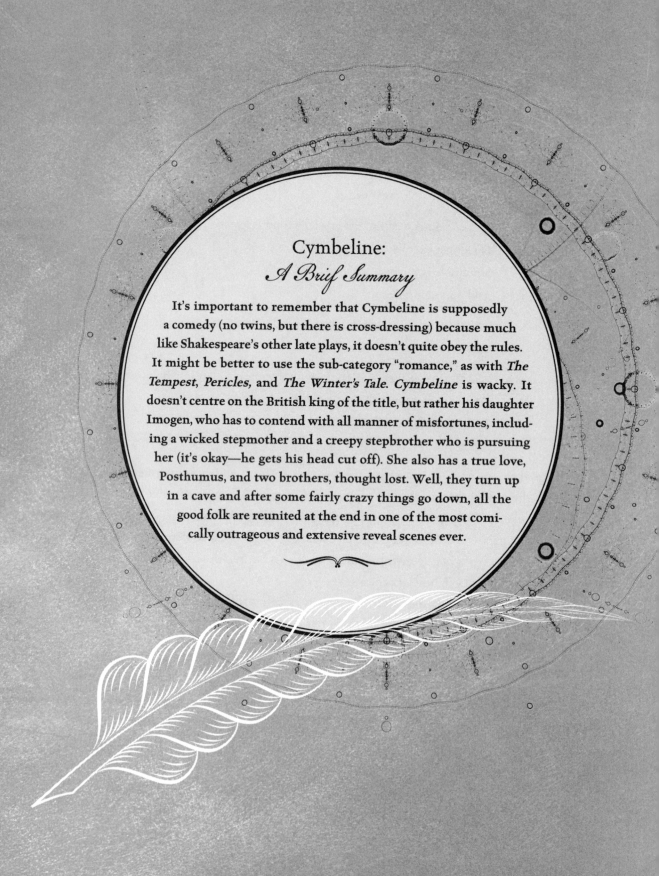

Cymbeline:
A Brief Summary

It's important to remember that Cymbeline is supposedly a comedy (no twins, but there is cross-dressing) because much like Shakespeare's other late plays, it doesn't quite obey the rules. It might be better to use the sub-category "romance," as with *The Tempest*, *Pericles*, and *The Winter's Tale*. *Cymbeline* is wacky. It doesn't centre on the British king of the title, but rather his daughter Imogen, who has to contend with all manner of misfortunes, including a wicked stepmother and a creepy stepbrother who is pursuing her (it's okay—he gets his head cut off). She also has a true love, Posthumus, and two brothers, thought lost. Well, they turn up in a cave and after some fairly crazy things go down, all the good folk are reunited at the end in one of the most comically outrageous and extensive reveal scenes ever.

Exercise: Shakespeare's Ghosts Tarot Spread

An incredibly brief introduction to tarot for the uninitiated: Tarot is a popular system of divination that has its historical and philosophical roots in the Renaissance. A traditional deck today consists of 78 cards, divided into 22 major arcana and 56 minor arcana. The major arcana evolved from designs that were in circulation around the courts of Shakespeare's time, most prevalently in Italy. To have a set of these cards produced for you, often very ornate and gilded, was a sign of prestige and wealth. The minor arcana are similar in structure to modern-day playing cards, and indeed playing cards' four suits of hearts, diamonds, clubs, and spades evolved from tarot's cups, pentacles, wands, and swords, respectively. These four suits relate to the four elements (water, earth, fire, and air), and the qualities of those elements relate to everyday life. Water/cups relates to the emotions, intuition, and compassion; earth/pentacles relates to practical and material concerns such as money, the home, and health; fire/wands relates to willpower, drive, and action; and air/swords relates to the mental realm of anxieties, dreams, and logic. Tarot's major arcana relate to the archetypal and universal forces at work in our lives.

If you do not already own a pack of tarot cards, there are many thousands of designs to choose from, with themes to suit almost any realm of interest—including Shakespeare! If you would like to try this exercise without a tarot deck, you may use ordinary playing cards and look up divinatory meanings online or in a book of playing card divination, but the range of meanings in traditional systems of playing card divination are much more limited and tend to the mundane.

A tarot spread is a way to lay out multiple cards within a reading to add focus and clarity to that reading. The following tarot spread is inspired by the preceding section and is designed to help you look more deeply into what you are being called to do at this time and what might be supporting you, as well as what might be holding you back. The cards are placed roughly in the shape of a dagger, with any card (chosen either consciously or drawn from the deck at random) to represent yourself or your querent at the hilt and the outcome at the point, with pairs of cards exploring themes represented by the ghosts of each play placed together. Shuffle your cards while focusing on either your own life or on your querent, then lay them out as follows:

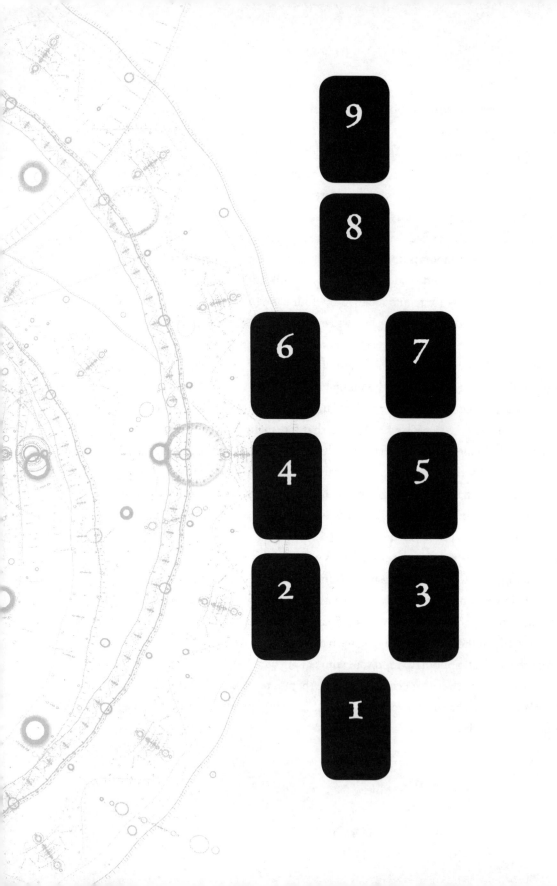

1. SWEET PRINCE: Choose a significator. (This is to represent either yourself, if you are reading for yourself, or your querent. You can choose this by going through your deck and picking the card you think fits best, or you can shuffle and draw randomly along with the rest of the cards.)

2. THE GHOST OF HAMLET'S FATHER: What/who is calling you to action at this time?

3. "REMEMBER ME...": What action are you being called to?

4. RICHMOND'S TENT: What blessing are you being offered?

5. RICHARD'S TENT: What is holding you back?

6. THE GHOST OF BANQUO: What is haunting you from your past?

7. BURY CAESAR: How can this be laid to rest?

8. THE DREAM OF POSTHUMUS: What is supporting you?

9. ACT V: Likely outcome.

Example Reading

1. SWEET PRINCE: I picked a card at random to represent my querent and got the Ten of Cups. Cups represent the element of water within the tarot, so here we have someone highly swayed by that element and all their emotions. There is a longing for belonging and prioritising home, contentment, and community.

2. THE GHOST OF HAMLET'S FATHER: Temperance. This is a major arcana card, meaning that it represents a powerful universal force in the querent's life. It's one of only two majors in this spread and shows that the call to action is coming from a very powerful place. In the case of Temperance, this is not so much an external calling as an internal calling, the angel of Temperance representing the higher spiritual self of the querent. Temperance is a call to healing, to seek balance.

3. "REMEMBER ME...": Three of Swords. Swords are connected to the element of air and the mental realm, but the Three of Swords is traditionally the card of heartbreak or the sense of losing a part of oneself. The previous card gave a good sense of the nature of the call to action, and this cements it further. The querent has become separated from their sense of spiritual path and higher self, and in order to feel whole again, they must reconnect and heal that wound.

4. RICHMOND'S TENT: Knight of Wands. The blessing being offered here is the passion and energy to succeed. Wands connect to the element of fire and hence the power of will, creative drive, and passion. There is a boost being offered, and the querent now feels they have the will to fight for what they believe in and the power to make the necessary changes.

5. RICHARD'S TENT: Nine of Cups. This card is traditionally known as the wish card, so it is peculiar to think of it in a challenging position! Either this means that there isn't really any opposing factors or that the querent is expecting things to be too easy, that the universe will simply fix things for them so long as they make it clear that is what they want, and this expectation of ease may trip them up.

6. THE GHOST OF BANQUO: Princess/Page of Cups. There is a very childlike innocence to this card, which suggests that the ghosts which are haunting the querent stem from their own childhood and unresolved issues. This results in a longing to return to a more carefree way of being, with none of the pressures or responsibilities of adulthood.

7. BURY CAESAR: Two of Pentacles. Pentacles stand for the element of earth and the physical realm. In a perfect response to the previous

card, the Two of Pentacles is saying that it is time to fully embrace adult responsibilities and the work that must be done to attain the goal. By doing the work, we learn just how much we are capable of at once! The seeds of the future may be planted, but which seeds those will be must be chosen.

8. THE DREAM OF POSTHUMUS: The Sun. Here is the only other major arcana in the spread, and it is the most overwhelmingly positive and straightforward card in the pack! It's wonderful to see it here in a supporting position, lending strength to the other supporting card of the Knight of Wands. The fiery energy of the Sun is of a higher level and hearkens back in that sense to the higher calling of Temperance, the two majors in this spread complementing each other nicely. The Sun casts positive energy on all cards around it and thus the final card must be read with this in mind.

9. ACT V: Seven of Swords. This is a tricksy card and often indicates there are events happening behind the scenes that the querent is unaware of. It's sometimes known as the thief card, and it may feel to the querent that opportunities have been taken from them or they have sometimes cheated themselves out of the chance to reach their goal. It seems the cards are reluctant to give a clear answer on outcome, other than that the querent must face challenges from the past again and again until they make the right choice. They must find the courage within to seek what has been hidden from them. With the support from higher powers that they have on their side and clear guidance from their higher self, they will likely eventually succeed.

…And we fairies, that do run,
By the triple Hecate's team,
From the presence of the sun,
Following darkness like a dream,
Now are frolic…

A MIDSUMMER NIGHT'S DREAM
ACT 5, SCENE 1

SIX

Fairies

e've already noted the significant crossover between ghosts and fairies within Shakespeare's works, reflecting the folklore of the time, but in A *Midsummer Night's Dream*, arguably the most famous work of literature to feature fairies, he makes the distinction clear. We are not dealing with the unsettled (and unsettling) spirits of the dead here, but with beautiful immortal beings of an otherworldly and powerful nature, yet strongly connected to the same natural world as mortal folk.

A Midsummer Night's Dream:
A Brief Summary

There's three worlds in this play, and they all weave together. You have the world of the Athenians, in which King Theseus has taken his prisoner, Hippolyta, Queen of the Amazons, as his wife, and there is a courtship dispute between four young people. Lysander and Hermia are in love, but Hermia's father has promised her to Demetrius, who used to be engaged to Hermia's best friend, Helena…meanwhile in Fairyland, the King and Queen of Fairy are involved in a long-term dispute over a changeling boy that Titania has taken in that Oberon wants for…I'm not sure why he wants him. Probably best not to overanalyse that. Anyway, Oberon resolves to use magic to get his own way and have vengeance upon Titania for denying him, so he sends Puck, a prankster hobgoblin, to find a flower whose juice will make her fall in love with the first thing she sees. That's where the next world comes in, the amateur performers who are all common tradespeople (or "rude mechanicals" as Puck calls them) who are hoping their play will get chosen to be performed before Theseus and Hippolyta at their wedding. One of these actors, Bottom, is a bit of an ass, so Puck, coming across them in the woods, decides to literally give him the head of an ass. Titania, under enchantment, falls for Bottom, the fairies also interfere with the young human lovers, but it all works out in the end and the rude mechanicals get to perform *Pyramus and Thisbe* at the wedding. Huzzah!

PUCK: My fairy lord, this must be done with haste,

　For night's swift dragons cut the clouds full fast,

　And yonder shines Aurora's harbinger;

　At whose approach, ghosts, wandering here and there,

　Troop home to churchyards: damned spirits all,

　That in crossways and floods have burial,

　Already to their wormy beds are gone;

　For fear lest day should look their shames upon,

　They willfully themselves exile from light

　And must for aye consort with black-brow'd night.

OBERON: But we are spirits of another sort:

　I with the morning's love have oft made sport,

　And, like a forester, the groves may tread,

　Even till the eastern gate, all fiery-red,

　Opening on Neptune with fair blessed beams,

　Turns into yellow gold his salt green streams.

(ACT 3, SCENE 2)

Titania

Fairies were incredibly fashionable in Shakespeare's time, in part due to the popularity of Spenser's epic poem *The Faerie Queene*, of which the first three books were published in 1590, a few years before it is thought Shakespeare wrote *Dream*. Some, such as scholar Frances Yates, have argued that, like Spenser, Shakespeare was also drawing parallels with the English court and his fairies with Titania being a representative of Queen Elizabeth in the same way as Spenser reflected various aspects of the Virgin Queen in his work.

Yates maintained that Shakespeare's fairies did not have English folkloric origins, but instead their roots were

> in Arthurian legend and the white magic of Christian Cabala…to read Shake-speare's fairy scenes without reference to the contemporary build-up of the Virgin Queen as the representative of pure religion is to miss their purpose as an affirmation of adherence to the Spenserian point of view, a very serious purpose disguised in fantasy (Yates 1979, 174).

It certainly makes sense that Spenser's work would be influential on the choice of topic, but if we choose to believe that this is the sole inspiration and that Titania is meant to represent Elizabeth I, not only do we miss much of the esoteric and folkloric richness of the work, but we're left with a bit of a problem when we consider her humiliation at the hands of Oberon and her unwitting taking of the ass-headed Bottom as lover (though there is a theory that this may have been a jibe at one of her courtly suitors at the time). Titania is far from a chaste queen; she is a passionate being with great appetite for the sensual pleasures of the world, whose powers are tied to the cycles of the moon and all the forces of nature. When we first meet Titania, it has already been explained in a meeting between a fairy in her service and Puck, who is in the service of Oberon, the fairy king, that the immortal couple have been long absorbed in a feud over a change-ling boy that Titania refuses to give over to Oberon. Since they are immortal and not governed by time as mortal folk are, we cannot tell how long this may have been going on, but we are given a poetic description of the ravages that this imbalance in their relationship have wrought upon the earth:

> TITANIA: … Therefore the moon, the governess of floods,
> Pale in her anger, washes all the air,
> That rheumatic diseases do abound:
> And thorough this distemperature we see
> The seasons alter: hoary-headed frosts
> Far in the fresh lap of the crimson rose,
> And on old Hiems' thin and icy crown
> An odorous chaplet of sweet summer buds
> Is, as in mockery, set: the spring, the summer,
> The childing autumn, angry winter, change
> Their wonted liveries, and the mazed world,
> By their increase, now knows not which is which:
> And this same progeny of evils comes
> From our debate, from our dissension;
> We are their parents and original.
> (ACT 2, SCENE 1)

These are certainly no petty sprites that we are witnessing here, and nor, I would posit, are they to be seen as merely symbolic of earthly sovereigns, but in the richly layered tapestry that Shakespeare so often weaves, there is a deeply mythic and esoteric undercurrent. As Thomas Keightley observes in *The Fairy Mythology*, "Shakespeare, having the Faerie Queen before his eyes, seems to have attempted a blending of the elves of the village with the Fays of romance" (Keightley 1870, 325), and, as with many of the medieval romantic Fay characters, Titania's true roots lie in the ancient goddesses.

What's in a Name?

Ovid's hefty influence on Shakespeare's work shows itself again. Titania is a name taken from *Metamorphoses*, an epithet given to those goddesses who are born of the pre-Olympian primal forces, the Titans (Ovid is, of course, also his source for the tale of Pyramus and Thisbe, which is enacted by the rude mechanicals). This directly ties her origins to the goddess Diana (a granddaughter of the Titans), who is mentioned frequently in Shakespeare's plays, and that power over which she rules, the moon.

The moon or moonshine/light is mentioned no less that thirty-eight times during the course of the play, including its opening lines:

> THESEUS: Now, fair Hippolyta, our nuptial hour
> Draws on apace; four happy days bring in
> Another moon: but, O, methinks, how slow
> This old moon wanes! she lingers my desires,
> Like to a step-dame or a dowager
> Long withering out a young man revenue.

> HIPPOLYTA: Four days will quickly steep themselves in night;
> Four nights will quickly dream away the time;
> And then the moon, like to a silver bow
> New-bent in heaven, shall behold the night
> Of our solemnities.

Hippolyta is no ordinary mortal but an Amazon, and her description of the moon as a silver bow instantly invokes the huntress Diana. Hippolyta and Theseus are the mortal counterparts of Titania and Oberon, and traditionally they would have been played by the same actors. Just as the moon reflects the light of the sun, so mortal and immortal realms are reflected in each other and inextricably linked—as he goes on to demonstrate more dramatically when Titania describes the chaos that their dispute has caused in the world of Nature, affecting both Fairy and humanity. Those of us who work within Fairy wisdom traditions know this to be true.

The World Soul

The association of Titania and Hippolyta with the moon, as well as with the balance of Nature herself, leads to an even deeper possibility. The moon was regarded as the seat of the world soul in Neoplatonic philosophy, which Shakespeare almost certainly would have been familiar with. Though the term "world soul" appears to have been coined by Plato, a similar concept exists through many philosophies around the globe: a feminine force that conveys energy from the ultimate cosmic source above into the centre of the planet and radiates that energy into all beings. Diana was often equated with Hecate, who is named as the world soul in the ancient Chaldean Oracles, which would also have been available to Shakespeare as a source of wisdom and inspiration. The implication for interpretation of the witches and Hecate in *Macbeth* and their deeper meaning will be explored in the next chapter.

Diana and Witchcraft

When attempting to piece together Shakespeare's knowledge and opinion of magic, it is very interesting to note that, in the time he was writing, Diana as goddess and queen of the fairies was closely associated with witchcraft and the practice of sorceries that were becoming more and more dangerous to be associated with. In 1597, the well-known *Daemonologie* by King James VI of Scotland (soon to become James I of England) had this to say about fairies:

> That fourth kind of spirit which by the gentiles was called Diana and her wandering court, and amongst us was called the Fairy (as I told you) or to our good neighbours, was one of the sorts of illusions that was most widespread in the time of Papistry…[and goes on to say] the devil eluded the senses of various simpleminded creatures, in making them believe that they saw and heard such things as were nothing so indeed (James I 2016, 87).

Titania as Goddess

Old World beliefs were intrinsically tied in with Catholicism, which in turn was associated with simple-mindedness and susceptibility to the devil's wiles. However, whilst *A Midsummer Night's Dream* may be a comedy, with much of the farce derived from the antics of the Fairy realm, Shakespeare shows us that these are powerful beings not to be mocked or trifled with. It is one of several examples throughout his works where he has chance to mock magical beliefs but instead treats them with affection, reverence, and respect. Lest we think the queen of Fairy any less than a goddess, the author reminds us of her divine status with her line "his mother was a votaress of my order" (act 1, scene 2) and also her words when she first seduces the transformed Bottom in act 3, scene 1:

> Out of this wood do not desire to go:
>
> Thou shalt remain here, whether thou wilt or no.
>
> I am a spirit of no common rate;
>
> The summer still doth tend upon my state…

Oberon/Oberyon/Auberich/Elberich

But what of her partner, "jealous Oberon"? T. F. Thiselton-Dyer explains Oberon in his exhaustive work *Folk-lore of Shakespeare*, which was originally published in 1883:

> Oberon first appears in the old French romance of "Huon de Bordeaux," and is identical with Elberich, the dwarf king of the German story of Otuit in the "Heldenbuch." The name Elberich, or, as it appears in the "Nibelungenlied," Albrich, was changed, in passing into French, first into Auberich, then into Auberon and finally became our Oberon (Thiselton-Dyer 2017, 5).

It could be that Shakespeare first encountered Oberon from these sources, or perhaps he first came across our fairy king through a brief mention in Spenser's work, which, as we've already noted, was immensely popular at the time. Another contemporary appearance of Oberon was in Robert Greene's *The Scottish History of James IV*, which may have been performed before Shakespeare wrote *A Midsummer Night's Dream*. In the original German and French tales, he was described as being a dwarf or an elf that was beautiful yet diminutive in stature. Robert Greene's Oberon is an "antic." So where does the powerful and regal figure we are now familiar with come from? Is he purely an invention of the author?

"There sleeps Titania"

Oberon in the Grimoires

A source that is rarely mentioned when one reads about Shakespeare's influences is the grimoires, practical manuals of ritual and natural magic that are often added to over the ages with handwritten notes by practitioners. Natural magic includes the charting of correspondences (that is, the qualities of plants and objects within nature that resonate with certain planets, times of day, organs of the body, etc.) and the nature of certain herbs, plants, and stones and how to find and use them. Ritual magic involves often complex and precise procedures to summon spirits to perform tasks, answer questions, or petition God (or, if dealing with a Pagan pantheon, gods or goddesses) directly. The majority of grimoires from Shakespeare's time are strongly based within the Christian tradition, often hearkening back to Catholicism (which had a much stronger foundation in ritual practice) and often using phrases or psalms from the Bible.

As demonstrated in the grimoires, the different kinds of spirits that may be summoned through ritual magic include demons, angels, pagan gods, and, of course, fairies—including kings and queens of Fairy.

Oberon, or rather Oberion/Oberyon, appears in three grimoires that are currently in published form and available to the public. *The Grimoire of Arthur Gauntlet*, also known by its less catchy identifying number as Sloane MS 3851, is thought to have been written around 1620–30 and gives details of a ritual to conjure Oberion "in likeness of a beautiful man like a soldier personally in the air or in a Glass" (Rankine 2011, 261). Confusingly, in the invocation itself the command is made that he should "appear in the Air In the likeness of a Boy of 7 years of age."

Sloane MS 3824/3825, aka *The Book of Treasure Spirits* (Rankine 2009), conjures Oberion together with his queen Mycob to command the "Seven Sisters Lilia, Rostilia, Foca, Folla, Africa, Julia, Venulla" in order to aid in locating treasure. The connection of fairies to treasure in folklore is hinted at in act 3, scene 3 of *The Winter's Tale*, when the Old Shepherd finds the gold that was left with baby Perdita and exclaims "This is fairy gold, boy, and 'twill prove so."

The Book of Oberon

The most impressive tome of this type to feature Oberion was published by Llewellyn in 2015 under the name *The Book of Oberon*, which, as authors Harms and Peterson point out in their introduction, is a far better title than Folger Manuscript. This extremely impressive collection of magical workings and drawings was indeed found in the world-famous Folger Shakespeare Library in Washington, DC, as it hails from the time when Shakespeare was alive and working, more specifically around a decade before he wrote A *Midsummer Night's Dream*. In the introduction the authors ask, "How much knowledge of the folk traditions surrounding Oberion might Shakespeare have known?" and come to the conclusion that any connection is unlikely because his functions in the play are "fertility and marital bliss against the wide range of capabilities listed in the Offices of Spirits." They also note that Shakespeare's Oberon is a mature man rather than a small boy, which is the appearance requested of Oberon in the conjuration (much like in the aforementioned *Grimoire of Arthur Gauntlet*), "in fair form like a child of three years of age" (Harms and Peterson 2015, 472).

However, if we look at the description of Oberion and his powers in the Offices of Spirits, we can see many similarities with the Oberon we know:

> Oberyon is a king; he appeareth as a king with a crown on his head. He is under the government of the sun and moon. He teacheth a man knowledge in physic and he showeth the nature of stones, herbs and trees and of all metals. He is a great and mighty king and he is king of the fairies. He causeth a man to be invisible (Ibid., 207).

He demonstrates his knowledge of herb lore in act 2, scene 1 with the purple flower he sends Puck to find to use against Titania:

> Fetch me that flower; the herb I shew'd thee once:
> The juice of it on sleeping eye-lids laid
> Will make or man or woman madly dote
> Upon the next live creature that it sees…

He also has the power to make himself invisible (which, due to obvious limitations of the abilities of Elizabethan stagecraft, is simply indicated by him declaring himself invisible!), so potentially we can theorise he would be able to share that knowledge with others if required. As to the variance in size/age, this seems to be as much an inconsistency within the grimoires as between them and Shakespeare, though the childlike appearance in the conjurations is in keeping with the German literary source material. Perhaps the conjurations specify that he appear as a child so that he is not too intimidating? As to whether the folklore, grimoire, or literary appearance was established first, it is unclear.

In truth, all we can do is theorise as to whether or not Shakespeare may or may not have had access to documents of this kind. *The Book of Oberon* is certainly contemporary to his time, and the fact that the knowledge in grimoires stems from folk traditions and would have been passed down through generations only makes it more likely that he would have encountered it somewhere—we just can't say for certain where. We do know that the folk knowledge of Oberon (or various versions of his name) was around for a long time before that, not only through the German and French literary references but also through an account shared in the introductions to both *The Book of Oberon* and *The Grimoire of Arthur Gauntlet*:

> Indeed we see precedents for the conjuration of Oberion in a court record
> from 1444 which describes a man being pilloried for summoning a "wicked
> spyryte the whyche was callyd Oberycom" (Rankine 2011:19).

This is perhaps the oldest recorded mention of this conjuration, with others appearing on records after this date. Of course, we cannot know how far back the practice of conjuring the fairy king under this name may have gone, as presumably many were sensible enough not to get caught or were in such times and places that it would not have been recorded.

For He's a Jolly Goodfellow

Whilst there are a few possible sources for Titania and Oberon, both in name and nature (and the truth is likely to be that they are a combination of a number of these plus Shakespeare's powerful imagination and the message he wished to imbue the play with), Puck, aka Robin Goodfellow, is a figure straight out of English folklore.

> English Folks-lore generally, had but very imperfect and immature ideas on
> the nature, attributes, and action of our favourite sprite, till Shakespeare cre-
> ated the wondrous birth ; and so excellent was the formation, so beautiful and
> various the play of colour and refraction, that his contemporaries and succes-
> sors seized the new fairy world he had produced, to revel in with almost equal
> powers of invention and fancy (Bell 1852, 155).

Puck and the fairies

As William Bell observes, there are no literary sources that we know of from which Shakespeare derived his Puck, yet the creation of this much-beloved character set a template for further appearances in the popular entertainment and literature of the time. Shakespeare's influence can almost certainly be seen in the appearance of Puck in Ben Jonson's masque of 1612, *Love Restored*, and even more so in John Milton's pastoral poem *L'Allegro*. Most famously in modern times we find *Puck of Pook's Hill* by Rudyard Kipling to be a rich mixture of folklore and Shakespeare's creation. But where did Shakespeare receive his inspiration for this iconic character that would go on to inspire so many? As always, we must look to the treasures contained within the text itself. There is much to be gleaned from the first meeting we witness between Puck and one of Titania's fairy retinue in act 2, scene 1:

> FAIRY: Either I mistake your shape and making quite,
> Or else you are that shrewd and knavish sprite
> Call'd Robin Goodfellow: are not you he
> That frights the maidens of the villagery;
> Skim milk, and sometimes labour in the quern
> And bootless make the breathless housewife churn;
> And sometime make the drink to bear no barm;
> Mislead night-wanderers, laughing at their harm?
> Those that Hobgoblin call you and sweet Puck,
> You do their work, and they shall have good luck:
> Are not you he?

> PUCK: Thou speak'st aright;
> I am that merry wanderer of the night.
> I jest to Oberon and make him smile
> When I a fat and bean-fed horse beguile,
> Neighing in likeness of a filly foal:
> And sometime lurk I in a gossip's bowl,
> In very likeness of a roasted crab,
> And when she drinks, against her lips I bob
> And on her wither'd dewlap pour the ale.

The wisest aunt, telling the saddest tale,

Sometime for three-foot stool mistaketh me;

Then slip I from her bum, down topples she,

And "tailor" cries, and falls into a cough;

And then the whole quire hold their hips and laugh,

And waxen in their mirth and neeze and swear

A merrier hour was never wasted there.

In this exchange we get a clear description of the sorts of pranks that are popularly associated with fairies in folklore, but we also get a sense of the folkloric tradition that if you are good to the "good people," then they will be good to you. It seems clear that the name "Goodfellow" is connected to the tradition of calling fairy beings and devils names that appeal to their better nature in an effort to avoid their darker aspect or accidentally draw their attention by calling their true name. Robin Goodfellow sounds like a specific name, but it was, in fact, more of a generic name given to hobgoblins or some (relatively benign) versions of the devil. He was certainly known for the kind of mischievous country pranks listed here and for his merry, resounding laughter. "Puck" is no more specific a name either, deriving from the Irish *pouka* or Welsh *pwca*, a wild, shapeshifting, often malignant being who became a devil in medieval times. Similar beings of strikingly similar names can be found throughout ancient Scandinavian, Germanic, and Celtic lands, so we cannot be sure of exactly where Shakespeare found his inspiration to include this name for his hobgoblin character. These days we tend to think of Robin Goodfellow and Puck of being simply different names for the same being, and yet this appears to be entirely down to Shakespeare (unless another instance exists that is lost), as previously they were quite separate, yet obviously sharing some similarities. Robin Goodfellow was a merry hobgoblin prankster, whereas Puck was a darker and sometimes quite frightening figure. Until Shakespeare's play, neither were popularly associated with the Fairy kingdom either.

As Thistelton-Dyer observes in *Folk-lore of Shakespeare*, the sources for Shakespeare's inspiration for this most iconic of fairy characters are as elusive and slippery as the shapeshifter himself:

> Time has dealt so harshly with the memory of poor Robin that we might also imagine his spirit was still leading us astray over massive volumes of antiquity, in a delusive search after documents forever lost (Thistelton-Dyer 2017, 6).

However, a likely contemporary source is Reginald Scot's *Discoverie of Witchcraft*, which, by setting out to refute witches and magic in great detail, ironically manages to provide us with one of the most exhaustive grimoires of the age. It was published in 1584 and not only mentions Robin Goodfellow repeatedly (suggesting that he is closely connected to the lustful spirits called incubi) but lists some of the pranks he is known for as well as "sweeping the house at midnight" for the payment of a bowl of milk, directly linking to Puck's line in the play, "I am sent with broom before, to sweep the dust behind the door" (act 5, scene 1). We can also find a chapter in *The Discoverie of Witchcraft* that details the transformation of an unfortunate individual into an ass (book 5, chapter 3). It is interesting to note that the medieval pouka was said to sometimes appear with the head of an ass, which instantly brings to mind probably the most famous magical transformation in theatre: Bottom the weaver being given the head of an ass by Puck as part of Oberon's scheming vengeance on his queen.

The Famous Ass Head

It's not made clear in the text how Puck is able to transform Bottom, as it happens offstage, but it happens quickly and without Bottom himself noticing, so it would seem that it is an inherent magic that Puck possesses as he goes on to boast about his own shapeshifting skills immediately afterwards:

> Sometime a horse I'll be, sometime a hound,
>
> A hog, a headless bear, sometime a fire;
>
> And neigh, and bark, and grunt, and roar, and burn,
>
> Like horse, hound, hog, bear, fire, at every turn.
>
> (ACT 3, SCENE 1)

The forms he describes himself changing into are, like the ass, all references to his folkloric origins as the large, hairy sort of fae being that is closely associated with the classic devil. The mention of being a fire suggests a connection with will-o'-the-wisps, small fires that appear over marshlands and are reputed to lead travellers either to safety or more often to their doom. In folklore the pouka were thought to carry lanterns to similar effect or use their shapeshifting abilities to lead people astray, often over the edge of cliffs or to similarly unpleasant ends. This brings to mind the tradition of being pixy-led, and indeed it's possible that the words *pixie/pixy* and *pouka* come from the same root. When we think of A *Midsummer Night's Dream* as being light and frivolous enter-tainment suitable for children, the darker side is often overlooked, which of course also includes potions that make people love against their will, which we might now refer to as date rape drugs.

Returning to the ass head, there are several sources besides folklore and the afore-mentioned *Discoverie of Witchcraft* that may have inspired the bard. It's most likely that he would be familiar with a number of them, but the most obvious source is his old favour-ite Ovid, which we already know he drew from regularly and within this particular play is the source of *Pyramus and Thisbe*, the play within a play. In book XI of *Metamorphoses*, we read of Midas speaking out against the judgement of Apollo and being punished with the ears of an ass as a result, which he is forced to conceal to avoid humiliation. However, there is another *Metamorphoses* that Shakespeare would likely have read, and that is the famous work by Apuleius known also as *The Golden Ass*.

> …the hair on my body turned to bristles, and my soft skin hardened to hide,
> my fingers and toes merged with hands and feet, squeezing together into indi-
> vidual hooves, and a long tail shot from the tip of my spine. Now my face was
> enormous, my mouth immense, my nostrils gaped, and my lips hung down.
> My ears too were ludicrously long and hairy. The only consolation I found
> in my wretched transformation was that though I could no longer embrace
> Photis, at least my member had grown (*The Golden Ass*, book 3).

Whilst on the surface it appears that *The Golden Ass* is an erotic comedy, there is a deep undercurrent of esoteric wisdom contained within. The "hero" of this tale, Lucius, undergoes a number of trials that are an initiatory journey leading him towards a deeper devotion of the goddess Isis. With the obvious strong connections between Isis and Diana, and remembering how we have already noted the conflation of Titania and Diana, it makes sense that this text would have been the chief source for Shakespeare's comedy transformation. How much of an initiation Bottom undergoes during his time as Tita-nia's lover remains uncertain, but it is interesting to muse upon how he emerges from his experience with fresh inspiration to write a play himself, *Bottom's Dream*. Within the Fairy tradition, as we see in such ballads as *Thomas the Rhymer*, lovers of the Fairy Queen emerge back into the mortal realm with certain poetic gifts, and perhaps this may be true of our favourite "rude mechanical"?

Titania and Bottom

Romeo and Juliet:
A Brief Summary

One of the things that makes *Romeo and Juliet* such a remarkable and moving play is that it's a comedy for the whole first half. Romeo and Juliet are young people from rival households who fall in love and get married in secret; Juliet has a comedy nurse and Romeo has his manic friend Mercutio. The seeds of tragedy are present, however…Juliet is supposed to marry Paris, a match deemed more suitable by her parents, and the rivalry between the houses means that violence on the streets is commonplace. Juliet's cousin Tybalt seeks out Romeo for a fight; Mercutio intervenes, fights on his behalf, and receives a mortal wound. Romeo then kills Tybalt in a rage. End of first half, the actors playing Mercutio and Tybalt spend the rest of the play in the bar and definitely don't miss their curtain call (yes, this happened to me when I played Mercutio, hush), Romeo is banished, the priest that marries them comes up with a ridiculous plan that almost works but doesn't, and the tragic suicide of the two young lovers shocks the opposing families into making peace.

Size and Powers of Shakespeare's Fairies

From A *Midsummer Night's Dream*, we gather a variety of facts about folkloric beliefs of
the time. The fairy king and queen are so powerful that they may be considered godlike,
their minions diverse and capable of being both human size and tiny enough to "creep
into acorn cups." They are seen to be capable of both blessings and curses, and have good
knowledge of herblore. We can gauge from the jealous arguments between Oberon and
Titania that they frequently take human lovers, though we can't be sure if this is true
of the lesser fairies such as Cobweb and Mustardseed, and Oberon's servant Puck is a
powerful being in his own right, with shapeshifting abilities and roots in the folklore of
the devil himself. Yet Shakespeare's portrayal is often blamed for the Victorian flower
fairy and the diminutive, disempowered fairy of later traditions. This may more likely
be traced to another of his works and the famous Queen Mab speech that Mercutio
delivers in *Romeo and Juliet* act 1, scene 4:

> O, then, I see Queen Mab hath been with you.
>
> She is the fairies' midwife, and she comes
>
> In shape no bigger than an agate-stone
>
> On the fore-finger of an alderman,
>
> Drawn with a team of little atomies
>
> Athwart men's noses as they lie asleep;
>
> Her wagon-spokes made of long spiders' legs,
>
> The cover of the wings of grasshoppers,
>
> The traces of the smallest spider's web,
>
> The collars of the moonshine's watery beams,
>
> Her whip of cricket's bone, the lash of film,
>
> Her wagoner a small grey-coated gnat,
>
> Not so big as a round little worm
>
> Prick'd from the lazy finger of a maid;
>
> Her chariot is an empty hazel-nut
>
> Made by the joiner squirrel or old grub,
>
> Time out o' mind the fairies' coachmakers.
>
> And in this state she gallops night by night…

Falstaff gets a beating

As with Puck, it appears that Shakespeare was something of a theatrical trendsetter, as this is the first known appearance of Queen Mab in literature. It's uncertain what his source or inspiration was for this, but if we return to the grimoires, it's possible the name is derived from the fairy Mycob who appears in the *Book of Oberon* and indeed is partnered with Oberon himself as fairy queen. Another possible source of inspiration, and indeed that which is most popularly cited, is the mighty Irish goddess Medb. Since Mercutio is jesting with Romeo about the illusion of love at the time, how seriously can we take the fact that this fairy queen is so diminished of stature? People who describe this speech as twee have perhaps not fully understood its darker connotations, and it is not clear that in the context it was delivered at the time how seriously it was to be taken. Is the reference to size another of Mercutio's jokes that has been lost and misinterpreted as the centuries have passed? Perhaps the shrinking of fairies is directly connected to the same shift in philosophies we have already discussed in the previous chapter when discussing Hamlet's ghost.

Whilst the fairies of A *Midsummer Night's Dream* are shown to be powerful shapeshifters capable of appearing as either human sized or tiny, it seems that the popularity of the play meant that other writers of the period latched onto the perception of fairies as being at least child-sized, if not smaller. This was a tamer, easier, gentler fairy for times in which humanist philosophy was on the rise and magic was perceived as a dangerous practice and was, as occult beliefs grew out of fashion, something to be mocked. It is difficult to say for certain, but no matter their size, they remain a potent influence within the works.

Merry Wives and an Unfortunate Herne the Hunter

Taking the corner of the human-sized fairy, we have another of Shakespeare's comedies, *The Merry Wives of Windsor*. The story goes that Queen Elizabeth was so taken with the shenanigans of Sir John Falstaff, corpulent mentor of debauchery to the heir apparent in plays *Henry IV, Parts* I and II, that she demanded he get his own play—the Renaissance equivalent of a spin-off series, if you will. In this most English of Shakespeare's comedies, Falstaff has been relentlessly pursuing two married women, Mistresses Ford and Page. After a series of escalating pranks devised by the two women, Mistress Ford invites Falstaff to a nighttime rendezvous in Windsor Park, requesting that he disguise himself as Herne the Hunter, antlers and all. There the two women conspire to dress as fairies, along with many of the local children and other characters, to pinch him, mock him, terrify him, and teach him the error of his ways. Of course, the "fairies" of this play are merely humans in disguise, but they are readily accepted by Falstaff, the target of their foolery, as the real deal. Not only that, but through this playful mockery of Falstaff, we are given insight into English folkloric belief of the time:

> HOSTESS QUICKLY: Fairies, black, grey, green, and white,
> You moonshine revellers and shades of night,
> You orphan heirs of fixed destiny,
> Attend your office and your quality.
> Crier Hobgoblin, make the fairy oyes.

> PISTOL: Elves, list your names; silence, you airy toys.
> Cricket, to Windsor chimneys shalt thou leap:
> Where fires thou find'st unraked and hearths unswept,
> There pinch the maids as blue as bilberry:
> Our radiant queen hates sluts and sluttery.

> FALSTAFF: They are fairies; he that speaks to them shall die:
> I'll wink and couch: no man their works must eye.
> (ACT 5, SCENE 5)

One of the first things to note about this extract is the listing of the colours of fairies as "black, grey, green, and white," which could simply refer to their clothing but may also refer to their overall tone, in this case represented by masks or "vizards" as part of the disguise. This is strongly reminiscent of a line from Hecate's song from Middleton's *The Witch* (circa 1613): "white spirits, black spirits, grey spirits, red spirits," which was transposed into Shakespeare's *Macbeth*, possibly by Middleton himself at an unknown date prior to the publishing of the folio in 1623. (Though it is impossible to know for certain, it seems most likely that the song and the character of Hecate were introduced to bring the play into trend with the popular Jacobean form of songs, dances, and masques and also to preserve aspects of Middleton's play, which was suppressed by the government as dangerous satire.) This in turn shows a clear influence from the work of Reginald Scot and his *Discourse of Devils and Spirits* (often credited to *The Discoverie of Witchcraft*):

> Titty and Tiffin, Suckin and Pidgin, Liard and Robin, &c. his white-spirits and
> blackspirits, gray-spirits and red-spirits, Devil-toad and Devil-lambe, Devilscat
> and Devils-dam (Scot 1665, chapter 33).

In her work *Elizabethan Fairies* (1930), Minor White Latham makes the point that the costumes of the fairies in *Merry Wives* are clearly described as being specifically "green and white" and that the other colours therefore must refer to the complexions of the fairies. She goes on to give other examples from the period from literature where fairies are described as being of various colours, including black, white, grey, red, green, and blue. From this we can discern that the fairies of Shakespeare's time were beyond human portrayals of race and indeed could be quite alien in appearance.

The other insights from this segment include a hatred of dirt and messiness ("sluts and sluttery") and that the fairies are so powerful that to look upon them might mean death.

The Spirits of The Tempest

Aside from *A Midsummer Night's Dream*, the most densely spirit-populated of Shakespeare's plays must be *The Tempest*, and yet apart from the famous invocation "Ye elves of hills, brooks, standing lakes and groves," which we will look at in more detail later, the spirits are not referred to as fairies and appear more along the lines of conjured grimoire spirits. However, though we have already looked at the spirit Ariel from this perspective in earlier chapters, it's important to remember that Ariel appears to be a native spirit of the island, and as Peter Dawkins observes, "Ariel can also be described as a Puck or Robin Goodfellow" (Dawkins 2000, 70). Ariel does not necessarily share Puck's inherent disposition for pranking and seems to be a far more efficient servant, but he does share a similar role in relation to Prospero as Puck does to Oberon.

In his extraordinary work *Shakespeare and the Goddess of Complete Being*, Ted Hughes posits that Ariel's natural form is that of a flower spirit, who could then certainly be compared to the lesser fairies of *A Midsummer Night's Dream*. However, Ariel seems to have much more power than this would imply. Hughes notes that Ariel sings "where the bee sucks, there suck I" and that he lives in a cowslip. If this is to be taken to have more meaning beyond the conveying of rural idyll, the symbolism of this becomes pertinent. Shakespeare also references the herb cowslip in *Cymbeline* and (in description but not named) in his poem *Venus and Adonis*, where it is the flower of the slain Adonis, described as resembling his "pale cheeks, and the blood which in round drops upon their whiteness stood." This is a return to the theme of red and white polarity, seen in the alchemical process and Fairy lore, female and male, queen and king, goddess and god joined together—just as Ariel is an hermaphroditic spirit and the means by which Prospero works his will. Powerful indeed.

Exercise: Meditation Journey to Meet Titania and Oberon

Find a quiet space where you can sit uninterrupted. You may wish to record the visualisation in order to listen and follow the directions if you think you will have difficulty recalling. Keep a notebook and pen nearby in case you need to make notes afterwards.

Sit comfortably with your legs uncrossed and take deep breaths, relaxing your body as much as possible. Close your eyes and see yourself in the room as you are now, and then see yourself being surrounded by a white mist. This mist feels safe and welcoming as it covers you until all you can see is white. Soon the white mist begins to disperse, and you see that you are standing on verdant grass under a twilight sky. You are in a forest clearing. There are stars in the sky, but you do not recognise the constellations. A short distance ahead of you, you see a grassy bank. As you look down, you notice a purple flower the colour of the twilit sky: a wild pansy growing at your feet. Soon you notice more and more flowers in front of you, and they start to form a path leading to the top of the bank. Follow the path of purple flowers.

When you reach the top of the bank, you see two figures side by side on thrones that appear to be living wood growing from the bank, the roots old and deep. In the left-hand throne, you see a powerful fairy queen dressed all in white and wearing a silver crescent crown. She holds a shining silver chalice in her hand. In the right-hand throne, you see a beautiful fairy king wearing red robes, with a crown with golden antlers on his head and holding a golden acorn in his hand.

They look upon you warmly and welcome you.

Titania, for it is she, speaks: "Well met by starlight, humble mortal. What brings you to our realm?"

In your own words, you explain that you wish to work with the Fairy realm to right the wrongs that humankind has done to the world and help restore nature's balance.

Oberon, for it is he, speaks: "As above, so below. As we have healed our rift, so must you before it is too late. What will you offer that order may be restored?"

You notice that you too are holding a small object in your hand, which represents how you may be of service. Explain in your own words what you offer.

Titania speaks: "We accept your offering. Step forward, and place it in the chalice."

She holds out the chalice, and you do as she asks.

Oberon speaks: "Now take this sacred seed into the world with you. Plant it within your heart and let it grow. The acorn within you, if nourished, may become part of a mighty forest."

Oberon presents you with the golden acorn and you hold it to your heart, where it is absorbed.

Titania sprinkles you with silver water from the chalice and speaks once more: "Blessings of the moon, that you may grow in insight, empathy, and understanding."

Oberon speaks once more: "Blessings of the sun, that your actions may be true and that you will remain strong and resolute."

They nod their farewells, and you may bid them farewell as you wish.

You return down the path of purple flowers to the clearing where you began.

The white mist returns until all is white. It then clears and you see yourself as you were, sitting in the room. You may open your eyes when ready, and make any notes you wish to make.

The weird sisters, hand in hand,
Posters of the sea and land,
Thus do go about, about:
Thrice to thine and thrice to mine
And thrice again, to make up nine.

MACBETH

ACT I, SCENE 3

SEVEN

Witches

When most people think of Shakespearean witches, their minds turn instantly to *Macbeth* and the three "weird sisters." It remains one of Shakespeare's most popular plays, is often taught in schools, and nary a fringe festival goes by without a few postapocalyptic interpretations of "the Scottish play." It's fair to say that as a result of this, *Macbeth* has gone a way towards moulding how witches are portrayed within popular culture, but just how typical were they at the time? And are they simply old ladies with a penchant for prophecy or do they represent something deeper and more significant?

On the surface there are descriptions within the text that do seem to relate directly to some of the more outlandish claims about witches at the time. There is an almost throwaway line where they are

Macbeth:
A Brief Summary

After a victorious battle on behalf of King Duncan, Macbeth and Banquo come across three "weird sisters" on the Scottish moorland who prophecy that Macbeth will be king and Banquo will be the father of kings. Pretending to laugh it off, Macbeth takes a bit of an interpretive leap and decides this means his needs to murder the king, and his wife agrees. It all goes rather downhill from that point on, although Macbeth is crowned king after the not-very-convincingly covered-up murder and he realises that there's a whole bunch of other people he needs to kill to maintain his position, including his friend Banquo, who makes a post-death guest appearance at a celebratory banquet. The three sisters on the heath tell Macbeth that he will not be defeated until Birnam Wood itself rises against him and that he can be harmed by no man born of woman, and bless him, he's just not bright enough to question why they're so specific about this. Poor Lady Macbeth goes mad and kills herself offstage (or dies by misadventure—it's not clear), and Macbeth defends his tyrannical throne until the seemingly impossible happens and soldiers bearing branches from Birnam Wood succeed in piercing his defences and Macduff reveals he was "untimely ripp'd" from his mother's womb. It's head on a stick time for Maccers before the rightful heir, Malcolm, claims the throne.

noted to have beards, are described as "wither'd and wild in their attire" (act 1, scene 3), and are seen to summon winds. Reginald Scot's *Discoverie of Witchcraft* details ointments made from grotesque ingredients such as "the bowels and members of children" that would allegedly enable flight. These we know better today as hallucinogenic mixtures derived from fungi to enable astral travel or journeying, but here it is being shown literally. However, none of these details, presumably topical additions to the story to appease the interests of James I, have much bearing on their function in the plot.

Macbeth is, of course, a famously bloody play, full of many murders and the tragic downfall of one who was once thought honourable. It is often the witches and Lady Macbeth who get the blame for all this bloodshed as the corrupting female influence on Macbeth's noble male mind. But why is this?

Three...Witches?

Firstly, let's look at the nature of the three witches. From the very opening, they are established as being otherworldly in nature, not bound by physical laws. Though they perhaps fit the stereotypical description of witches at the time (which we'll also question later), they clearly possess qualities beyond mere mortal practitioners of the Craft. They are described as being able to vanish "into the air," seem to dwell in the wilds, and function as a sort of triple-formed hive mind. But in terms of what they actually do—what dastardly deeds are performed or urged by them—well...they don't. Other than a summoning of a storm for vengeance purposes early on, which has no bearing on the main plot, our three sisters merely prophesy, conjure visions, and stir ingredients into a cauldron. Even the ingredients seem less dubious when you learn that many of the sinister-sounding names are simply folk terms for herbs (for example, "eye of newt" is a folk name for mustard seed). There's no mention of bloody deeds when they inform Macbeth that he shall be Thane of Cawdor and subsequently king, yet his mind instantly strays towards violent means:

> This supernatural soliciting
>
> Cannot be ill, cannot be good: if ill,
>
> Why hath it given me earnest of success,
>
> Commencing in a truth? I am Thane of Cawdor:

Macbeth receiving the weird sisters' prophecy
that he will be king of Scotland

If good, why do I yield to that suggestion

Whose horrid image doth unfix my hair

And make my seated heart knock at my ribs,

Against the use of nature? Present fears

Are less than horrible imaginings:

My thought, whose murder yet is but fantastical,

Shakes so my single state of man that function

Is smother'd in surmise, and nothing is

But what is not.

(ACT 1, SCENE 3)

It is also extremely interesting to note that the only time the weird sisters are referred to as witches in the text is when one of them recounts being insulted by a sea captain's wife. We know that, as with many of the historical plays, Shakespeare's chief source for *Macbeth* was Holinshed's *Chronicles*, in which Macbeth and Banquo meet three "creatures of the elderwood, nymphs or fairies" (Holinshed 1577, 268), not "witches" at all. A contemporary account of a performance of *Macbeth* from 1611, written by renowned astrologer Simon Forman, recalls the plot flawlessly, including this fascinating detail:

> There was to be observed first how Macbeth and Banquo, 2 noblemen of Scotland, riding through a wood, there stood before them 3 women fairies or nymphs, and saluted Macbeth, saying 3 times unto him, "Hail Macbeth, king of Codon [Thane of Cawdor], for thou shall be a king but shall beget no kings," etc. Then said Banquo, "What, all to Macbeth, and nothing to me?" There said the nymphs, "Hail to thee, Banquo, thou shall beget kings, yet be no king."

It is important to note that in Shakespeare's time witches and fairies were strongly linked, with the power of witches said to derive from visitations with fairies or even fairy queens before the shift in politics and religion brought more emphasis onto the devil and evil dealings, as this extract from James I's *Daemonologie* demonstrates:

> PHI.: But how can it be then, that sundrie Witches haue gone to death with that confession, that they haue ben transported with the Phairie to such a hill, which opening, they went in, and there saw a faire Queene, who being now lighter, gaue them a stone that had sundrie vertues, which at sundrie times hath bene produced in judgement?

EPI:. I say that, euen as I said before of that imaginar rauishing of the spirite foorth of the bodie. For may not the deuil object to their fantasie, their senses being dulled, and as it were a sleepe, such hilles & houses within them, such glistering courts and traines, and whatsoeuer such like wherewith he pleaseth to delude them. And in the meane time their bodies being senselesse, to conuay in their hande any stone or such like thing, which he makes them to imagine to haue receiued in such a place (James I 2016, 75).

The Power of Three

The triple-formed nature of our "secret black and midnight hags" hearkens back to world myths of the Fates, including the Moirai of Greek mythology and the Norns of Norse belief, and this is indeed the function that our three "witches" of the Scottish play fulfil, awakening Macbeth to his dark destiny. However, it is important to remember the strong link between the Fates and Fairy, as the very root of the word *fairy* is in the Latin for "fate"—*Fata*, and many fairy queens throughout myth and romance are depicted as triple-formed, triple-aspected, or appearing in threes. Three is a sacred number within Fairy lore, but what is the deeper meaning behind it and our three weird sisters in *Macbeth*?

Hecate the Fairy Queen

The appearance of Hecate as leader of the witches in *Macbeth* has always been a bit of an oddity and the subject of some academic debate, which thus far has been unable to come to a satisfactory conclusion. Many assert that she is a late addition by Middleton, either in collaboration with Shakespeare or after his death, along with the songs from Middleton's *The Witch*, which were added at some point before the publication of the folio, most likely to update it to the current trends in theatre and to appeal to James I. Indeed, she does not further the plot and is often cut in modern productions, but what if there is a meaning to Hecate's inclusion? If Shakespeare meant for her to be there, then he will have had good reason for it, and if it's not a story reason, then it must be to deepen the symbolic significance and impact of the overall play. Shakespeare's Hecate and Middleton's are of such different tones and motivations that it seems likely that she was at least a collaboration, if not entirely Shakespeare's, but not simply a late insertion of Middleton's. On that basis, why is she there?

Although it's unclear if the Hecate of *Macbeth* is simply a name or if she is intended to represent the goddess Hecate, it can be no coincidence that Hecate is a triple goddess, reflected in the triplicity of the weird sisters, and her appearance emphasises the importance of this triplicity. We've already seen that Ovid was a huge influence on Shakespeare's works, and Hecate as the goddess or queen of witches is certainly a strong presence throughout *Metamorphoses*. There are, however, other perspectives to consider. In keeping with our three witches originally being faeries, it is interesting to note that in Scottish lore Hecate was often equated with Nicneven, a queen of Fairy who dwelt within the mountain Ben Nevis, and it is likely that Shakespeare would have known this. (And let's not forget that in A *Midsummer Night's Dream*—see the quote that begins chapter 6—Puck refers to himself and all faeries as being ruled by "triple Hecate," meaning the moon as opposed to the sun, but a notable use of the name.) One of the best-known associations of the goddess Hecate is that of the triple crossroads, which is reminiscent of the traditional Scottish fairy ballad *Thomas the Rhymer*. Based on a real historical figure of the thirteenth century, the ballad (based on the original romance, which dates to the fifteenth century, so was known to Shakespeare's time) tells how Thomas is taken by the Queen of Elfland into her kingdom and passes through strange lands on the way, including the triple crossroads of "fairlies three," which are the roads to Heaven, Hell, and Fairy.

Hecate rules over the triple realms of Earth, Sea, and Sky, so again we can find this in the weird sisters, who call themselves "posters of the sea and land" and have the power to vanish "into the air."

When we look deeper into the mystery of this triple-formed goddess, our weird sisters, and triple fairies throughout myth and folklore, we find some valuable avenues of wisdom to explore. Do the three forms represent the triple nature of the soul? Celtic tradition holds that the soul is contained within three cauldrons located in the centre, the heart, and the head. (Is it taking this too far to note our "witches" dance around a cauldron like "elves and fairies in a ring"?) Platonic philosophy, prevalent in the Renaissance, has a parallel concept of a triple soul, consisting of an earthly, intellectual, and spiritual component. Also popular in Shakespeare's time, the Kabbalah expresses this same concept in Nephesh, Ruach, and Neshamah. Nor is it a stretch to relate our three sisters to the universal cycle of life, death, and rebirth, themes firmly reflected in the play; indeed, some modern versions on film and stage interpret them as "maiden, mother, crone."

Anima Mundi

Since we know that the three weird sisters started out as fairy beings and have more in common with their natures as described than they do with earthly witches, and that they are ruled by a mysterious figure known as Hecate, in order to delve into the deepest aspect of their mystery, we must take a moment to explore the true nature of Fairy women and another aspect they share with the goddess Hecate: that is, as expressions of the anima mundi, or world soul. Hecate is associated with the world soul through the ancient text fragments known as the Chaldean Oracles and her strong association/equation with Diana; as noted earlier in this chapter, this is an association shared with Shakespeare's most famous fairy queen, Titania. But why are fairies so closely linked with the world soul?

Folklore tells us that the origins of Fairy are that some fallen angels did not wish to follow Lucifer all the way to hell, but settled in the hollow places of the earth. In other words they are celestial energy which has fallen into the earth that performs an important function in the sublunar realm of conveying cosmic energy into the earth and then back into the cosmos; that is that they are regulators of an essential process whereby there is a constant flow of animating spirit within all living things—the function of the world soul. Goddesses perceived as manifestations of the world soul all share a connection with the moon, which in Platonic philosophy was seen as the seat of the world soul and the intermediary lens by which the soul is conveyed between the pure spiritual source of the sun and the material realm of the earth. This lunar association is strong in both Diana and Hecate, of course, both of whom were known as fairy queens and often equated in Shakespeare's time, and both known as manifestations of the world soul. Wisdom goddesses, fairy queens, and all manifestations of the world soul also have one significant and pertinent trait in common: the gift of prophecy, which is the chief gift and function of the weird sisters of *Macbeth*.

The Rhythm of Magic: Catalectic Trochaic Tetrameter

The witches of *Macbeth* and the faeries of *A Midsummer Night's Dream* have a surprising amount in common, including the rhythm of their speech! In both plays, Shakespeare breaks away from his usual iambic pentameter verse rhythm (ba-DUM, ba-DUM, ba-DUM, ba-DUM, ba-DUM; ten beats, five emphases, designed to resonate with the beating of the heart and echo natural speech) and adopts the "rhythm of magic," or catalectic (lacking a beat at the end) trochaic (the emphasis is on the first beat of each pair) tetrameter (eight beats as opposed to ten, making a shorter line):

☞ "When shall we three meet again?" (*Macbeth* act 1, scene 1)

☞ "Now the hungry lion roars" (*Midsummer Night's Dream*, act 5, scene 1)

The fact that there should be eight beats but each line lacks one not only has the effect of feeling slightly unnatural (or supernatural), but also means, of course, that each line is seven beats long, a number that we have already noted is extremely significant in Hermetic belief and practice, and is also important in Fairy lore.

Witchcraft in the Comedies and Histories

Since the word *witch* is uttered but one solitary time in *Macbeth*, it is interesting to note that overall there are seventy-three mentions of witches and/or witchcraft (by name) in Shakespeare's plays, and the majority of the more significant occurrences are in the comedies and histories, most particularly *The Merry Wives of Windsor* and the *Henry* VI trilogy. From *The Merry Wives of Windsor*:

> MISTRESS FORD: I would my husband would meet him in this shape: he cannot abide the old woman of Brentford; he swears she's a witch; forbade her my house and hath threatened to beat her.
>
> MISTRESS PAGE: Heaven guide him to thy husband's cudgel, and the devil guide his cudgel afterwards!
>
> MISTRESS FORD: But is my husband coming?
>
> MISTRESS PAGE: Ah, in good sadness, is he; and talks of the basket too, howsoever he hath had intelligence.
>
> MISTRESS FORD: We'll try that; for I'll appoint my men to carry the basket again, to meet him at the door with it, as they did last time.
>
> MISTRESS PAGE: Nay, but he'll be here presently: let's go dress him like the witch of Brentford.
>
> (ACT 4, SCENE 2)

As in the climactic fairy-filled scene of this comedy that we have already looked at, that popular rotund figure of jest Falstaff, thinking to pursue two married women, instead finds himself repeatedly and hilariously put in his place. Here Mistresses Ford and Page have conspired to dress him in old woman's clothes so that he will be beaten by Mistress Ford's husband. According to Thiselton-Dyer, the witch of Brentford was "an actual personage…of whose vaticinations must have been traditionally well known to an audience of the time." He goes on to observe that she also has a mention in *Westward Ho*, written by Dekker and Webster in 1604. There's little hint of the eerie abilities displayed by *Macbeth's* witches here, though as portrayed by Falstaff she does share the trait of facial hair, noted within the scene by Hugh Evans as he states:

> By the yea and no, I think the 'oman is a witch
>
> indeed: I like not when a 'oman has a great peard;
>
> I spy a great peard under his muffler.
>
> (ACT 4, SCENE 2)

It is uncertain whether the use of "his" instead of "her" here indicates that he recognises Falstaff's true identity.

Falstaff makes previous mention of witchcraft in *Henry IV, Part I*, when he remarks:

> …I am bewitched with the
>
> rogue's company. If the rascal hath not given me
>
> medicines to make me love him, I'll be hanged; it
>
> could not be else: I have drunk medicines.
>
> (ACT 2, SCENE 2)

Yet in both these instances, though they are comic, the comedy is at Falstaff's expense and not directed at witchcraft or its practitioners as was popular with many playwrights of the time. The closest Shakespeare comes to being disparaging or sceptical of the practice of magic is in *Comedy of Errors*:

> ANTIPHOLUS OF SYRACUSE: They say this town is full of cozenage,
>
> As, nimble jugglers that deceive the eye,
>
> Dark-working sorcerers that change the mind,
>
> Soul-killing witches that deform the body,

Disguised cheaters, prating mountebanks,

And many such-like liberties of sin.

(ACT 1, SCENE 2)

The town in question is, of course, Ephesus, renowned for its ancient pagan temples and remarkable legacy of learning and culture. There are several mentions of magic and witchcraft throughout the play as two sets of long-lost twins repeatedly cause each other to be caught in farcical situations, often resulting in accusations of possession when an individual's behaviour seems erratic—because of course they have been mistaken for their twin!

Historical Conjurations

Joan of Arc's story is well known: that of a young French peasant girl who, aided by visions and saintly voices, became a great military leader, her sad ending coming in flames, tied to the stake for witchcraft. Unfortunately, her first portrayal on stage, in Shakespeare's *Henry VI, Part I*, is far from favourable and has oft been criticised by public, critics, and academics alike. It is transparent propaganda and perhaps as it is one of Shakespeare's earliest plays (and most likely written in collaboration with a mentor, possibly Marlowe), it is very strongly rooted in the tone of his source material, Holinshed's *Chronicles*, which is naturally somewhat anti-French. Digging beneath the layers of propaganda, in Joan we find a very different kind of witch character. Very human, very flawed, young and vulnerable. Though she is shown as able to summon spirits, those spirits turn from her when she needs them most:

> JOAN LA PUCELLE: The regent conquers, and the Frenchmen fly.
>
> Now help, ye charming spells and periapts;
>
> And ye choice spirits that admonish me
>
> And give me signs of future accidents.
>
> [Thunder]
>
> You speedy helpers, that are substitutes
>
> Under the lordly monarch of the north,
>
> Appear and aid me in this enterprise.
>
> [Enter Fiends]

A Brief History of the Histories

When we talk about Shakespeare's history plays, we mean the plays that cover the English rulers from King John to Richard III, though they were not written in chronological order (although to be fair, there's debate over the order Shakespeare wrote many of his plays, other than early, mid, and late). It's thought that *Henry VI, Part II & III* came first, followed by *Part I*, then *Richard III*, then *Richard II*, followed by *King John* and then *Henry IV, Part I & II* and then *Henry V*. At least the last three are in some sort of coherent order! To watch with a through line, you can pretty much ignore *King John* as it's a standalone play, but you can follow the rise and fall (and many deaths) of characters in this order: *Richard II*, *Henry IV, Part I & II*, *Henry V*, *Henry VI, Part I, II & III*, and *Richard III*. For just the War of the Roses (so named for the dispute between the houses of York, the white rose, and Lancaster, the red rose), then it's the *Henry VI* plays plus *Richard III*.

This speedy and quick appearance argues proof

Of your accustom'd diligence to me.

Now, ye familiar spirits, that are cull'd

Out of the powerful regions under earth,

Help me this once, that France may get the field.

[They walk, and speak not]

O, hold me not with silence over-long!

Where I was wont to feed you with my blood,

I'll lop a member off and give it you

In earnest of further benefit,

So you do condescend to help me now.

[They hang their heads]

No hope to have redress? My body shall

Pay recompense, if you will grant my suit.

[They shake their heads]

Cannot my body nor blood-sacrifice

Entreat you to your wonted furtherance?

Then take my soul, my body, soul and all,

Before that England give the French the foil.

[They depart]

See, they forsake me! Now the time is come

That France must vail her lofty-plumed crest

And let her head fall into England's lap.

My ancient incantations are too weak,

And hell too strong for me to buckle with:

Now, France, thy glory droopeth to the dust

(ACT 5, SCENE 3)

Yet the ill-fated Joan is not the only one to burn for witchcraft in the *Henry* VI trilogy. Margery Jourdain and Robert Bolingbroke are a sorcerous duo paid by the Duchess of Gloucester to perform the forbidden act of conjuring spirits and casting the king's horoscope. Here the conjurer Bolingbroke evokes the requisite atmosphere:

BOLINGBROKE: Patience, good lady; wizards know their times:

Deep night, dark night, the silent of the night,

The time of night when Troy was set on fire;

The time when screech-owls cry and ban-dogs howl,

And spirits walk and ghosts break up their graves,

That time best fits the work we have in hand.

(*Henry* VI, *Part* II, ACT 1, SCENE 4)

Jourdain and Bolingbroke are based on real historical figures who did indeed work for the Duchess of Gloucester on occasion. Margery Jourdain (or Jourdemayne) was also known as "the witch of Eye," and after several trials for witchcraft from which she was released after promising to commit no further witchcraft, she was finally convicted of plotting to bring down Henry VI by witchcraft in 1441 and burned at the stake.

These witches are shown to be clearly mortal, indeed career magicians making a living. However, as in *Macbeth*, the predictions made by the summoned spirit all prove true—that is, that the king will be deposed by one who in turn will die a violent death (Richard, duke of Gloucester, later Richard III), that Suffolk will die by water, and that castles are not the best place for Somerset to hang out.

Sycorax

A witch, and one so strong that

could control the moon.

—*The Tempest*, ACT 5, SCENE 1

Since Sycorax has supposedly already died before the events of the play, she never appears in person, and yet her presence is keenly felt. She is mother to Caliban, a supposed demi-devil whom Prospero has enslaved, whose father is alleged to be no less than the Patagonian demon-god Setebos, a name Shakespeare presumably encountered in Magellan's accounts of his circumnavigating the globe. The "New World" was incredibly fashionable at the time, and it appears that Shakespeare found it more important to include exotic names and locations than to adhere to any real sense of geography, as Sycorax is described as having been banished for unknown heinous acts of sorcery from

Argier, or Algiers (North Africa), yet worships a god from an entirely different region. (Since the location of the island is also unspecified, this only adds to the mythic nature of the tale and a reminder that it's better to be interpreted symbolically than literally!) We can presume she was meant to be dark-skinned and yet she is also described as a "blue-eyed hag" (act 1, scene 2). Her powers are described as being almost goddess-like, not only in her imprisoning Ariel in a pine tree for twelve years, but she is also described by Prospero, whom we should take as a reliable source, as being able to "control the moon."

Other than contemporary accounts of shipwrecks and exploration of the New World, there is no known source for *The Tempest*, hence Sycorax's origins remain mysterious. It has been noted that a chief source of inspiration may well have been the sorceresses Circe and Medea, both of whom were devotees of Hecate. Indeed, Ted Hughes explores this possibility at length, comparing Prospero to Ulysses and naming Ariel as the equivalent of the flower through which the sorceress's magic is neutralised. It is an appealing and poetic interpretation, and of course we already know that Ovid was Shakespeare's favourite source of mythic content.

In his indispensable work *Prospero's Island*, Noel Cobb notes that Sycorax can be broken down and translated to mean "pig-raven," which might again imply a Circe reference since she was most famous for turning intruding sailors into pigs. Cobb takes a Jungian approach in his analysis, declaring Sycorax as the "neglected feminine which has turned fierce and vengeful." He also observes that "much has been written on the possible sources for Sycorax and many attempts have been made to figure out exactly who she is" (Cobb 1984, 67).

In my own undergraduate thesis (writ many, many moons ago!), I theorised that through Shakespeare's plays there is a struggle between male and female and a particular issue with mother figures, noting that in *The Tempest*, thought to be his final play, the perfected daughter (Miranda) has only a father and no mother, and the deformed son (Caliban) has only a mother and no father, with Sycorax embodying all fears of powerful women and their ability to reproduce.

However, previous scholars and academics have not considered that Shakespeare may have looked to the grimoires as a possible source.

Back to the Grimoires...

Returning to *The Book of Oberon* and indeed to the conjuration of Oberyon himself, we see four advisors to Oberyon listed that must be called upon: "Storax, Carmelion, Caberyon" and "Severion." Storax bears a striking similarity to the name Sycorax, and this becomes even more apparent when we consider other grimoire sources. In *The Grimoire of Arthur Gauntlet* we see the same list of advisors but with a different spelling: "Scorax" (Rankine 2011, 261). It is thought that the alternative spelling of "Storax" is a mutation of "Scorax," possibly resulting from the frequent use of the resin of the same name as a ritual ingredient. The most concrete proof of all comes from Daniel Harms and Joseph H. Peterson's most recent grimoire publication, *Of Angels, Demons & Spirits*. This transcription of a seventeenth-century grimoire contains the following mention:

> ...and by all masses and alms that were made in the Church of God, and by the seven planets of heaven, by the sun and its angel, Sycoracem or Storax, by Saturn and its angel Malathym, by Jupiter and its angel Phytoneum (Harms and Peterson 2019, 77).

The exactness of a name found nowhere else previously in literature plus the spirit's direct association with Oberon, already featured in the works, suggests extremely strongly that Shakespeare at the very least had access to and was familiar with grimoires, was inspired by their contents, and consciously chose to use them in his work.

So Sycorax, in name at least, was an angel of the sun, which seems in direct contradiction to the context in which she appears in Shakespeare's play. Did he simply take the name because it sounded cool? (Let's face it, it does.) Or can we read more into this secret knowledge? Although on first description we are led to believe that Sycorax and Prospero are contrasting in nature, Prospero reveals himself to be more akin to Sycorax than he would like to admit. He threatens Ariel with the exact same punishment that Sycorax inflicted him with, and for the same amount of time: twelve years imprisoned in the pine tree. They were both banished to the island, both with a child of the opposing gender. If Noel Cobb is correct in his assertion that Sycorax is Prospero's neglected feminine aspect, a furious dark goddess, then the integration of this quality is implied in Prospero's final acceptance of her son, Caliban: "This thing of darkness I acknowledge mine" (act 5, scene 1). Is it reading too much into this symbolism to suggest if she is an angel of the sun but is portrayed as dark, that she represents Sol Niger, the beginning of the alchemical process? Her arrival on the island is, after all, key to the events of the play and could be seen to be the magical seed of its overall process. If we look once again at the line "one so strong as could control the moon," this takes on an even more potent meaning.

With the exception of *Comedy of Errors*, where the mentions of witchcraft seem mostly down to comedic xenophobia and confusion on the part of the Syracusian characters, Shakespeare portrays the subject with clear reverence. Even when painted in a negative light, the powers claimed by the witches are shown to be real and worthy of respect, as indeed are ghosts and fairies, as we have seen through the explorations of the preceding chapters.

Exercise: World Soul Visualisation

We've explored the Platonic concept of the world soul through our discussion of the witches of *Macbeth* and in the preceding chapter regarding fairies. Here is an exercise to help you connect more deeply with the concept. It will also help to develop your spiritual and energetic connection to the world and your fellow luminous beings of all kinds that inhabit it (very valuable to performers—this will help increase your connection, awareness, and hence your charisma and stage presence).

☞ You will need a white candle/tealight with appropriate holder

   and

☞ A clear surface/shrine/ safe outdoor location

TIMING: Anytime, but full moon would be most powerful.

In a space where you know you will not be disturbed and you can safely light a candle, either sit or stand comfortably in front of your candle, take three deep breaths, and release the thoughts and worries of the day, then light the candle as you say

> O for a Muse of fire, that would ascend
> The brightest heaven of invention!

Take three more deep breaths as you sit and observe the light from the candle.

Keep your breathing steady.

Be aware of the rays of light touching you and how its energy becomes part of your energy field. Stay with this awareness for three more breaths.

Expand your awareness to other things touched by the light. You are all connected by these rays of light. Hold this awareness for another three breaths.

Now imagine there are no barriers between the light of the candle and all you can see. It is all touched by and connected by this energy. Contemplate this for three breaths.

How far can you visualise this connection spreading? You become aware of the light of the candle as a great pillar of light that stretches both to the beyond above and out of vision into infinity and down into the below, out of sight and beyond awareness. It expands in all directions beyond limit and connects everything it touches with the same illuminating energy, with no diminishing over distance or time.

Closing your eyes, imagine that the candle exists within your solar plexus (your centre). Feel how the energy connects to all things as if you are at the centre of a great web. Expand this awareness as much as you are able to, taking all the time you need.

As you expand this awareness, you become aware that all living things have their own candles at their centres, sparks of the same great light, a pillar that extends from above to below, from below to above, in a continuous flow and renewal of life-force, of soul.

Hold this awareness for at least three breaths.

When you feel it is time, slowly withdraw your awareness a stage at a time, taking three breaths again at each stage. Feel your awareness returning to yourself and the space you are in but retain knowledge of the connection.

Open your eyes and return your awareness to the candle flame.

Three deep breaths, knowing your internal flame is ever lit. You may extinguish the candle when you are ready.

If you wish, you may recite Sonnet 29, with the thought that whilst at times we may feel disconnected from those around us and from the world, in truth we are all one with the divine:

When, in disgrace with fortune and men's eyes,
I all alone beweep my outcast state,
And trouble deaf heaven with my bootless cries,
And look upon myself, and curse my fate,
Wishing me like to one more rich in hope,
Featur'd like him, like him with friends possess'd,
Desiring this man's art and that man's scope,
With what I most enjoy contented least;
Yet in these thoughts myself almost despising,
Haply I think on thee, and then my state,
Like to the lark at break of day arising
From sullen earth, sings hymns at heaven's gate;
For thy sweet love remember'd such wealth brings
That then I scorn to change my state with kings.

Methinks I am a prophet
new inspired…
RICHARD III
ACT 2, SCENE 1

EIGHT

Oracles and Omens, Prophecies and Portents

It's not only witches and conjurors that have the power to make predictions in Shakespeare's plays. Prophecies may be declared by anyone from a queen to a character with one line called Peter from Pontefract. Dreams reveal secrets of the future (usually doom-ridden), the land itself appears to cry out when its rulers are corrupt, and to disrespect an oracle brings grievous consequences. In this chapter we'll explore some of the many examples of prophecy, omens, and oracular insight, and we'll discuss what the implications might be about Shakespeare's worldview.

Prophets and Omens in the Histories

Shakespeare's history plays were not written or performed in chronological order. Although we can't be certain, it appears that the *Henry VI* trilogy of plays were amongst the earliest to be performed, around 1591–92, followed by his first big hit, *Richard* III, in 1593. Then he went back in time with *Richard* II in 1595, flashed back even further to *King John* in 1596, then continued the progression with *Henry IV, Part I* in 1596–7 and *Part II* the next year. *Henry V* completed the War of the Roses in 1599, with *Henry VIII* marking the end of his writing career (as far as we know) in 1613.

Through all these plays, with the exception of *Henry V*, there is a connecting theme of prophecies, dreams, and omens, reflecting the fascination with such prognostication in Shakespeare's time. Prophesying was taken extremely seriously as an everyday and accepted element of politics in Elizabethan England, and Geoffrey of Monmouth's *Prophesies of Merlin* was particularly popular. King Henry VIII took a prophecy about his daughters (that Elizabeth would marry a Frenchman or Scotsman and Mary would marry a Spaniard) so seriously that he had them poisoned, but thankfully they were able to recover. People would circulate rumours of prophecies in an attempt to bring down monarchs, including predictions of death.

In 1563 a law called the "Act agaynst fonde and phantasticall Prophesyes" was passed to stop circulation of false prophecies that said Elizabeth I's reign was to be brief and her life short. Elizabeth used prophecy to her political advantage, one of the reasons why she kept Dee as such a close advisor. Prophecies that were circulated around the people could take on a potent political punch. We don't now tend to think of the history plays as being particularly magical, perhaps because our modern mindset discounts the prophetic or supernatural elements as irrelevant, but to Shakespeare's audience they would have been expected and treated as important aspects of the plot.

King John

This adds important context to such events as King John immediately sentencing a common man to death for speaking prophecies about his imminent fall from power, as he dare not let such opinion spread:

> PHILIP THE BASTARD: But as I travell'd hither through the land,
> I find the people strangely fantasied;

> Possess'd with rumours, full of idle dreams,
>
> Not knowing what they fear, but full of fear:
>
> And here a prophet, that I brought with me
>
> From forth the streets of Pomfret, whom I found
>
> With many hundreds treading on his heels;
>
> To whom he sung, in rude harsh-sounding rhymes,
>
> That, ere the next Ascension-day at noon,
>
> Your highness should deliver up your crown.
>
> KING JOHN: Thou idle dreamer, wherefore didst thou so?
>
> PETER OF POMFRET: Foreknowing that the truth will fall out so.
>
> (*King John*, ACT 4, SCENE 2)

Poor Peter has only one line before he is dragged off to death, but his voice is instantly replaced by the voice of the land and even the cosmos itself as peculiar visions of five moons are seen in the sky, connected to the death of young Arthur (nephew of the French king, with claims to the English throne), striking John to the heart with dread and causing instant panic and regret. Whilst he is relieved to find that young Arthur remains alive (though poor Arthur then dies rather stupidly after falling from a roof in a failed escape attempt), King John is later poisoned and much military power on both sides of the conflict is lost to flooding. Perhaps the previous omen of the five moons, since the moon is "governess of floods," portended to this occurrence.

Richard II

Kings and queens are not always just the subject of prophecy but may prophesy themselves, and often these seem a combination of both prediction and curse, with those who find themselves at the bottom of Fortune's wheel reminding those at the top that it must turn again.

In the final act of *Richard* II, the deposed king pronounces a searing prophecy to Bolingbroke's closest ally, declaring that the future will see them become enemies:

> RICHARD II: Northumberland, thou ladder wherewithal
>
> The mounting Bolingbroke ascends my throne,
>
> The time shall not be many hours of age

More than it is ere foul sin gathering head

Shalt break into corruption: thou shalt think,

Though he divide the realm and give thee half,

It is too little, helping him to all;

And he shall think that thou, which know'st the way

To plant unrightful kings, wilt know again,

Being ne'er so little urged, another way

To pluck him headlong from the usurped throne.

The love of wicked men converts to fear;

That fear to hate, and hate turns one or both

To worthy danger and deserved death.

(ACT 5, SCENE I)

Henry IV, Part I & II

This prophecy fulfils itself and comes back to haunt Bolingbroke, now the ailing Henry IV, as he despairs at the enmity between himself and his once-close friend. He repeats almost exactly the words as spoken by Richard, though he was not there. Presumably since it was a prophecy of some import, it had been written down and shown to him or spoken to him and he has held it in his memory.

HENRY IV: …You, cousin Nevil, as I may remember—

When Richard, with his eye brim full of tears,

Then check'd and rated by Northumberland,

Did speak these words, now prov'd a prophecy?

'Northumberland, thou ladder by the which

My cousin Bolingbroke ascends my throne'—

Though then, God knows, I had no such intent

But that necessity so bow'd the state

That I and greatness were compell'd to kiss—

'The time shall come'—thus did he follow it—

'The time will come that foul sin, gathering head,

Shall break into corruption' so went on,

> Foretelling this same time's condition
> And the division of our amity.
> (*Henry IV, Part II*, ACT 3, SCENE I)

The Earl of Warwick, seeing his king so disturbed, offers a rational counterpoint for the source of the prophecy in an attempt to calm Henry's fears that he might be under a divine curse.

> EARL OF WARWICK: There is a history in all men's lives,
> Figuring the natures of the times deceas'd;
> The which observ'd, a man may prophesy,
> With a near aim, of the main chance of things
> As yet not come to life, who in their seeds
> And weak beginning lie intreasured.
> Such things become the hatch and brood of time;
> And, by the necessary form of this,
> King Richard might create a perfect guess
> That great Northumberland, then false to him,
> Would of that seed grow to a greater falseness;
> Which should not find a ground to root upon
> Unless on you.
> (*Henry IV, Part II*, ACT 3, SCENE I)

Hotspur is another character sceptical of supernatural prediction who tires of the "great magician" Glendower's boasting of the portents that accompanied his birth, such as the earth shaking and the heavens being full of "fiery shapes":

> I cannot choose: sometime he angers me
> With telling me of the mouldwarp and the ant,
> Of the dreamer Merlin and his prophecies,
> And of a dragon and a finless fish,
> A clip-wing'd griffin and a moulten raven,
> A couching lion and a ramping cat,

And such a deal of skimble-skamble stuff

As puts me from my faith.

(*Henry IV, Part I,* ACT 3, SCENE I)

This is an example of symbolic Galfridian prophecy, which uses animals as symbols to obscure the direct truth, which originated with Geoffrey of Monmouth ("Galfridian" is based upon Geoffrey's Latin name, Galfridus Monemutensis). Of course, Hotspur is making direct reference here to Geoffrey of Monmouth's work *The Prophecies of Merlin,* which was popular in Shakespeare's time. It's an example of Shakespeare taking a contemporary reference and placing it into a historical character's mouth. The other manner of prophecy is called Sibyllic, which originated in Europe and used initials and letters to signify people. The ill-fated Duke of Clarence (whose first name is George) refers to this manner of prophecy in the opening scene of *Richard* III, when he tells his brother Richard that their elder brother, King Edward IV,

…hearkens after prophecies and dreams;

And from the cross-row plucks the letter G.

And says a wizard told him that by G

His issue disinherited should be.

However, these prophecies have been planted by Richard himself in order to poison the king's mind against Clarence and ultimately dispose of him and get closer to the throne. Cunning indeed, but lest we should believe all prophecies to be so false, Richard's bloody clamber to power through the War of the Roses is littered with curses and prophecies that do come to pass.

The War of the Roses

Some of these predictions take the form of dreams, such as the haunting of both Richard and his rival Richmond in their tents the night before the Battle of Bosworth, as discussed in chapter 5. One of the most beautifully horrifying predictive dreams is Clarence again, who not only dreams of his death, but unknowingly picks out the one who is to blame:

DUKE OF CLARENCE: Methought that Gloucester stumbled;

and, in falling,

> Struck me, that thought to stay him, overboard,
> Into the tumbling billows of the main.
> Lord, Lord! methought, what pain it was to drown!
> What dreadful noise of waters in mine ears!
> What ugly sights of death within mine eyes!
> Methought I saw a thousand fearful wrecks;
> Ten thousand men that fishes gnaw'd upon;
> Wedges of gold, great anchors, heaps of pearl,
> Inestimable stones, unvalued jewels,
> All scatter'd in the bottom of the sea:
> Some lay in dead men's skulls; and, in those holes
> Where eyes did once inhabit, there were crept,
> As 'twere in scorn of eyes, reflecting gems,
> Which woo'd the slimy bottom of the deep,
> And mock'd the dead bones that lay scatter'd by.
> (*Richard* III, ACT I, SCENE 4)

Of all of Richard's victims, it is the women who bite back most vociferously, with the triad of Lady Anne, his own mother the Duchess of York, and Queen Margaret all firing curses at him. Margaret's curses take the form of prophecies, and the line is blurred as to where the intent lies between them when she is targeting others. In act I, scene 3, she warns the current queen, Elizabeth, of what is to come:

> QUEEN MARGARET: Poor painted queen, vain flourish of my fortune!
> Why strew'st thou sugar on that bottled spider,
> Whose deadly web ensnareth thee about?
> Fool, fool! thou whet'st a knife to kill thyself.
> The time will come when thou shalt wish for me
> To help thee curse that poisonous bunchback'd toad…
> …O, but remember this another day,
> When he shall split thy very heart with sorrow,
> And say poor Margaret was a prophetess!

Richard's close ally Buckingham scoffs at her predictions in act 1 but later comes to realise the truth of them when he is cast aside by Richard, repeating her words.

Margaret is not the only prophetess of the War of the Roses. *Henry VI, Part I* is dominated by the presence of the charismatic Joan of Arc, described by the King of France as:

> Divinest creature, Astraea's daughter,
>
> How shall I honour thee for this success?
>
> Thy promises are like Adonis' gardens
>
> That one day bloom'd and fruitful were the next.
>
> France, triumph in thy glorious prophetess!
>
> Recover'd is the town of Orleans:
>
> More blessed hap did ne'er befall our state.
>
> (ACT 1, SCENE 6)

Astraea is an ancient Greek goddess of Justice and purity whose name means "star-maiden" and was popularly identified with Elizabeth I, so this is a bold title to choose. However, Shakespeare has been criticised for his portrayal of Joan, who seems to become weak and cowardly when faced with her own death. She is, of course, only very young, and also French. He could never be seen politically to portray the French in too much of a positive light!

Henry VIII and the Birth of Elizabeth I

Shakespeare's prophecies catch up with his own lifetime in the last scene of one of his very last collaborative plays, *Henry VIII*, which was penned with John Fletcher. The extreme nostalgia for the reign of Elizabeth is demonstrated by this divine oracle delivered by Archbishop Cranmer on the birth of Elizabeth to her father the king:

> She shall be loved and fear'd: her own shall bless her;
>
> Her foes shake like a field of beaten corn,
>
> And hang their heads with sorrow: good grows with her:
>
> In her days every man shall eat in safety,
>
> Under his own vine, what he plants; and sing
>
> The merry songs of peace to all his neighbours:

God shall be truly known; and those about her

From her shall read the perfect ways of honour,

And by those claim their greatness, not by blood.

Nor shall this peace sleep with her: but as when

The bird of wonder dies, the maiden phoenix,

Her ashes new create another heir,

As great in admiration as herself;

So shall she leave her blessedness to one,

When heaven shall call her from this cloud of darkness,

Who from the sacred ashes of her honour

Shall star-like rise, as great in fame as she was,

And so stand fix'd: peace, plenty, love, truth, terror,

That were the servants to this chosen infant,

Shall then be his, and like a vine grow to him:

Wherever the bright sun of heaven shall shine,

His honour and the greatness of his name

Shall be, and make new nations: he shall flourish,

And, like a mountain cedar, reach his branches

To all the plains about him: our children's children

Shall see this, and bless heaven.

(*Henry* VIII, ACT 5, SCENE 5)

This is an example of prophecy channelled not from ancient gods or spirits but from the Christian deity by a Christian clergyman. It is both a deeply political message and a spiritual message, with Elizabeth painted as the phoenix that is both an alchemical symbol connected to the philosopher's stone and a symbol of the hopes that Shakespeare and others placed on the rebirth of her Golden Age. The phoenix was often associated with Elizabeth during her reign, but since this was obviously written after her death, the heir that hopes were resting on was James I's son, Henry, whose beliefs were close to the old occult philosophy as opposed to the restricting beliefs of his pious father, but he was sadly to die young and thus be unable to fulfil these hopes.

Macbeth

Who can impress the forest, bid the tree
Unfix his earth-bound root? Sweet bodements!

—*Macbeth*, ACT 4, SCENE 1

Shakespeare's most prophecy-driven plot is without a doubt *Macbeth*, with the mysterious "weird sisters" giving him two triple-aspected prophecies that embolden him to indulge his darkest urges. In their first encounter they call him by a title he already has, one that he will shortly be given, the Thane of Cawdor, and one that is further off, the ultimate ambition of the crown. The latter would be more unbelievable were it not for the first two, and as soon as he is made Thane of Cawdor his thoughts turn to what steps he must take to gain the crown. As we have discussed in the previous chapter, the dark will to attain it by blood was already innate within his mind, and the prophecy of the witches only served to quicken it, not to implant the desire, as some would have it. Sadly, the prophecies being proven true also means that his friend Banquo, whom the witches promise will be the father of kings despite never being king himself, is also placed in the way of his ambition and quickly becomes a target.

Despite being bloodily despatched, the image of Banquo reappears, first as a ghost (which as we've discussed may or may not be a manifestation of a guilty conscience) and secondly as the head of a procession of kings in the last of a second set of prophecies, which are delivered by the "masters" of the witches, whose nature is not revealed.

The second set of prophecies, which are answers to the direct questions he asks, reveal once again that the witches are not the source of evil in the play, but that it is in his own heart. His response to "none of woman born shall harm Macbeth" (a tricksy response, since Macbeth doesn't realise that Macduff was "untimely ripp'd" from his mother's womb) is firstly that Macduff should be allowed to live if no one can harm Macbeth, but then shortly after he sends killers after Macduff's whole family, children included. The witches then follow with another prediction that boosts his narcissistic tendencies—that he "will never vanquished be until Great Birnam Wood to high Dunsinane hill shall come against him" (act 5, scene 1). If he was merely acting under the inspiration of the witches, then his supposed invulnerability would prevent him having to commit more atrocities to remain in power, but he does them anyway, which brings about his downfall.

The King's Evil

An interesting detail that is often skipped over or cut from performance in *Macbeth* (understandably, as it doesn't further the plot) is how the evils of the Scottish king contrast with the divinely sourced magic of the English king, as discovered by Malcolm and Macduff when they have their lengthy political discussion:

> MALCOLM: 'Tis call'd the evil:
> A most miraculous work in this good king;
> Which often, since my here-remain in England,
> I have seen him do. How he solicits heaven,
> Himself best knows: but strangely-visited people,
> All swoln and ulcerous, pitiful to the eye,
> The mere despair of surgery, he cures,
> Hanging a golden stamp about their necks,
> Put on with holy prayers: and 'tis spoken,
> To the succeeding royalty he leaves
> The healing benediction. With this strange virtue,
> He hath a heavenly gift of prophecy,
> And sundry blessings hang about his throne,
> That speak him full of grace.
>
> (ACT 4, SCENE 3)

This is a detail that derives from the source material, Holinshed's account of Edward the Confessor, and Shakespeare's inclusion of it is a nod to James I, who believed himself the inheritor of the supposedly divine powers of Edward the Confessor. "The evil" seems a strange name for it, but as Thiselton-Dyer informs us, the "King's Evil" was "a common name in years go by for scrofula, because the sovereigns of England were supposed to possess the power of curing it" (Thiselton-Dyer 2017, 104). Presumably this sort of magical healing and prophecy was acceptable, or perhaps he feared others having access to this kind of power. One rule for some and another for others is a principle that still abides.

"Beware the Ides of March"

Ill Portents

The "weird sisters" are not the only source of supernatural tidings in the Scottish play, but the land itself seems to cry out at the death of King Duncan, with ill portents that are understood by the common people as a sign that all is not well, with great storms and unnatural acts such as the king's horses bolting and then eating each other.

Consequences of Ignoring Omens

This can be compared to the omens witnessed in Rome in the early scenes of *Julius Caesar*, which Cassius interprets as Nature mirroring the qualities of the current ruler as a warning from the heavens:

> CASSIUS: ...Why all these fires, why all these gliding ghosts,
>
> Why birds and beasts from quality and kind,
>
> Why old men fool and children calculate,
>
> Why all these things change from their ordinance
>
> Their natures and preformed faculties
>
> To monstrous quality,—why, you shall find
>
> That heaven hath infused them with these spirits,
>
> To make them instruments of fear and warning
>
> Unto some monstrous state.
>
> Now could I, Casca, name to thee a man
>
> Most like this dreadful night,
>
> That thunders, lightens, opens graves, and roars
>
> As doth the lion in the Capitol,
>
> A man no mightier than thyself or me
>
> In personal action, yet prodigious grown
>
> And fearful, as these strange eruptions are.
>
> (ACT I, SCENE 3)

Julius Caesar has one of the most famous prophecies of all literature—"Beware the Ides of March"—and the consequences of his not heeding the warnings are brutal, as is usually the case in Shakespeare's tragedies. Prophecies are to be taken seriously, and if they are ignored or disrespected, even accidentally, there is always a dire price to pay;

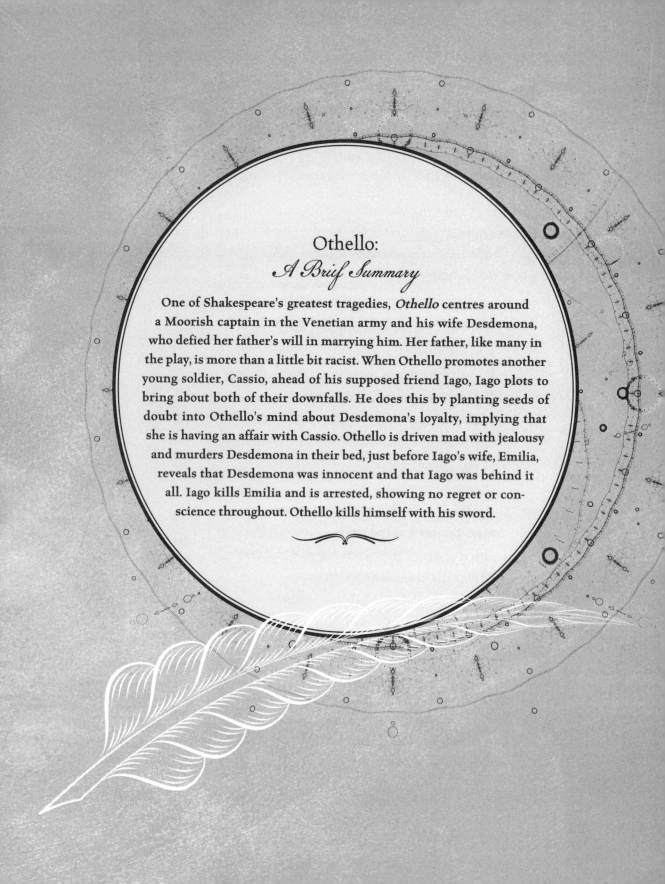

Othello:
A Brief Summary

One of Shakespeare's greatest tragedies, *Othello* centres around a Moorish captain in the Venetian army and his wife Desdemona, who defied her father's will in marrying him. Her father, like many in the play, is more than a little bit racist. When Othello promotes another young soldier, Cassio, ahead of his supposed friend Iago, Iago plots to bring about both of their downfalls. He does this by planting seeds of doubt into Othello's mind about Desdemona's loyalty, implying that she is having an affair with Cassio. Othello is driven mad with jealousy and murders Desdemona in their bed, just before Iago's wife, Emilia, reveals that Desdemona was innocent and that Iago was behind it all. Iago kills Emilia and is arrested, showing no regret or conscience throughout. Othello kills himself with his sword.

Othello gifts a handkerchief to Desdemona as a wedding gift that contains a potent charm. Emilia takes it under her husband, Iago's, instruction, not realising its significance, and even Desdemona is not fully aware of the danger of losing it until it is already too late:

> OTHELLO: That is a fault.
>> That handkerchief
>> Did an Egyptian to my mother give;
>> She was a charmer, and could almost read
>> The thoughts of people: she told her, while
>> she kept it,
>> 'Twould make her amiable and subdue my father
>> Entirely to her love, but if she lost it
>> Or made gift of it, my father's eye
>> Should hold her loathed and his spirits should hunt
>> After new fancies: she, dying, gave it me;
>> And bid me, when my fate would have me wive,
>> To give it her. I did so: and take heed on't;
>> Make it a darling like your precious eye;
>> To lose't or give't away were such perdition
>> As nothing else could match.
>
> DESDEMONA: Is't possible?
>
> OTHELLO: 'Tis true: there's magic in the web of it:
>> A sibyl, that had number'd in the world
>> The sun to course two hundred compasses,
>> In her prophetic fury sew'd the work;
>> The worms were hallow'd that did breed the silk;
>> And it was dyed in mummy which the skilful
>> Conserved of maidens' hearts.
>
> (ACT 3, SCENE 4)

197

Apollo's Angry

In *The Winter's Tale* Leontes faces dire retribution from the god Apollo after denying the truth of the Oracle from Delphi that proved Hermione and Camillo's innocence. The inclusion of the oracle is almost word for word exactly as is written in the source material, Robert Greene's *Pandosto*:

> Suspicion is no proof; jealousy is an unequal Judge; Bellaria is chaste; Egistus blameless; Franion a true subject; Pandosto treacherous; his babe an innocent, and the king shall live without an heir if that which is lost be not found (Greene 1588).

> Hermione is chaste;
> Polixenes blameless; Camillo a true subject; Leontes
> a jealous tyrant; his innocent babe truly begotten;
> and the king shall live without an heir, if that
> which is lost be not found.
> (*The Winter's Tale*, ACT 3, SCENE 2)

There is also an excellent description of the witnessing of the oracle that is paraphrased from the source material, describing the sacrifices and "ear-deafening voice o' the oracle, Kin to Jove's thunder" (act 3, scene 1), which corresponds with historical accounts in which the Pythia (the name given to the priestess who delivers the oracle) speaks with the voice of the god Apollo.

However, the denial of the oracle by Leontes is entirely Shakespeare's addition. In the original story, King Pandosto is instantly struck by remorse upon hearing the oracle, knowing it must be true. His queen genuinely dies, no resurrection or statue, also Shakespeare's magical touch. The bear that pursues and consumes Antigonus is a symbol of Diana, twin of the god Apollo whose oracle has been denied. It is clear that Shakespeare wished to emphasise the importance of respecting magical practices, especially those derived from the gods.

Exercise: Bibliomancy

Bibliomancy is a simple divination technique using any book, traditionally a bible, but in our case let's use *The Complete Works of Shakespeare*. There are two different possible methods.

Book Method

Holding a question in your mind and the book in your hands, call on inner guidance and turn to a random page. Without looking, let your finger land on a line. Within that passage there should be some advice or answer to your question.

Online Method

If you need to use an online copy of the works (this is an alternative if you don't have access to a copy of the complete works or your own copy has been worn in so that it tends to open in the same place), you can use an online random number generator to determine your answer—www.opensourceshakespeare.org is an excellent online resource. Remember to hold your question clearly in your mind. It will help to speak it aloud every time you generate a number.

☞ Go to random.org or another random number generator and set your parameters to 1–37. This number will determine your play.

1	All's Well That Ends Well
2	As You Like It
3	Comedy of Errors
4	Love's Labour's Lost
5	Measure for Measure
6	Merchant of Venice
7	Merry Wives of Windsor
8	Midsummer Night's Dream
9	Much Ado about Nothing
10	Taming of the Shrew

35	Timon of Athens
36	Titus Andronicus
37	Troilus and Cressida

☞ Act: Parameters are 1–5 as there are always five acts.

☞ Scene: Set parameters to number of scenes in your act.

☞ Line: Set parameters to number of lines in your scene (these should be marked at regular intervals).

☞ You have your answer! If it doesn't make immediate sense, note the whole passage and meditate on its meaning.

Exercise: Rhapsodomancy Cut-Up Technique

Rhapsodomancy is the name for using poetic works for divination.

☞ Firstly, decide on a Shakespeare speech or poem that is on the same subject as your divination question. (If you're uncertain, then search for keywords that relate.)

☞ Once you have your speech or poem, write it out clearly in block capitals.

☞ Now cut up the speech into individual words.

☞ Put all your words into a container and shake it to mix them while thinking of your question.

☞ Now draw out seven words at random and see if you can make a phrase. This is your answer.

By the sacred radiance of the sun,
The mysteries of Hecate
and the night…
KING LEAR
ACT I, SCENE I

NINE

Invocation

*I*nvocation is the act of calling in or on the powers of gods, spirits, or other external forces (such as the planets, stars, or Nature herself), rooted in the Latin word *invocare*, meaning "to call on." It is sometimes confused with the magical act of evocation, which is the act of conjuring a spirit into an external space, which we will also mention in this chapter. Agrippa describes what is required for the crafting of an effective invocation:

> …in composing verses, and orations, for the attracting of virtue of any star, or deity, you must diligently consider what virtues any star contains, as also what effects, and operations, and to infer them in verses, by praising, extolling, amplifying, and setting forth those things which such a kind of star is wont to cause by way of its influence, and by vilifying and

dispraising those things which it is wont to destroy, and hinder, and by supplicating, and begging for that which we desire to get, and by condemning and
detesting that which we would have destroyed, and hindered: and after the
same manner to make an excellent oration, and duly distinct by articles, with
competent numbers, and proportions.

He goes on to say that in order to effectively invoke, we must also call upon them

by their wonderful things, or miracles, by their courses, and ways in their
sphere, by their light, by the dignity of their kingdom, by the beauty and
brightness that is in it, by their strong and powerful virtues, and by such like
as these (Agrippa 1993, 216).

Not all invocations have to be as involved as this, and there are varying degrees and
types of invocation, but it is worth bearing the above details in mind when you come
to write your own or as an aid to recognising invocation when you come across one in
a play. We can't know if Shakespeare has direct experience of invocation used in ritual
beyond the usual prayers and invocations of the church, but his experience of invocation in literature would have been a mixture of his source material, such as Ovid, and
classical texts such as the Orphic Hymns, which means he was drawing on sources that
were already composed for use in ritual. As an example of the Orphic Hymns and effective classical invocation structure, here is the Orphic Hymn to Pallas Athena (Taylor
1824, 120), who is particularly relevant to our topic as goddess of the arts and because
she is also known as "Spear-Shaker"!

> Only-Begotten, noble race of Jove, blessed and fierce, who
>   joy'st in caves to rove:
> O, warlike Pallas, whose illustrious kind, ineffable and effable
>   we find:
> Magnanimous and fam'd, the rocky height, and groves, and
>   shady mountains thee delight:
> In arms rejoicing, who with Furies dire and wild, the souls of
>   mortals dost inspire.
> Gymnastic virgin of terrific mind, dire Gorgons bane,
>   unmarried, blessed, kind:

Mother of arts, imperious; understood, rage to the wicked.,
  wisdom to the good:

Female and male, the arts of war are thine, fanatic, much-
  form'd dragoness [Drakaina], divine:

O'er the Phlegrean giants rous'd to ire, thy coursers driving,
  with destruction dire.

Sprung from the head of Jove [Tritogeneia], of splendid
  mien, purger of evils, all-victorious queen.

Hear me, O Goddess, when to thee I pray, with supplicating
  voice both night and day,

And in my latest hour, peace and health, propitious times,
  and necessary wealth,

And, ever present, be thy vot'ries aid, O, much implor'd, art's
  parent, blue eyed maid.

Ye Elves…

In *The Tempest*, Prospero's invocation to the spirits of the land in act 5, scene 1, which begins "Ye Elves of hills, brooks, standing lakes and groves," is almost certainly directly inspired by Medea's invocation to Hecate from Ovid's *Metamorphoses*. Here is that invocation from the sixteenth-century Arthur Golding translation that Shakespeare would have been familiar with, with the strong similarities to Prospero's speech in bold:

O trustie time of night

Most faithfull unto privities, O golden starres whose light

Doth jointly with the Moone succeede the beames that blaze by day

And thou three headed Hecate who knowest best the way

To compasse this our great attempt and art our chiefest stay:

Ye Charmes and Witchcrafts, and thou Earth which both
  with herbe and weed

Of mightie working furnishest the Wizardes at their neede:

**Ye Ayres and windes: ye Elves of Hilles, of Brookes,
  of Woods alone,**

Of standing Lakes, and of the Night approche ye
   everychone.
Through helpe of whom (the crooked bankes much
   wondring at the thing)
I have compelled streames to run cleane backward to
   their spring.
By charmes I make the calme Seas rough, and make
   the rough Seas plaine,
And cover all the Skie with Cloudes and chase them
   thence againe.
By charmes I raise and lay the windes, and burst the
   Vipers jaw.
And from the bowels of the Earth both stones and trees
   doe draw.
Whole woods and Forestes I remove: I make the
   Mountaines shake,
And even the Earth it selfe to grone and fearfully to quake.
I call up dead men from their graves: and thee lightsome Moone
I darken oft, though beaten brasse abate thy perill soone.
Our Sorcerie dimmes the Morning faire, and darkes the
   Sun at Noone.
The flaming breath of firie Bulles ye quenched for my sake
And caused their unwieldie neckes the bended yoke to take.
Among the Earthbred brothers you a mortall war did set
And brought asleepe the Dragon fell whose eyes were never shet.
By meanes whereof deceiving him that had the golden fleece
In charge to keepe, you sent it thence by Jason into Greece.
Now have I neede of herbes that can by vertue of their juice
To flowring prime of lustie youth old withred age reduce.
I am assurde ye will it graunt. For not in vaine have shone

These twincling starres, ne yet in vaine this Chariot all alone

By drought of Dragons hither comes.

(Rouse and Golding 1904, Book 7, 147)

Now here is Shakespeare's speech for comparison with the equivalent sections again in bold:

Ye elves of hills, brooks, standing lakes and groves,

And ye that on the sands with printless foot

Do chase the ebbing Neptune and do fly him

When he comes back; you demi-puppets that

By moonshine do the green sour ringlets make,

Whereof the ewe not bites, and you whose pastime

Is to make midnight mushrooms, that rejoice

To hear the solemn curfew; **by whose aid,**

Weak masters though ye be, I have bedimm'd

The noontide sun, call'd forth the mutinous winds,

And 'twixt the green sea and the azured vault

Set roaring war: to the dread rattling thunder

Have I given fire and rifted Jove's stout oak

With his own bolt; the strong-based promontory

Have I made shake and by the spurs pluck'd up

The pine and cedar: graves at my command

Have waked their sleepers, oped, and let 'em forth

By my so potent art. But this rough magic

I here abjure, and, when I have required

Some heavenly music, which even now I do,

To work mine end upon their senses that

This airy charm is for, I'll break my staff,

Bury it certain fathoms in the earth,

And deeper than did ever plummet sound

I'll drown my book.

Throughout this book we have seen how Ovid was one of Shakespeare's most frequently used sources for stories, and this speech follows the same structure of calling on spirits of the landscape, boasting of effects they can cause on the elements, the uprooting of trees, and even the raising of the dead. Both speeches are written in a way that would be considered an effective invocation technique by a trained magician.

Since invocation is essentially the art of crafting phrases that attract the gods and other spiritual powers, Shakespeare's genius is particularly suited to this art, and his works all contain many examples of the different forms that invocation may take, from simple prayers to blessings and curses to full invited possession. I have also included charms within this section, as though they do not always call upon a divine energy, they do channel that energy in order to render a similar effect and are usually used by people or beings that inherently possess a power of spiritual connection that does not require naming in the moment.

We will divide this chapter into sections according to the different types and purposes of invocation, with explanations of what each involves and examples from Shakespeare's works.

Prayer and Petitioning

Prayer is a common source of invocation, which may be as simple or as complex as the moment demands. In prayer we directly petition the gods, Nature, planets, or other external force to come to our aid, but we do not necessarily draw any of their power within us. We are asking the external force to strengthen the spirit of our cause or to do work for us that we cannot do ourselves. This might be as simple as an exclamation of "Heaven help me!" or as involved as the following prayer from *Henry* V:

> O God of battles! steel my soldiers' hearts;
> Possess them not with fear; take from them now
> The sense of reckoning, if the opposed numbers
> Pluck their hearts from them. Not to-day, O Lord,
> O, not to-day, think not upon the fault
> My father made in compassing the crown!
> I Richard's body have interred anew;

And on it have bestow'd more contrite tears

Than from it issued forced drops of blood:

Five hundred poor I have in yearly pay,

Who twice a-day their wither'd hands hold up

Toward heaven, to pardon blood; and I have built

Two chantries, where the sad and solemn priests

Sing still for Richard's soul. More will I do;

Though all that I can do is nothing worth,

Since that my penitence comes after all,

Imploring pardon.

(ACT 4, SCENE 1)

The above shows how an aspect of a god might be called upon to suit the need of the moment. In this instance we can presume that Henry is calling upon the Christian god, but it could equally be a plea to Mars, god of war. He is calling on the martial aspect of his god to strengthen the will and hearts of his soldiers before the Battle of Agincourt. Although he is calling on his god to empower his soldiers, it is not a theurgical invocation. He is much more concerned with seeking forgiveness and good favour than he is with listing and calling upon the virtues and qualities of his god.

Prayer to Diana

Another example of penitent prayer may be found in *Much Ado About Nothing* where the Divine Feminine, most likely Diana or Hecate, is being called upon to forgive the supposed death of the innocent Hero. This prayer takes the form of a sung hymn (therefore, it has a different structure and rhythm from an iambic speech), but note it is still directed towards forgiveness rather than the qualities of the goddess:

Pardon, goddess of the night,

Those that slew thy virgin knight;

For the which, with songs of woe,

Round about her tomb they go.

Midnight, assist our moan;

Help us to sigh and groan,

Heavily, heavily:

Graves, yawn and yield your dead,

Till death be uttered,

Heavily, heavily.

(ACT 5, SCENE 3)

Don't Try This One at Home, Kids

We find a rather unique approach to prayer in *Titus Andronicus* where Titus writes petitions to all the gods and wraps them around arrows that he shoots towards the heavens in the hope of instant answer. This is a sign of his ebbing relation to sanity:

And, sith there's no justice in earth nor hell,

We will solicit heaven and move the gods

To send down Justice for to wreak our wrongs.

Come, to this gear. You are a good archer, Marcus;

[He gives them the arrows]

"Ad Jovem," that's for you: here, "Ad Apollinem":

"Ad Martem," that's for myself:

Here, boy, to Pallas: here, to Mercury:

To Saturn, Caius, not to Saturnine;

You were as good to shoot against the wind.

To it, boy! Marcus, loose when I bid.

Of my word, I have written to effect;

There's not a god left unsolicited.

(ACT 4, SCENE 3)

Presumably he was not aware of the most important aspect of prayer, or indeed any form of magic—that the energy, intent, and focus must be behind the words in order for them to be effective, as in this example from *Hamlet*:

CLAUDIUS: My words fly up, my thoughts remain below.

Words without thoughts never to heaven go.

(ACT 3, SCENE 3)

Witnessing

Calling upon external spiritual forces to witness a promise or add potency to a sworn oath is also an act of invocation. Needless to say, there are many examples of this in the plays. It heightens the emotional stakes in a scene, and in a ritual context, calling upon the gods to witness a promise means you'd better be sure to keep that promise or the consequences will be on your head! Lovers are the most prolific swearers of divine oaths to prove their love is true, so often in Shakespeare this is at first sight. Here, Ferdinand swears endless and unprecedented love for Miranda in *The Tempest*:

> O heaven, O earth, bear witness to this sound
>
> And crown what I profess with kind event
>
> If I speak true! if hollowly, invert
>
> What best is boded me to mischief! I
>
> Beyond all limit of what else i' the world
>
> Do love, prize, honour you.
>
> (ACT 3, SCENE 1)

We have no reason to doubt his sincerity in this instance, and at the very least his love lasts long enough to get Miranda off the island and headed to a new life. Romeo, of course, also swears. We know that he has made many a sworn oath of love to others before Juliet since Shakespeare chooses to show us that he is infatuated with another woman, Rosaline, before he meets her. Therefore, we have good reason, along with Juliet, to wish him to swear on something more constant than the moon:

> ROMEO: Lady, by yonder blessed moon I swear
>
> That tips with silver all these fruit-tree tops—
>
> JULIET: O, swear not by the moon, the inconstant moon,
>
> That monthly changes in her circled orb,
>
> Lest that thy love prove likewise variable.
>
> ROMEO: What shall I swear by?
>
> JULIET: Do not swear at all;
>
> Or, if thou wilt, swear by thy gracious self,
>
> Which is the god of my idolatry,
>
> And I'll believe thee.
>
> (ACT 2, SCENE 2)

It's not only lovers who are taken to swearing oaths, of course, and those who have need to add extra punch to their promises because they have proven unreliable in the past may ask for divine witnessing to prove their sincerity. In *Henry IV, Part II*, when the young Hal thinks his father has died and that it is his time to take on the weight of the crown, his father (who is just about still alive) catches him trying on the crown and thinks that his son wishes him gone:

> God witness with me, when I here came in
>
> And found no course of breath within your Majesty,
>
> How cold it struck my heart! If I do feign,
>
> O, let me in my present wildness die,
>
> And never live to show th' incredulous world
>
> The noble change that I have purposed!
>
> (ACT 4, SCENE 5)

Shakespeare does not allow a broken oath to go unpunished. In *Pericles* when Pericles leaves his baby daughter with the governor of Tarsus and his wife to raise alongside their own daughter, a solemn pact is made, with divine powers called to witness it:

> CLEON: Fear not, my lord, but think
>
> Your grace, that fed my country with your corn,
>
> For which the people's prayers still fall upon you,
>
> Must in your child be thought on. If neglection
>
> Should therein make me vile, the common body,
>
> By you relieved, would force me to my duty:
>
> But if to that my nature need a spur,
>
> The gods revenge it upon me and mine,
>
> To the end of generation!
>
> PERICLES: I believe you;
>
> Your honour and your goodness teach me to't,
>
> Without your vows. Till she be married, madam,
>
> By bright Diana, whom we honour, all
>
> Unscissor'd shall this hair of mine remain,
>
> Though I show ill in't. So I take my leave.

> Good madam, make me blessed in your care
>
> In bringing up my child.
>
> (ACT 3, SCENE 2)

However, when Marina grows up to be more full of grace, intelligence, and beauty than their own daughter, they plot to have her killed. Though she survives, the gods still take their vengeance in act 5, scene 3:

> For wicked Cleon and his wife, when fame
>
> Had spread their cursed deed, and honour'd name
>
> Of Pericles, to rage the city turn,
>
> That him and his they in his palace burn;
>
> The gods for murder seemed so content
>
> To punish them; although not done, but meant.

Blessing and Cursing

In order to effectively bless or curse, you must be acting as a channel for a source of spiritual power. We have already noted (in chapter 2) how Feste, ruled by Mercury as all fools are, also gives out the blessings of Mercury. Fools and kings, though they may seem on opposite ends of the social scale, both have a sort of divinity, although of course the divinity of kings through the cultures of the world is better known. In *King Lear* this divine connection is made clear, but in a corrupted form, as Lear uses his divine connection to curse rather than to bless.

From the very first scene of *King Lear*, we see a king whose mental and spiritual decline is evidenced by his liberal and vicious curses on those closest to him, starting with his most precious daughter, Cordelia. When she refuses to pander to his narcissistic request for her to verbally shower him with adoration, he snaps and calls on the powers of Hecate, Apollo, and all the planets to land a curse upon her head, banishing her from his sight:

> Let it be so! thy truth then be thy dower!
>
> For, by the sacred radiance of the sun,
>
> The mysteries of Hecate and the night;
>
> By all the operation of the orbs

An 1881 engraving of King Lear

From whom we do exist and cease to be;

Here I disclaim all my paternal care,

Propinquity and property of blood,

And as a stranger to my heart and me

Hold thee from this for ever. The barbarous Scythian,

Or he that makes his generation messes

To gorge his appetite, shall to my bosom

Be as well neighbour'd, pitied, and reliev'd,

As thou my sometime daughter.

(ACT I, SCENE I)

The ever-loyal and honourable Kent tries to counteract Lear's curse with a blessing: "The gods to their dear shelter take thee, maid, That justly think'st and hast most rightly said," and warns Lear of his misuse of power: "Now by Apollo, King, Thou swear'st thy gods in vain," but of course he does not have the instant and powerful divine connection of a king and is cursed and banished himself by Lear.

Soon Lear is turning his curses onto Goneril, the eldest of his daughters, when she refuses to house a hundred of his rowdy knights. In this instance he calls on Nature herself as goddess:

Hear, Nature, hear! dear goddess, hear!

Suspend thy purpose, if thou didst intend

To make this creature fruitful.

Into her womb convey sterility;

Dry up in her the organs of increase;

And from her derogate body never spring

A babe to honour her! If she must teem,

Create her child of spleen, that it may live

And be a thwart disnatur'd torment to her.

Let it stamp wrinkles in her brow of youth,

With cadent tears fret channels in her cheeks,

Turn all her mother's pains and benefits

To laughter and contempt, that she may feel

How sharper than a serpent's tooth it is
To have a thankless child!

(ACT 1, SCENE 4)

In act 2, scene 4, Lear uses his ability to curse as a passive threat to attempt to keep his remaining daughter in line, with little effect but to further alienate them.

I do not bid the Thunder-bearer shoot
Nor tell tales of thee to high-judging Jove.
Mend when thou canst; be better at thy leisure.

Presumably they've dealt with bullying behaviour from him their whole lives and when we realise what they have endured, we may afford them more sympathy than they are usually subject to. Nature herself seems angered by Lear's abuse of her power, and a wild storm rages around him as he leaves the safety of his daughter's house. His daughters make no effort to bring him safely back inside but instead Regan observes:

O, sir, to wilful men,
The injuries that they themselves procure,
Must be their schoolmasters.

Lear willingly joins with the storm, raging with it and commanding it to grow in strength. Shakespeare may be teaching us here that curses will always come back to you if they are unjust. It is another example of "the king and the land are one" and also the alchemical process of dissolution as the storm purges both his fury and what seems to be the remainder of his rational mind, giving himself over to the process so that in the end, he can be reunited with the pure Cordelia, very briefly, and then eternally in death.

In a more positive moment of royal divine connection, in the final scene of *The Winter's Tale*, when Hermione's statue is brought to life (or she is brought out of her sixteen-year period of hiding), she does not speak until she comes to bless her daughter, making her blessing all the more potent, as though she has been saving the power of the words within her to allow them to carry the full force of her love:

You gods, look down
And from your sacred vials pour your graces
Upon my daughter's head!

(ACT 5, SCENE 3)

Queen Hermione's statue

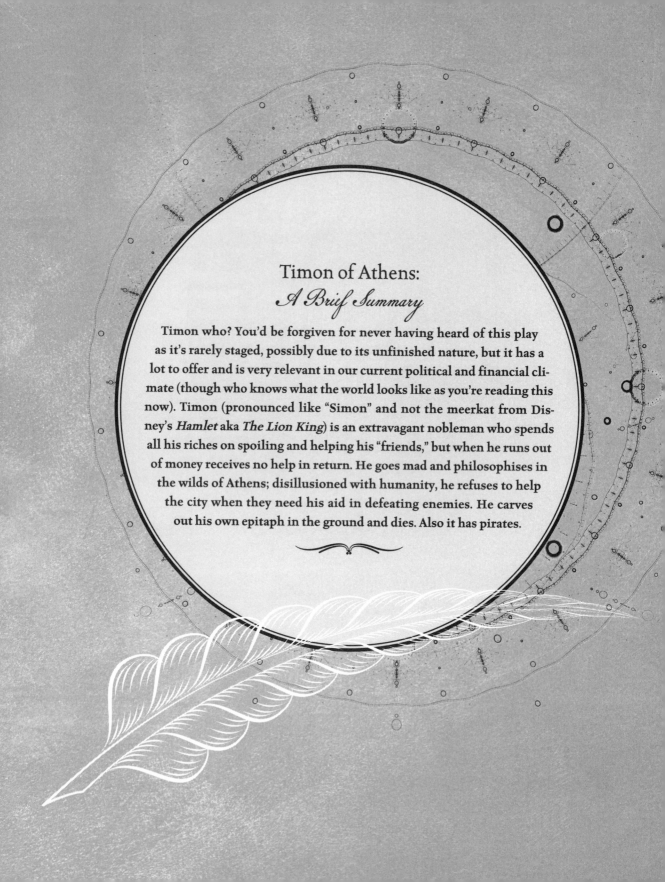

Timon of Athens:
A Brief Summary

Timon who? You'd be forgiven for never having heard of this play as it's rarely staged, possibly due to its unfinished nature, but it has a lot to offer and is very relevant in our current political and financial climate (though who knows what the world looks like as you're reading this now). Timon (pronounced like "Simon" and not the meerkat from Disney's *Hamlet* aka *The Lion King*) is an extravagant nobleman who spends all his riches on spoiling and helping his "friends," but when he runs out of money receives no help in return. He goes mad and philosophises in the wilds of Athens; disillusioned with humanity, he refuses to help the city when they need his aid in defeating enemies. He carves out his own epitaph in the ground and dies. Also it has pirates.

Curses on All Humanity

Parental passion is potent indeed, and so when love turns to grief and cursing, it is apocalyptic in its scope, as in this passage from *Henry* IV, *Part* II, when Northumberland learns of the death of his son, Harry "Hotspur" Percy. He does not call on the gods but on the chthonic force of Nature herself, having presumably lost faith in the divine:

> Let heaven kiss earth! Now let not Nature's hand
> Keep the wild flood confin'd! Let order die!
> And let this world no longer be a stage
> To feed contention in a ling'ring act;
> But let one spirit of the first-born Cain
> Reign in all bosoms, that, each heart being set
> On bloody courses, the rude scene may end
> And darkness be the burier of the dead!

Whilst Northumberland's intent is a nihilistic vision of a violent end of existence for all the world, steeped in war and destruction, *Timon of Athens* brings us a curse upon all mankind rooted in the corruption of humanity that Timon has come to know and loathe:

> O blessed breeding sun, draw from the earth
> Rotten humidity; below thy sister's orb
> Infect the air! Twinn'd brothers of one womb,
> Whose procreation, residence, and birth,
> Scarce is dividant, touch them with several fortunes;
> The greater scorns the lesser: not nature,
> To whom all sores lay siege, can bear great fortune,
> But by contempt of nature.
> Raise me this beggar, and deny 't that lord;
> The senator shall bear contempt hereditary,
> The beggar native honour.
> It is the pasture lards the rother's sides,
> The want that makes him lean. Who dares, who dares,

In purity of manhood stand upright,

And say "This man's a flatterer?" if one be,

So are they all; for every grise of fortune

Is smooth'd by that below: the learned pate

Ducks to the golden fool: all is oblique;

There's nothing level in our cursed natures,

But direct villany. Therefore, be abhorr'd

All feasts, societies, and throngs of men!

His semblable, yea, himself, Timon disdains:

Destruction fang mankind!

(*Timon of Athens*, ACT 4, SCENE 3)

Fairy Blessings

When one is already a magical being, one does not need to call on divine powers but can weave a blessing much like a charm, as in this wholesome blessing from the end of *Midsummer Night's Dream*:

Now, until the break of day,

Through this house each fairy stray.

To the best bride-bed will we,

Which by us shall blessed be;

And the issue there create

Ever shall be fortunate.

So shall all the couples three

Ever true in loving be;

And the blots of Nature's hand

Shall not in their issue stand;

Never mole, hare lip, nor scar,

Nor mark prodigious, such as are

Despised in nativity,

Shall upon their children be.

With this field-dew consecrate,

Every fairy take his gait;

And each several chamber bless,

Through this palace, with sweet peace;

And the owner of it blest

Ever shall in safety rest.

Trip away; make no stay;

Meet me all by break of day.

(ACT 5, SCENE 1)

Evocation/Conjuration

Whilst invocation is the act of calling in, evocation is the act of calling forth—that is, rather than calling on the powers of a spirit/deity/planet/other external spiritual force, it involves directly summoning and commanding a being. The word *conjure* has its roots in the Latin verb *jurare*, meaning "to swear," so it means "with a sworn oath," which isn't always necessarily magical when we see it used in Shakespeare's plays, as both magical and non-magical uses of the word were still common. When we see a character conjuring another character in a mundane context, they are not making magical allusions, they are simply asking them to swear to something.

Conjurors

There are a few characters within Shakespeare's plays with the power to command spirits. Prospero may be the first to spring to mind, naturally, and his (mostly) benevolent connection with his conjured spirit Ariel. It is a portrait designed to evoke the idealised Renaissance magus, a perfected John Dee, pedestalised by Shakespeare after his disgraced demise. We are given a description of another conjuror, Sycorax, as a malevolent contrast, with a description of how she imprisoned Ariel in a tree because he would not follow her base commands. However, Prospero then threatens a return to imprisonment in an oak tree when Ariel appears reluctant to obey:

> PROSPERO: …it was mine art,
>
> When I arrived and heard thee, that made gape
>
> The pine and let thee out.
>
> ARIEL: I thank thee, master.

Ariel from *The Tempest*

PROSPERO: If thou more murmur'st, I will rend an oak

    And peg thee in his knotty entrails till

    Thou hast howl'd away twelve winters.

    (ACT 1, SCENE 2)

This would have appeared less morally ambiguous to an audience more familiar with the processes of this kind of magic, some of whom may have had an understanding that threatening conjured spirits to get them to obey is par for the course.

Prospero also uses his skill in conjuration to bless his daughter's betrothal by summoning spirits to portray goddesses, who in turn invoke spirits to attend and bless the couple in act 4, scene 1:

> You nymphs, call'd Naiads, of the windring brooks,
> With your sedged crowns and ever-harmless looks,
> Leave your crisp channels and on this green land
> Answer your summons; Juno does command:
> Come, temperate nymphs, and help to celebrate
> A contract of true love; be not too late.

After our discussion about the nature of *Macbeth's* three "witches," we can add further weight to the argument that they are spirits or fairy beings by the fact that Macbeth conjures them when he desires further information in act 4, scene 1:

> I conjure you, by that which you profess,
> Howe'er you come to know it, answer me:
> Though you untie the winds and let them fight
> Against the churches; though the yesty waves
> Confound and swallow navigation up;
> Though bladed corn be lodged and trees blown down;
> Though castles topple on their warders' heads;
> Though palaces and pyramids do slope
> Their heads to their foundations; though the treasure
> Of nature's germens tumble all together,
> Even till destruction sicken; answer me
> To what I ask you.

It is not only the magic-steeped, fantastical tales that contain conjurers, but also the more down-to-earth historical plays, showing how it was a normal part of culture at the time. We've already looked at the two conjurers Margery Jourdain and Roger Bolingroke, who in *Henry VI, Part II* are hired to summon spirits to perform divination. They are preceded in Part I by the fiery and charismatic French general Joan of Arc, or Joan la Pucelle as she is referred to in Shakespeare's play. Though she claims divine inspiration, it becomes clear that her power is sourced from wicked spirits who abandon her when the tide turns against her. Shakespeare reveals more of his knowledge of magical working by showing that she summons them by their master, "the monarch of the north."

> You speedy helpers, that are substitutes
> Under the lordly monarch of the north,
> Appear and aid me in this enterprise.
> (ACT 5, SCENE 3)

Demons and angels have a hierarchy and may be commanded by calling upon those higher in the ranks, and it was thought that malignant spirits were located in the north. There are a number of instances of Shakespeare dropping in nuggets of demonology knowledge into his plays, often incidentally with no bearing on plot. Demon names mentioned in the plays that were from grimoires of the time include Amaimon and Barbason, both mentioned in *Merry Wives of Windsor*, further showing that Shakespeare was using grimoires as a source for his plays.

In *Henry IV, Part I*, the magician Glendower claims to be able to command spirits and is roundly mocked by young Harry "Hotspur," one of many examples where the shift in beliefs at the time was personified in his characters:

> GLENDOWER: I can call spirits from the vasty deep.
> HOTSPUR: Why, so can I, or so can any man;
>   But will they come when you do call for them?
> GLENDOWER: Why, I can teach you, cousin, to command
>   The devil.
> HOTSPUR: And I can teach thee, coz, to shame the devil
>   By telling truth: tell truth and shame the devil.
>   If thou have power to raise him, bring him hither,

And I'll be sworn I have power to shame him hence.

O, while you live, tell truth and shame the devil!

(ACT 3, SCENE 1)

Theurgy

The ultimate aim of theurgy is henosis, or union with the divine. Full theurgical invocations call upon the divine power to enter into the invoker and bring them closer to perfection and awareness that "all is one." Whilst Prospero is certainly practicing theurgy, we only ever see him invoking elemental spirits and powers of nature. Ariel may be either angelic or elemental (though the text would seem to suggest elemental in contradiction to the angelic name), but we do not see Prospero invoke higher powers. Whilst "Ye elves" is an excellent example of invocation that we have already identified the classical inspiration for and underlying Hecate connection, we can find some excellent examples of classical theurgical invocation in one of Shakespeare's collaborative works, *Two Noble Kinsmen*, which is an adaptation of Chaucer's *The Knight's Tale*. Though this work is co-written with Fletcher, it is generally agreed that the prime author of the final act in which the invocations appear is Shakespeare.

In the final act of *Two Noble Kinsmen*, two warriors who were once close friends are now rivals for the affection of Emilia, and it is decided that they must fight to the death to decide the victor. One invokes Mars, god of war, the other invokes Venus, goddess of love, and then Emilia invokes Diana, that whoever truly loves her should be the victor since she cannot choose. Whilst the second half of these invocations turns to prayer, the first half focuses on invoking the god/dess by calling upon their qualities and deeds. Since this play is not well-known, I have included the invocations here in full:

ARCITE'S INVOCATION TO MARS

> Thou mighty one, that with thy power hast turned
>
> Green Neptune into purple, whose approach
>
> Comets prewarn, whose havoc in vast field
>
> Unearthèd skulls proclaim, whose breath blows down
>
> The teeming Ceres' foison, who dost pluck
>
> With hand armipotent from forth blue clouds

The masoned turrets, that both mak'st and break'st
The stony girths of cities; me thy pupil,
Youngest follower of thy drum, instruct this day
With military skill, that to thy laud
I may advance my streamer, and by thee
Be styled the lord o' th' day. Give me, great Mars,
Some token of thy pleasure.

Here they fall on their faces as formerly, and
there is heard clanging of armor, with a short
thunder, as the burst of a battle, whereupon
they all rise and bow to the altar.

O, great corrector of enormous times,
Shaker of o'er-rank states, thou grand decider
Of dusty and old titles, that heal'st with blood
The Earth when it is sick, and cur'st the world
O' th' pleurisy of people, I do take
Thy signs auspiciously, and in thy name
To my design march boldly.

Palamon's Invocation to Venus

Hail, sovereign queen of secrets, who hast power
To call the fiercest tyrant from his rage
And weep unto a girl; that hast the might
Even with an eye-glance to choke Mars's drum
And turn th' alarm to whispers; that canst make
A cripple flourish with his crutch, and cure him
Before Apollo; that mayst force the king
To be his subject's vassal, and induce
Stale gravity to dance. The polled bachelor,
Whose youth, like wanton boys through bonfires,
Have skipped thy flame, at seventy thou canst catch,

And make him, to the scorn of his hoarse throat,
Abuse young lays of love. What godlike power
Hast thou not power upon? To Phoebus thou
Add'st flames hotter than his; the heavenly fires
Did scorch his mortal son, thine him. The huntress,
All moist and cold, some say, began to throw
Her bow away and sigh. Take to thy grace
Me, thy vowed soldier, who do bear thy yoke
As 'twere a wreath of roses, yet is heavier
Than lead itself, stings more than nettles.
I have never been foul-mouthed against thy law,
Ne'er revealed secret, for I knew none—would not,
Had I kenned all that were. I never practiced
Upon man's wife, nor would the libels read
Of liberal wits. I never at great feasts
Sought to betray a beauty, but have blushed
At simp'ring sirs that did. I have been harsh
To large confessors, and have hotly asked them
If they had mothers—I had one, a woman,
And women 'twere they wronged. I knew a man
Of eighty winters—this I told them—who
A lass of fourteen brided; 'twas thy power
To put life into dust. The agèd cramp
Had screwed his square foot round;
The gout had knit his fingers into knots;
Torturing convulsions from his globy eyes
Had almost drawn their spheres, that what was life
In him seemed torture. This anatomy
Had by his young fair fere a boy, and I
Believed it was his, for she swore it was,
And who would not believe her? Brief, I am

To those that prate and have done, no companion;

To those that boast and have not, a defier;

To those that would and cannot, a rejoicer.

Yea, him I do not love that tells close offices

The foulest way, nor names concealments in

The boldest language. Such a one I am,

And vow that lover never yet made sigh

Truer than I. O, then, most soft sweet goddess,

Give me the victory of this question, which

Is true love's merit, and bless me with a sign

Of thy great pleasure.

EMILIA'S INVOCATION TO DIANA

O sacred, shadowy, cold, and constant queen,

Abandoner of revels, mute contemplative,

Sweet, solitary, white as chaste, and pure

As wind-fanned snow, who to thy female knights

Allow'st no more blood than will make a blush,

Which is their order's robe, I here, thy priest,

Am humbled 'fore thine altar. O, vouchsafe

With that thy rare green eye, which never yet

Beheld thing maculate, look on thy virgin,

And, sacred silver mistress, lend thine ear—

Which ne'er heard scurrile term, into whose port

Ne'er entered wanton sound—to my petition,

Seasoned with holy fear. This is my last

Of vestal office. I am bride-habited

But maiden-hearted. A husband I have 'pointed,

But do not know him. Out of two I should

Choose one, and pray for his success, but I

Am guiltless of election. Of mine eyes,

Were I to lose one—they are equal precious—

I could doom neither; that which perished should

Go to 't unsentenced. Therefore, most modest queen,

He of the two pretenders that best loves me

And has the truest title in 't, let him

Take off my wheaten garland, or else grant

The file and quality I hold I may

Continue in thy band.

Here the hind vanishes under the

altar, and in the place ascends a rose

tree, having one rose upon it.

See what our general of ebbs and flows

Out from the bowels of her holy altar

With sacred act advances: but one rose.

If well inspired, this battle shall confound

Both these brave knights, and I, a virgin flower,

Must grow alone unplucked.

(Here is heard a sudden twang of instruments,

and the rose falls from the tree.)

The flower is fall'n, the tree descends. O mistress,

Thou here dischargest me. I shall be gathered;

I think so, but I know not thine own will.

Unclasp thy mystery!

(Two Noble Kinsman, ACT 5, SCENE 1)

As a co-written tragi-comedy, the play does not obey the usual structure of a Shake-speare play since Arcite does actually perish from his wounds, but in true Shakespear-ean spirit, it is love and the invocation to Venus that wins the day, and Emilia and Palamon are married.

Lady Macbeth

Possession/Full Embodiment

Invited spiritual possession is a form of invocation. Whilst in the pursuit of henosis or for certain ritual purposes such as oracular work a magician, priest, or priestess might fully embody a deity, it is unusual to call upon lower levels of being for this purpose. It is more common that negative spiritual entities might take up residence in vulnerable and sensitive people without permission. However, in act 1, scene 5, Lady Macbeth invites these very spirits to inhabit her body to enable her to commit inhuman acts:

> …Come, you spirits
>
> That tend on mortal thoughts, unsex me here,
>
> And fill me from the crown to the toe top-full
>
> Of direst cruelty! make thick my blood;
>
> Stop up the access and passage to remorse,
>
> That no compunctious visitings of nature
>
> Shake my fell purpose, nor keep peace between
>
> The effect and it! Come to my woman's breasts,
>
> And take my milk for gall, you murdering ministers,
>
> Wherever in your sightless substances
>
> You wait on nature's mischief! Come, thick night,
>
> And pall thee in the dunnest smoke of hell,
>
> That my keen knife see not the wound it makes,
>
> Nor heaven peep through the blanket of the dark,
>
> To cry "Hold, hold!"

To what extent her invocation is successful is up for debate and is a matter that is open for interpretation in performance.

Another character that seems to either pretend to be possessed or is genuinely possessed due to his extreme circumstances, making him open to spiritual attack (again open to interpretation), is Edgar in *King Lear*. In his madness, whether feigned or genuine, he mentions the names of various demons as mentioned in Samuel Harsnett's *A Declaration of Egregious Popish Impostures* (1603):

A Note for Actors

If you do start to practice magical techniques as part of your work, or indeed just as something to bear in mind considering the potency and construction of these passages—please try not to curse each other. Or the audience. Or technical equipment!

Early in my MFA at Exeter, after having been very much immersed in the esoteric but not working in theatre for over ten years, I was very excited to work on a piece which used parts of *The Tempest* to create a short piece about Ariel returning at the end of the play to drag Prospero off to hell for his cruel treatment of the spirits of the land. I had mashed this up using bits of text from throughout the play, including many of Caliban's curses, and also parts of Marlowe's *Doctor Faustus*. I was playing Ariel and having a marvellous time throwing these terrific curses around. However, we were supposed to film the piece to share and after directing some of this vitriol directly at the camera, it turned off. Had the battery run out? Nope. Was the memory card full? Nope, there was some other problem. It was a new memory card, a reliable make, but when I took it to the tech department they removed it and found that it had basically melted and was not salvageable. They said they'd never seen anything like that happen before. Oops.

Obviously you want to convey all the energy and intent of the curse towards your target, but as you do so, visualise the actual energy grounding through your feet down into the ground whilst only *performing* casting it outwards.

Both stile and gate, horseway and footpath. Poor Tom hath been
scar'd out of his good wits. Bless thee, good man's son, from
the foul fiend! Five fiends have been in poor Tom at once: of
lust, as Obidicut; Hobbididence, prince of dumbness; Mahu, of
stealing; Modo, of murder; Flibbertigibbet, of mopping and
mowing, who since possesses chambermaids and waiting women. So,
bless thee, master!

(*King Lear*, ACT 4, SCENE 1)

The Power of Iambic Pentameter

Most of Shakespeare's invocations are written, like much of his speech, in blank or
rhymed verse, meaning they have ten beats per line, with an off-stress/stress rhythm,
like so:

O **God** of **bat**tles! **steel** my **sol**diers' **hearts**

This rhythm echoes the beat of our own hearts and carries the truth of our hearts.
When we hear someone speak in this rhythm, it feels familiar and sincere to us for this
reason, and heart speaks to heart. The beat does not need to be overemphasised, but with
a breath at the beginning of each line and time taken to speak with clarity, the energy
will carry through. Giles Block, "master of words" at Shakespeare's Globe, describes it as

> our secret rhythm, not one which the audience is really conscious of, but one
> which, beating in time with the audience's own hearts, subliminally creates a
> sympathetic bond between audience and actor (Block 2013, 8).

When combined with resonating your voice, this can be immensely powerful in
ritual. Think of the rhythm as being the hooves of the horses of a chariot that may carry
your words to the gods.

Exercise: Use Shakespeare's Words to Create an Invocation

Just as Shakespeare drew on various sources for his plays and used extracts from the work of others to make his work, so we should feel free to use Shakespeare's words in a fresh context to create something new. Whilst there are some speeches and invocations from his works that we can use as they are in ritual, we can also stitch together lines from different plays or poems that suit our purpose to create something new. In the final chapter I will guide you through the process of how you can create your own piece of ritual theatre using this technique and demonstrate with my own example. For now, let's start with writing a simple invocation using this stitching or "mash-up" technique.

The structure of an effective invocation needs:

- ☞ the naming of the god/goddess/planet/star/external spiritual force

- ☞ a listing and praising of their qualities

- ☞ (optional) a listing and praising of their deeds

- ☞ Repeated calling on them to hear you and attend

- ☞ The purpose of your request; e.g., teach us your mysteries; answer our question; bless this space; fill us with your wisdom

- ☞ (once the rite is finished) giving thanks and bidding farewell

Here are the suggested stages for creating an invocation using existing texts (in this instance, Shakespeare's works) in a fresh context:

- ☞ Decide the external force (god, goddess, planet, etc.) you wish to call upon and be clear about the purpose.

- ☞ Search Shakespeare's works for mentions of both the force and purpose of your invocation, and compile them all into a document so you can see them all clearly in one place.

- ☞ Plan out your invocation structure and find which bits of text fit best within it. You may use part phrases, it doesn't need to be complete lines, but you should try to keep to the iambic structure of ten beats per line if possible.

☞ Read aloud to see if it works; tweak as necessary.

☞ Using the sacred space exercise from chapter 2 to frame your invocation, perform your invocation in ritual. Make notes.

Here is an example invocation with the keywords that I searched for to find the phrases in bold. In some phrases "his" has been changed to "thy" for a more immediate address:

> Now blessed be the great **Apollo**!
>
> Wherever the **bright sun** of heaven shall shine,
>
> Your honour and the greatness of your name,
>
> The fire-robed god, Golden **Apollo**
>
> Thy voice is **music**, By your best **arrow**
>
> Now let me see your **archery**
>
> The show and seal of nature's **truth**
>
> My **oracle**, my prophet, bright **Apollo**
>
> **Answer** to what I shall ask you
>
> I pray you, **come**.

Exercise: An Invocation to a Shakespearean Character

You may wish to call upon the qualities of a particular character, either to increase understanding of the text or in your daily life to help with a situation you find challenging but that they would thrive in; for example, you could call upon Portia to help with a court case or Henry V to increase leadership skills.

Following the same principles and structure as a divine invocation, write a simple invocation to the character/s of your choice, using your own words or the stitching/mash-up technique. What physical qualities do they have that you can call them by? What deeds do they perform in the play? What is the nature of their personality; e.g., are they true of heart, sharp of mind, etc.? What task do you wish them to help you with?

Once your invocation is ready, perform it in ritual conditions and/or memorise it to use as a prayer when you need a boost to that quality.

O, mickle is the powerful
grace that lies
In herbs, plants, stones, and
their true qualities:
For nought so vile that on
the earth doth live
But to the earth some
special good doth give.
ROMEO AND JULIET
ACT 2, SCENE 3

TEN

Plants, Herbs, and Trees

*S*hakespeare's plays show evidence of extensive knowledge of plant lore, including magical, medicinal, and folkloric properties of plants. In this chapter we'll be looking at some of the most interesting mentions of plants both beneficent and toxic in the plays, and then each of those plants mentioned in Shakespeare's works for which we have a historical planetary correspondence from either the grimoires, Dee, Agrippa, or Culpeper are listed by their planet.

In *Othello* Iago uses the garden as a metaphor for the human body, explaining that, in essence, we become who we choose to be:

Our bodies are our gardens, to the which
our wills are gardeners: so that if we will plant
nettles, or sow lettuce, set hyssop and weed up
thyme, supply it with one gender of herbs, or
distract it with many, either to have it sterile with
idleness, or manured with industry, why, the power
and corrigible authority of this lies in our wills.

(ACT 1, SCENE 3)

If we presume he also applies this to personality and morals, then he becomes even more despicable through his conscious acknowledgement of choosing the path that he does. This passage gives us an insight into the mental workings of Shakespeare's most conscienceless villain.

Willow, Willow, Willow

The most poetic plant reference, however, belongs to the women of *Othello*, with the haunting lyrics of Desdemona's willow song as she readies herself for a fateful rest with her maid and friend, Emilia, in act 4, scene 3:

The poor soul sat sighing by a sycamore tree,
Sing all a green willow:
Her hand on her bosom, her head on her knee,
Sing willow, willow, willow:
The fresh streams ran by her, and murmur'd her moans;
Sing willow, willow, willow;
Her salt tears fell from her, and soften'd the stones;
Lay by these:—
[Singing]
Sing willow, willow, willow.

Willow, especially the weeping willow, was considered a token of grieving lovers, either in mourning for death or rejection. Desdemona sings this song as she fears that Othello's love has gone, but it is also a foreshadowing of her death at her husband's hands. The theme is revisited in the final moments of the play when Emilia is stabbed by her husband Iago for revealing the truth about his plots:

> What did thy song bode, lady?
> Hark, canst thou hear me? I will play the swan.
> And die in music.
> [Singing]
> Willow, willow, willow,—
> Moor, she was chaste; she loved thee, cruel Moor;
> So come my soul to bliss, as I speak true;
> So speaking as I think, I die, I die.
> (ACT 5, SCENE 2)

The grieving willow was not reserved only for tragedy but also featured in the history plays…

> Tell him, in hope he'll prove a widower shortly,
> I'll wear the willow garland for his sake.
> (*Henry* VI, ACT 3, SCENE 3)

And comedies…

> Troth, my lord, I have played the part of Lady Fame.
> I found him here as melancholy as a lodge in a
> warren: I told him, and I think I told him true,
> that your grace had got the good will of this young
> lady; and I offered him my company to a willow-tree,
> either to make him a garland, as being forsaken, or
> to bind him up a rod, as being worthy to be whipped
> (*Much Ado About Nothing*, ACT 2, SCENE 1)

Once we understand the meaning behind the willow, Viola's iconic speech that makes Olivia fall in love with her in her male guise makes more sense:

> Make me a willow cabin at your gate,
> And call upon my soul within the house;

Write loyal cantons of contemned love

And sing them loud even in the dead of night;

Halloo your name to the reverberate hills

And make the babbling gossip of the air

Cry out "Olivia!" O, You should not rest

Between the elements of air and earth,

But you should pity me!

(*Twelfth Night*, ACT I, SCENE 5)

It also adds even more poignance to Gertrude's description of Ophelia's death:

There is a willow grows aslant a brook,

That shows his hoar leaves in the glassy stream.

There with fantastic garlands did she come

Of crowflowers, nettles, daisies, and long purples,

That liberal shepherds give a grosser name,

But our cold maids do dead men's fingers call them.

There on the pendant boughs her coronet weeds

Clamb'ring to hang, an envious sliver broke,

When down her weedy trophies and herself

Fell in the weeping brook. Her clothes spread wide

And, mermaid-like, awhile they bore her up;

Which time she chaunted snatches of old tunes,

As one incapable of her own distress,

Or like a creature native and indued

Unto that element; but long it could not be

Till that her garments, heavy with their drink,

Pull'd the poor wretch from her melodious lay

To muddy death.

(*Hamlet*, ACT 4, SCENE 7)

Gertrude's speech evokes a vivid picture of Ophelia's death that has inspired artists for centuries. It includes a number of wildflowers called by their old folk names, some of which would be regional and we can't be entirely certain of what they are. It's

Ophelia in *Hamlet*

thought that "crowflowers" might be a wetland flower called ragged robin and that "long purples" or "dead-men's fingers" are a wild orchid called *Orchis mascula*, which are indeed long and purple. We can easily imagine what the "grosser name" might pertain to. This phallic flower contrasts with the daisy, which represents virginity, highlighting the conflicted and split nature of Ophelia's mind. Nettles were sometimes an ingredient in love potions, as were rosemary and pansies, the first of the herbs she gives out in her madness:

> OPHELIA: There's rosemary, that's for remembrance.
> Pray you, love, remember. And there is pansies, that's for
> thoughts.
> LAERTES: A document in madness! Thoughts and
> remembrance fitted.
> OPHELIA: There's fennel for you, and columbines.
> There's rue for you, and here's some for me. We may call it
> herb of grace o' Sundays. O, you must wear your rue with a
> difference! There's a daisy. I would give you some violets,
> but they wither'd all when my father
> died. They say he made a good end.
> (ACT 4, SCENE 5)

Rosemary was chiefly known, and still is, for its memory-improving quality and was associated with remembering the dead. It would be cast upon the coffin during funeral rites, appropriate here as Ophelia has just lost her father. The association with pansies is in the name, which originates in the French word *pensée*, meaning literally "thought." Fennel was a symbol of flattery in Shakespeare's time, and columbine represented forsaken love. Rue not only carries the meaning of its name, connected with grief and suffering as befits Ophelia's circumstance, but also she points out the name "herb grace o' Sundays," a name earned by the herb's use in exorcism rites. Violets are associated with both Jupiter and Venus, hope and love, so her talking of them dying with her father is deeply symbolic. In her madness she has chosen these flowers with full awareness of their symbolism and message.

In a scene very reminiscent of this, but in a far more joyous context, Perdita gives out flowers she feels suits each guest at their shepherd's celebration:

> PERDITA: Reverend sirs,
>
> For you there's rosemary and rue; these keep
>
> Seeming and savour all the winter long:
>
> Grace and remembrance be to you both,
>
> And welcome to our shearing!
>
> POLIXENES: Shepherdess,
>
> A fair one are you—well you fit our ages
>
> With flowers of winter.
>
> PERDITA: Here's flowers for you;
>
> Hot lavender, mints, savoury, marjoram;
>
> The marigold, that goes to bed wi" the sun
>
> And with him rises weeping: these are flowers
>
> Of middle summer, and I think they are given
>
> To men of middle age. You're very welcome…
>
> …Now, my fair'st friend,
>
> I would I had some flowers o' the spring that might
>
> Become your time of day; and yours, and yours,
>
> That wear upon your virgin branches yet
>
> Your maidenheads growing: O Proserpina,
>
> For the flowers now, that frighted thou let'st fall
>
> From Dis's waggon! daffodils,
>
> That come before the swallow dares, and take
>
> The winds of March with beauty; violets dim,
>
> But sweeter than the lids of Juno's eyes
>
> Or Cytherea's breath; pale primroses
>
> That die unmarried, ere they can behold
>
> Bight Phoebus in his strength—a malady
>
> Most incident to maids; bold oxlips and
>
> The crown imperial; lilies of all kinds,

Florizel and Perdita from *The Winter's Tale*

> The flower-de-luce being one! O, these I lack,
>
> To make you garlands of, and my sweet friend,
>
> To strew him o'er and o'er!
>
> FLORIZEL: What, like a corse?
>
> PERDITA: No, like a bank for love to lie and play on;
>
> Not like a corse; or if, not to be buried,
>
> But quick and in mine arms.
>
> (*The Winter's Tale*, ACT 4, SCENE 4)

This wonderful segment not only shows flowers of different seasons connected to different ages of man but also drops hints as to planetary associations. Rosemary is something of an odd one out in that it's associated with funerals because of its qualities of remembrance but is ruled by the sun. Rue is one of Saturn's herbs, however, and most plants of bitter taste that are connected with death in some way are ruled by this planet. The summer flowers listed here are mostly ruled by the sun apart from mint, which comes under Mars, and savory, which is Mercury. Marigolds are a symbol of constancy so it is appropriate that she gives them to Camillo, whose nature is unwaveringly honourable. Perdita refers also to the fact that their petals open and close with the sun as if they are waking and sleeping, which Shakespeare also uses in his poem *The Rape of Lucrece*, which uses an extended metaphor of flowers to describe her beauty.

When Perdita comes to her young love, Florizel, she wishes that she has spring flowers to give him, but it is not the season. We have already noted that Shakespeare uses this moment to emphasise Perdita's role as Persephone within the mystery context of this play, as she talks of the flowers that the goddess was carrying when she was taken by Hades (Dis) to the underworld. One aspect of this myth is the transition from girlhood to womanhood, and Perdita is using this tale in a seductive context, as talk of dying in each other's arms is a reference to orgasm, "the little death."

Two young lovers who take this association rather too literally are the tragic Romeo and Juliet. The poison that Romeo takes is not named, but its effects are vividly described in act 5, scene 1:

> …let me have
>
> A dram of poison, such soon-speeding gear
>
> As will disperse itself through all the veins

That the life-weary taker may fall dead
And that the trunk may be discharged of breath
As violently as hasty powder fired
Doth hurry from the fatal cannon's womb.

Shakespeare uses similar language in *Henry* IV, Part II, act 4, scene 4, to describe the effects of aconite, so we might deduce from this that this is the same poison:

That the united vessel of their blood,
Mingled with venom of suggestion—
As, force perforce, the age will pour it in—
Shall never leak, though it do work as strong
As aconitum or rash gunpowder.

A Rose by Any Other Name…

Of course, the lives of our two iconic lovers are only too briefly filled with romance and joy before family conflict drives them to desperate ends. There is no more popular symbol for this love than the rose, and *Romeo and Juliet* gives us one of the most famous rose quotes in all literature:

'Tis but thy name that is my enemy;
Thou art thyself, though not a Montague.
What's Montague? it is nor hand, nor foot,
Nor arm, nor face, nor any other part
Belonging to a man. O, be some other name!
What's in a name? that which we call a rose
By any other name would smell as sweet;
So Romeo would, were he not Romeo call'd,
Retain that dear perfection which he owes
Without that title. Romeo, doff thy name,
And for that name which is no part of thee
Take all myself.

(ACT 2, SCENE 2)

The rose is by far the most frequently mentioned plant in the Shakespearean canon, used often to describe the bloom of beauteous youth in both men and women. It is interesting to note that not only is rose used in magical amplifications of love and beauty, including such simple concoctions as rose water, but that as medicine it can help maintain a healthy heart. In Paul Huson's excellent *Mastering Herbalism*, we learn that Culpeper recommended "the syrup of dried roses," which "comforts the heart, and resists putrefaction and infection" (Huson 2001, 140).

Sacred to Venus, rose's associations with love are powerful indeed, but it also has deep folkloric and emblematic connections to the land itself. From *Henry VI, Part I* through to the end of *Richard III*, we see Shakespeare's interpretation of what we now know as the War of the Roses due to the emblems of the white rose of York and the red rose of Lancaster. It is now thought that the red rose only became the emblem of Lancaster once the two were joined by Henry VII, but Shakespeare gives us a powerful imagined portrayal of the beginning of the conflict:

> PLANTAGENET: Since you are tongue-tied and so loath to speak,
>
>> In dumb significants proclaim your thoughts:
>>
>> Let him that is a true-born gentleman
>>
>> And stands upon the honour of his birth,
>>
>> If he suppose that I have pleaded truth,
>>
>> From off this brier pluck a white rose with me.
>
> SOMERSET: Let him that is no coward nor no flatterer,
>
>> But dare maintain the party of the truth,
>>
>> Pluck a red rose from off this thorn with me.
>
> (*Henry VI, Part I*, ACT 2, SCENE 4)

The white rose, or *rosa alba*, is thought to have been an emblem of England long before it was adopted by the House of York, and the red rose also became a symbol of the Rosicrucians. Also, for those who know their fairy lore, this plucking of roses is reminiscent of the ballad of Tam Lin, which dates as least as far back as Shakespeare's lifetime, so he may have known an early version:

> When she came to Carterhaugh
>
> Tam Lin was at the well,

And there she fand his steed standing,

But away was himsel.

She had na pu'd a double rose,

A rose but only twa,

Till upon then started young Tam Lin,

Says, Lady, thou's pu nae mae.

Why pu's thou the rose, Janet,

And why breaks thou the wand?

Or why comes thou to Carterhaugh

Withoutten my command?

(Francis James Child)

In the Fairy tradition as taught by R. J. Stewart, the "double rose" is one white and one red bloom, signifying a multilayered polarity including above and below, male and female, and the river of tears and the river of blood that run through the otherworld. This is similar to the white and red dragons of Merlin's teachings, and of course we have already learnt of the significance of these colours within alchemy (though in alchemy the queen is white and the king is red, whereas in Celtic lore the white is male and red is female). In *Well of Light*, R. J. Stewart talks of a teaching from folkloric ballads that is very reminiscent of the ending of *Romeo and Juliet*:

> …the basic plot appears to be simple: there are two lovers, and for various reasons depending on the ballad, first one dies, then the other. Though they are separated by the vagaries of life and love, they are united in death. They are buried near one another, and from the grave of one, a red rose grows, and from the other a white rose…The red and white rose plants intertwine in a true love's knot and the lovers are united beyond the grave (Stewart 2006, 114).

In Shakespeare's plays, as in history, the two roses are united by Henry VII as the conflict between Lancaster and York is resolved:

> And then, as we have ta'en the sacrament,
>
> We will unite the white rose and the red:
>
> Smile heaven upon this fair conjunction,
>
> That long have frown'd upon their enmity!
>
> (*Richard* III, ACT 5, SCENE 5)

We have no way of knowing to what extent Shakespeare was aware of the parallels of these aspects of his plays with fairy folklore and ballads, but we do know that he gave us one of the most beautiful depictions of fairies in the history of theatre, A *Midsummer Night's Dream*, which is rich with plant lore.

Love-in-Idleness

I know a bank where the wild thyme blows,

Where oxlips and the nodding violet grows,

Quite over-canopied with luscious woodbine,

With sweet musk-roses and with eglantine.

—A *Midsummer Night's Dream*, ACT 2, SCENE 1

As Oberon describes the sleeping place of Titania, he paints a scent picture with words. All of these flowers are known for their alluring fragrance, and burning incense or essential oils from these plants would be appropriate in any fairy working. Most of these plants are ruled by Venus, with love being the over-arcing theme of the play. The exception is eglantine, which is a plant of Jupiter, as befits a comedy. There is a dark and sinister edge to this family favourite, however, and that is the drug made from the flower known as love-in-idleness.

That very time I saw, but thou couldst not,

Flying between the cold moon and the earth,

Cupid all arm'd: a certain aim he took

At a fair vestal throned by the west,

And loosed his love-shaft smartly from his bow,

As it should pierce a hundred thousand hearts;

But I might see young Cupid's fiery shaft

Quench'd in the chaste beams of the watery moon,

And the imperial votaress passed on,

In maiden meditation, fancy-free.

Yet mark'd I where the bolt of Cupid fell:

A Midsummer Night's Dream

It fell upon a little western flower,

Before milk-white, now purple with love's wound,

And maidens call it love-in-idleness.

Fetch me that flower; the herb I shew'd thee once:

The juice of it on sleeping eye-lids laid

Will make or man or woman madly dote

Upon the next live creature that it sees.

(ACT 2, SCENE 1)

Folk names for plants change over the centuries and vary by region, with many now forgotten; however, it is popularly agreed that the plant Shakespeare is referring to is the wild pansy. Pansies' inclusion in magical love potions of the period make it an appropriate fit, and it's likely Shakespeare would have known of this association. The first half of this speech is a contemporary reference to Elizabeth I, in which Shakespeare is saying that many have tried to win her love but failed since she is so beloved of the virgin goddess Diana (here represented by the moon). He is also describing the Roman myth of the origin of the plant's powers, saying that the flower was hit by Cupid's arrow, changing from white to purple and taking on the power of the arrow to make people fall in love.

Love-in-idleness gets one other mention in the plays, and that is in act 1, scene 1 of *The Taming of the Shrew*:

TRANIO: I pray, sir, tell me, is it possible

That love should of a sudden take such hold?

LUCENTIO: O Tranio, till I found it to be true,

I never thought it possible or likely.

But see! while idly I stood looking on,

I found the effect of love in idleness;

And now in plainness do confess to thee,

That art to me as secret and as dear

As Anna to the Queen of Carthage was

Tranio, I burn, I pine, I perish, Tranio,

If I achieve not this young modest girl.

Counsel me, Tranio, for I know thou canst;

Assist me, Tranio, for I know thou wilt.

251

This is an earlier play than *Midsummer*, so perhaps Shakespeare made a mental note that such a potent plant would make a good future plot point.

In terms of magical plants whose folklore names have since been obscured or forgotten, one of the best examples is the "weird sisters" of *Macbeth* and their cauldron ingredients:

> Fillet of a fenny snake,
> In the cauldron boil and bake;
> Eye of newt and toe of frog,
> Wool of bat and tongue of dog,
> Adder's fork and blind-worm's sting,
> Lizard's leg and owlet's wing,
> For a charm of powerful trouble,
> Like a hell-broth boil and bubble.
> (ACT 4, SCENE 1)

On first examination this looks like a list of grotesque ingredients that the sisters of fate are stirring into their cauldron. They go on to include various other unsavoury body parts. However, with some knowledge of folk names for plants that still abide, we know that at least "eye of newt," "tongue of dog," and "adder's fork" are, in fact, herbs. "Eye of newt" is a folk name for mustard-seed, "tongue of dog" is a toxic herb more popularly known as hound's-tongue, and "adder's fork" is "adder's tongue," an herb that can help heal wounds. It's also possible that "toe of frog" is a type of buttercup. Since we know that many folk names for plants, especially region-specific names, have been lost or forgotten, then it is possible that far more of the seemingly horrendous cauldron ingredients are, in fact, plant-based.

MACBETH

Planetary Correspondences

We have already discussed the interconnectedness of all things within Hermetic beliefs, including that people can be considered to be ruled by a particular planet. In fact, the theory of correspondences applies to all things in nature, and so every plant also comes under the influence of a particular planet or combination of planets. This can be useful for magical practitioners; for instance, in making fragrances or incense to honour a particular planet or deity, or even just simply gathering flowers to place on a shrine or altar. The following lists are all plants that appear in Shakespeare's works, with correspondences compiled from a combination of Renaissance grimoire sources and Nicolas Culpeper's herbal, which dates to very slightly after Shakespeare's time. When plants appear in two lists, it is because they have been found under different planets in different sources, and they have qualities that seem to fit in both.

Sun

> Her eyes, like marigolds, had sheathed their light,
> And canopied in darkness sweetly lay,
> Till they might open to adorn the day.
> (*The Rape of Lucrece*)

☞ Ash tree, balsam, barley, bay, cabbage, clove tree, corn, marigold, marjoram, orange tree, palm tree, rosemary, saffron, thyme

These would all be good herbs to use in any magical working for success, happiness, or bringing knowledge to light, either by creating a charm bag (see the exercise at the end of this chapter), burning as incense, or leaving as an offering.

Moon

> When roasted crabs hiss in the bowl,
> Then nightly sings the staring owl…
> (*Love's Labours Lost*)

☞ Adder's tongue, almond, crab apple, gourd, lettuce, mistletoe, peony, pomegranate, poppy, reed, turnip

Deeply connected to the divine feminine, these plants are useful for any working with goddess energies, dream work, or the cycles of life.

Mars

> I peseech you heartily, scurvy, lousy knave, at my
> desires, and my requests, and my petitions, to eat,
> look you, this leek: because, look you, you do not
> love it, nor your affections and your appetites and
> your digestions doo's not agree with it, I would
> desire you to eat it.
> (*Henry V*)

☞ Bean, briar, burdock, fern, garlic, hawthorn, hemp, hound's-
tongue, leek, mint, mustard, nettle, nutmeg, onion, pepper,
poppy, radish, rhubarb, thistle, vine, wormwood

These plants all have an innate martial quality, making them suitable for works connected to ambition, drive, and competition.

Mercury

> Go to, sir; you were beaten in Italy for picking a
> kernel out of a pomegranate; you are a vagabond and
> no true traveller.
> (*All's Well That Ends Well*)

☞ Chamomile, clover, elder, filbert (hazel), hazelnut, honeysuckle
(woodbine), lavender, mushroom, pomegranate, rose (wild), savory

These are all herbs which may help with clear thought, travel, and communication.

Jupiter

> …to the dread rattling thunder
> Have I given fire and rifted Jove's stout oak
> With his own bolt
> (*The Tempest*)

☞ Aloe, cedar, cherry tree, daisy, elm tree, flax, mulberry, oak,
peony, plane tree, plum tree, quince, strawberry, white fig tree

Use these plants for any workings for abundance, leadership, and wisdom.

255

Venus

> So doth the woodbine the sweet honeysuckle
>
> Gently entwist...
>
> (A *Midsummer Night's Dream*)

☞ Almond tree, apple tree, box tree, clover, daffodil, daisy, honeysuckle, lemon tree, lily, medlar, mistletoe, myrtle, pansy, plantain, rose, thyme, violet

All these plants have connections to matters of the heart and may be used in related workings or as offerings to deities.

Saturn

> Not poppy, nor mandragora,
>
> Nor all the drowsy syrups of the world,
>
> Shall ever medicine thee to that sweet sleep
>
> Which thou owedst yesterday.
>
> (*Othello*)

☞ Aconite, cypress, elm tree, fennel, hebenon, hellebore, hemlock, mandragora (mandrake), moss, rue, weeping willow

Saturn plants are connected to death, and whilst some may have healing qualities and others are useful for magical work, please exercise caution when working with these plants and consult an expert or herbal. Many of these plants are highly toxic and even deadly! Hebenon was the poison used by Claudius to kill Hamlet's father, but there is some contention as to what plant it is, as the name is now lost. A likely candidate is yew.

Exercise: Create a Charm Bag for Inspiration

A charm bag is a small pouch to be worn upon your person, containing ingredients which are chosen and charmed to aid in a particular function. This charm bag uses herbs from The sun, Jupiter and Mercury in order to bring clear thought and inspiration.

You will need:

☞ a blue pen or quill and ink

☞ a small orange, pale blue, or purple pouch (made from natural material if possible)

☞ a palm-size square of paper (best quality possible)

☞ a small amount of dried rosemary, chamomile, and oak (any part)

☞ an orange, pale blue, or purple candle if possible; white if not

Set up an altar with everything that you need set out ready, and call in the directions as per your usual method or exercise given in chapter 2.

Light your candle. With your pen and paper, draw the planetary sigil for Mercury, with an added dot within the circle to represent the sun on one side and the sigil for Jupiter on the other.

Take three deep breaths and then, holding your hands over your ingredients, intone this charm (created using stitch technique):

> O for a Muse of fire, that would ascend
>
> The brightest heaven of invention,
>
> Apollo, Pallas, Jove, or Mercury,
>
> By inspiration of celestial grace,
>
> Let me be furnish'd with a mind so rare,
>
> To pluck bright honour from the pale-faced moon,
>
> And in a vision full of majesty,
>
> Witness the world that I create thee here!

Put all the ingredients into the pouch and tie it firmly closed. Now hold your pouch a safe distance above your candle and repeat the charm again, waving the pouch three times above the flame in a clockwise direction. Now hold it to your forehead and repeat the charm a third time. Give thanks and close the space.

Using this example as a template, you can now go on to create charm bags for other qualities you would like to focus on. You have already learned how to create invocations using the stitch technique in chapter 9, and planetary colour correspondences can be found in chapter 3. You may wish to use charm bags to enhance invocation work; for example, if you wish to work with the archetype of one of Shakespeare's characters, which herbs might you include? Look back to examples of which characters are ruled by which planets for inspiration, then choose from the list of herbs.

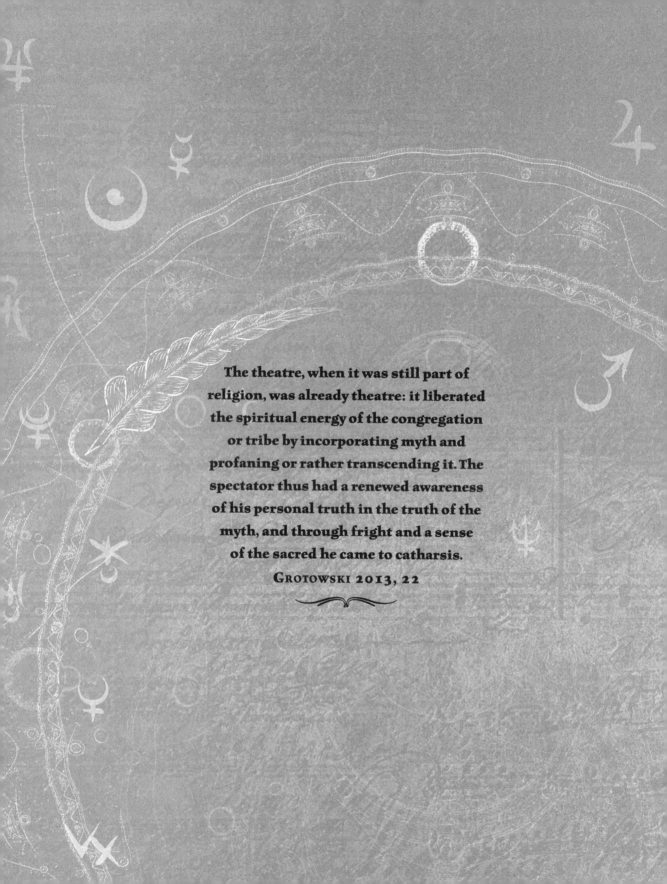

The theatre, when it was still part of
religion, was already theatre: it liberated
the spiritual energy of the congregation
or tribe by incorporating myth and
profaning or rather transcending it. The
spectator thus had a renewed awareness
of his personal truth in the truth of the
myth, and through fright and a sense
of the sacred he came to catharsis.

GROTOWSKI 2013, 22

ELEVEN

Shakespeare's
Modern Magicians

As we have seen, the magical content of Shakespeare is intrinsic to its most fulfilling interpretation, and there are many consciously channelling that knowledge in their work in theatre today. We will now look at current key figures whose practical work incorporates a spiritual and/or magical dimension to their understanding of Shakespeare.

The most direct link between Hermetic practices in theatre in Shakespeare's time and our own can be found on London's South Bank in the form of Shakespeare's Globe.

Masters of the Globe

The Globe is a unique and incredibly special place to those who love Shakespeare's works, and anyone who enters the space will attest to how truly magical it is. It is striking even from the outside, as you walk along the south bank of the River Thames and come across the circular white building with oak beams and thatched roof. When you enter the ground floor, you walk into a circular space lit by daylight (the outdoor space is only open in the summer season, other than for special events and courses), with the rectangular stage surrounded by gleaming gems of Hermetic iconography and the two striking pillars that support the roof of the stage.

The structure of the new Globe, due to scant archaeological evidence as to the design of the original building, was built according to Vitruvian principles, as are temples and Renaissance round churches. As previously discussed in relation to the original Globe theatres, the name and threefold structure of the heavens, earthly playing space and hell beneath are a direct reflection of the concept of microcosm and macrocosm. The iconography is Hermetic, including the seven planets above the stage, the zodiac in the heavens, and paintings of Apollo and Hermes on either side of the stage. The shared light of the playing space encourages the audience and actors to energetically engage with each other. Mark Rylance, first artistic director of the new Globe, was involved in its construction and performed a temple consecration on the site including an offering, the remains of which, as far as I know, still hang in a cigar box beneath the stage. A more in-depth study of the esoteric thinking behind the construction of Shakespeare's Globe is included later in this chapter.

Peter Dawkins and Mark Rylance

Mark Rylance's unofficial esoteric advisor during this process was his friend and spiritual mentor, Peter Dawkins. It was through Dawkins that Rylance first started to explore the mystery content of Shakespeare's work and eventually grew to adopt his viewpoint on the Shakespearean authorship question. This viewpoint—that the amount of hidden knowledge within Shakespeare's works is an indicator that they must have been penned by a more educated hand than William Shakespeare of Stratford (in this case, Francis Bacon at the head of a group of writers)—has been the cause of much controversy, resulting in Rylance being named by the Birthplace Trust as "anti-Shakespearean." In addition to his involvement in the early days of the Globe, Dawkins has also penned a number of books detailing the Cabbalistic teachings to be found in Shakespeare's plays and has run spiritual pilgrimages with Mark Rylance to explore the magic of the plays in the locations in which they are set. I visited him at his Banbury home in 2014 to learn more about how he feels we can utilise Shakespeare's hidden wisdom within theatre today (all his quotes in this chapter are from that interview).

Dawkins' first introduction to the mystery content of Shakespeare was through one of the most renowned founders of the New Age movement, Sir George Trevelyan. They were good friends when Peter lived and worked in Edinburgh as an architect, and when Trevelyan would visit him and his wife Sarah at their home, he would always make him read Shakespeare aloud. According to Peter, "I had no idea what he was doing…he was a mentor to me, he saw a potential in me that could be developed." In turn, Dawkins became a mentor to Mark Rylance when Rylance was performing as Hamlet at the RSC in Stratford in 1988. Together with Sir George Trevelyan, he was running weekend seminars looking at the alchemical content of the plays. After overhearing two of the attendees in conversation about the alchemical symbolism within *The Merchant of Venice* at the Dirty Duck, a pub well attended by the RSC actors, Rylance decided to attend the second part of the talk on Sunday morning and became fascinated by the ideas discussed.

Dawkins is also an expert practitioner of geomancy, the art of healing the landscape through the placing of structures and working with ancient structures such as stone circles that are already in place. It is this work that inspired Rylance to form his Phoebus Cart theatre company and tour sacred sites in Britain with an alchemically aware production of *The Tempest*, for which Dawkins was an advisor. He tells how he advised that they should perform the play as a magic circle around the outside of the audience, with altars set up in the four directions for the elements:

> It made too much magic really, because we had tempest after tempest after tempest! There was even a well-known critic at the time, who is normally renowned for criticising things very negatively, who said "Last night I was at a production of *The Tempest*, sitting in the middle of this circle and it was a tempest, and we just sat there for the full two and half hours, in this field, getting soaked to the skin—and it was wonderful!"

This tour ended with performances on the foundations of the Globe Theatre, and this connection with Sam Wanamaker led to Rylance being appointed as part of the artistic directorate and then as the first artistic director of the new Globe.

Of his involvement in the Globe's construction, Dawkins points out that his position as advisor was "unofficial" due to being considered a "heretic" for his position on the authorship debate. While he praises the research of the architects and advisors, which produced what he describes as "sacred architecture," he explained that they had "no idea" about the positioning of the pillars and the iconography, and that's where his advice became most useful:

> What's called as the right-hand pillar of the Cabala is the stage-right pillar, because being on the stage basically is the same as being in Solomon's temple, and the pillars are the entrance to that…Apollo is on the right because he is the Sun, the right-hand pillar is the light that gives the wisdom, and Mercury is the thinker…the intelligence that receives.

In Rylance's years as artistic director, Dawkins would also advise the actors when they were already a couple of weeks into rehearsal on the esoteric wisdom behind the play and their roles, and he also gave regular seminars on "The Wisdom of Shakespeare," the content of which can be found in his series of books, which includes *Twelfth Night*, *As You Like It*, *The Merchant of Venice*, and *The Tempest*. These books, and also the teachings given to actors and attendees at the seminars, map Shakespeare's plays and characters on the Qabalistic Tree of Life.

> It puts everything on a different level, the fundamental principle of Cabala and of Christianity. The other thing, which Mark has taken on board very much, it allows you, inwardly, to tune in to these great archetypes, these intelligences. To be able to tune in to these universal intelligences, then it works through you; you become a channel for it.

Although Dawkins and Rylance no longer run their seminars at the Globe, they have occasionally run spiritual pilgrimages that explore the esoteric content of Shakespeare's plays within the landscape they were set.

Richard Olivier

One of the first directors during this time to work with Rylance on the Globe stage was Richard Olivier, son of Laurence Olivier, who now runs a company called Olivier Mythodrama. This company runs workshops using the mytho-poetic structure of Shakespeare's plays to train future business and political leaders, inspired by work that Olivier did with Rylance on *Henry V* at Shakespeare's Globe. We had a brief but fascinating conversation via Skype in 2014 (all his quotes in this chapter are from that interview).

Prior to directing *Henry V*, Olivier had been running "men's mysteries" groups, which involved shamanic practices designed to empower men and their role in life. He brought this work to the rehearsals at the Globe, which, since they were working in original practice (a term meaning as close as possible to practices of Shakespeare's time, including cue-scripts and no women onstage) and were an all-male cast, were run as a "ritual men's group." Though most of the actors "took the lead from Mark Rylance," Olivier remembered that one or two

> didn't realise quite how unusual it was going to be…we did a whole expedition to an abandoned air force base where we set up camp for three days, where we lived through the play…we did what I call a mythodrama version of it…we lived through all the action both on-stage and off-stage.

On the night before the battle of Agincourt, the cast participated in a group sweatlodge, a powerful shamanic initiatory and healing tool, built for them by a sweatlodge master. Each member of the cast also ritually consumed a piece of earth brought from the battlefield at Agincourt, as Jenny Tiranami (the designer) had discovered in her research that soldiers would have done this on the night before battle. Olivier described this as "a way of grounding ourselves, both literally and metaphorically, in the play."

Glynn Macdonald

Work was done with the elements with master of movement Glynn Macdonald, with particular focus on fire, not only due to the first line being "O, for a Muse of fire," but also because they were interpreting it as "a play about inspiration, creative imagination, and leadership," according to Olivier. Glynn Macdonald's exercises, which work to embody elemental and archetypal forces, are proof that esoteric concepts can be grounded very much in the physical in an effective way and that there is much common ground between theatre training and magical practice. She also called the Globe an "alchemical cauldron" and taught actors and students at the Globe to embrace the energy of the pillars' sacred polarity.

Stewart Pearce

In addition to Glynn Macdonald's powerful work in movement, there was vocal work with Stewart Pearce, first master of voice at Shakespeare's Globe, where he held the post for ten years. Pearce also taught voice at Webber Douglas Academy of Dramatic Arts. He has since written a series of books and recorded accompanying audio CDs that teach an esoteric approach to voice work, including detailed practical exercises with the principal that "our voice is the window to our soul" (Pearce 2010, 72). Pearce brings an awareness of world spirituality together with expert knowledge of the anatomy of voice to create a workbook that enables the practitioner to use their voice as a tool to resonate not only in the physical realm but also in the mental/emotional and spiritual dimensions. His mystical yet practical approach, which emphasises alchemy, the planets, and the elements as sources of wisdom, fit comfortably within a Hermetic framework.

Shamanism at the Globe

Although Shakespeare's Globe can be seen as a Hermetic temple, much of the magical work that has taken place in a performance context has been shamanic in nature. Olivier tells us that African medicine man Malidoma Somé performed and taught the cast of *Henry V* a "war rhythm" on the djembe, and this drumbeat was used before performances to help create an authentic atmosphere of war, which Olivier recalls was "a very ritualistic and magical sound in that space…the Globe in a way became like a drum that was creating the energy for the performance."

Unlike Peter Dawkins and Mark Rylance, Richard Olivier does not consider the authorship of Shakespeare's plays to be of great importance when considering their hidden wisdom: "Personally I'm not as interested in it as a lot of people I know…for me the gift is that the work is here, that it is magic, and that it's still speaking to people four hundred years later." However, he does mention a possible Sufi influence, mentioning that when he and Mark Rylance met Prince Charles, the first question the royal asked them was whether they thought that Shakespeare had a Sufi teacher. Perhaps part of Shakespeare's universal appeal lies in the core of wisdom that runs throughout, upon which people can superimpose or identify their own beliefs.

Within his current work at Olivier Mythodrama, Olivier has kept the esoteric content more "masked" but hopes to be able to expand his practice and the minds of his clients by bringing in concepts like the sweatlodge in the future. His focus in using Shakespeare's texts and archetypal psychology to explore whether his clients are in alignment with their purpose is, however, still in keeping with the aim of using Shakespeare's wisdom for personal spiritual development. He has now taken a step back from mainstream theatre as it has been "something of an uphill struggle" to maintain the spiritual content of the work, and he is unaware of many people attempting to pursue it. We found ourselves in agreement that the audience should be made to feel as though they are a part of the story and that

> some of the Shakespeare myths were taken from ancient wisdom stories, infused with spiritual teaching that the audience may or may not understand when they see it…the work I wanted to do was put it back into a ritual context so hopefully people could get deeper insight into whatever mystery was waiting for them in the plays…based on the old Dionysian and Eleusinian mysteries.

The Magic of Immersive Theatre

Whether magically aware or not, the current trend in theatre practice is towards participatory, immersive experience, such as that offered by the new Bridge Theatre in London and other companies such as Punch Drunk who take over buildings, there being an understanding present that "if you live through a story, you gain insight into the wisdom that is hidden within the story," according to Olivier. It seems the time is ripe for an intentional sacred or magical element to be introduced. If the initiatory framework is indeed already inherent in the text, the "ritual" content need not be forced down the audience's throat so long as they are engaged on an energetic level and are somehow able to "live through the story."

Peter Brook

During our interview, Olivier identified Peter Brook as being one of the few living advocates in modern times of a spiritual dimension to Shakespeare's work in practice. Comically illustrating the point that anyone can find their culture's wisdom in Shakespeare's work, in his reflective book *The Quality of Mercy*, Brook recounts an anecdote in which a man who identified himself as being

> from one of the Islamic Republics in the South stood up after a talk and addressed the audience, stating in all confidence that in his language "Shake means Sheikh and Pir means a Wise Man. For us there is no doubt—over the years we have learnt to read secret messages. This one is clear" (Brook 2013, 3).

Certainly Brook's ideal of a "holy theatre" or "theatre of the invisible-made-visible" (Brook 1968, 47) has great resonance with the focus of this work, with the aim of a theatre that "not only presents the invisible but offers conditions that make its perception possible" (Brook 1968, 63).

Brian Bates

Olivier mentioned another practitioner whom I have also had the honour of working with, author and lecturer Brian Bates, who is a professor of psychology at the University of Sussex, also known for his work in reclaiming native Anglo-Saxon shamanic practices. His shamanic workshops feel very much like a drama class, and indeed he has worked extensively with actors on the magical and spiritual nature of performance. He has written a book on the subject called *The Way of the Actor*, which includes interviews with renowned actors such as Glenda Jackson, Anthony Sher, and Charlton Heston. Although it is not a practical manual, it does talk about simple techniques that, though not specifically Hermetic, may be tried in the rehearsal room to develop spiritual awareness within performance.

Wendy Jean Macphee

Another theatre practitioner who has put her years of experience and research of the magical content of Shakespeare into book form is Wendy Jean Macphee. In her fascinating and detailed work *Secret Meanings in Shakespeare*, she writes of how she translated her esoteric discoveries into performance with her company Theatre Set Up (sadly no longer extant). A theatre program for her 1989 production of *Cymbeline* lists planetary associations for each cast member, as well as the significance of every scene of the play in both alchemy and Celtic underworld initiation, with mention of assistance in interpretation of the latter by renowned spiritual teacher R. J. Stewart.

Grotowski and Artaud

Practitioners worthy of mention that are of modern times but no longer with us are Jerzy Grotowski and Antonin Artaud. Artaud was obsessed with the occult, but his vision lacked the grounding of sanity. The appeal of his work lies more in the idealised concept of what he was trying to achieve rather than the work itself, and he was never associated with Shakespeare. The emotional instability of Artaud's work seems incompatible with the aim of a spiritually disciplined and focused theatre.

Grotowski, however, has left a legacy with many qualities to aspire to:

> Art is a ripening, an evolution, an uplifting which enables us to emerge from
> darkness into a blaze of light (Grotowski 2013, 212).

Ted Hughes

There are also a number of writers who have insights into the mythic and esoteric content of Shakespeare's work who are not practitioners themselves, but whose work is of value and offers potential for practical exploration when combined with other methods. One of the most remarkable of these works is *Shakespeare and the Goddess of Complete Being* by poet and critic Ted Hughes. Inspired by the Robert Graves' iconic *White Goddess*, Hughes reveals insights into mythic symbolism and initiatory structure through a painstakingly close reading of the plays. Though criticised upon its release for being more of a reflection of the author's belief framework than that of the bard, it provides many valuable insights into the mythic treasures that may be found within Shakespeare's poems and plays.

Similar but less well known are the works of Beryl Pogson, student of Dr. Maurice Nicol, whose book *In the East My Pleasure Lies* interprets Shakespeare through the lens of "the Fourth Way," a Hermetic-inspired New Age spiritual path:

> …in the plays a Way of Return is indicated for Man towards his true destiny,
> which is the attainment of his Spiritual Being (Pogson 1999, 6).

Shakespeare's Globe: Museum Theatre or Hermetic Temple?

In 1949 a young American actor called Sam Wanamaker went to visit the site where the famous Globe Theatre, home of so many of Shakespeare's plays, had once stood. He was shocked to find that the only evidence of its existence was a bronze plaque on a brewery wall. He then made it his mission to reconstruct Shakespeare's famous theatre as close to the site as possible, and his extraordinary will and vision, with an extraordinary team behind him (including architect Theo Crosby of the Pentagram Design Group—yet another sign of the Globe's magic!) managed, with twenty-five dedicated years of work, to manifest the extraordinary institution that now stands on the South Bank. Sadly, he died the year before it was completed.

At the time of writing, Shakespeare's Globe on London's South Bank is in the midst of a highly successful summer season under the leadership of her new artistic director Michelle Terry. This is after previous artistic director Emma Rice's reign was cut short after complaints that her use of amplification and lighting was not in keeping with the purpose for which the theatre was built.

This revived a tendency for some academics, practitioners, and even the general public to be dismissive of the Globe as a flawed reconstruction and producer of "museum theatre," as if that were its only raison d'être. This is an echo of the dissenting voices that were much more commonly heard around the time of the new Globe's construction, the fear being that the Globe would be no more than "a sort of Shakespeareland, a Disneyesque heritage theme park for rubes and tourists" (http://www.edwardfox.co.uk/rylance.html). This was not an entirely unfounded fear, as this aspect appealed to a portion of the public who were keen to embrace the Globe as a place of pilgrimage, their Bardolatric tendencies manifesting in eccentric behaviours such as arriving at performances of the 1996 modern dress production of *Two Gentlemen of Verona* in Elizabethan dress (for which they were turned away). As Siobhan Keenan and Peter Davidson point out, this was "in direct contradiction to the stated aims of those who have worked for the project" (Mulryne 1997, 147).

These original aims were to build a space that would re-create as close as possible the environment in which Shakespeare's plays were first performed. Mark Rylance, first artistic director of the new Globe, called it "the most experimental space in England" and likened its construction to "someone discovering the original cello or the original violin and saying 'Mozart wrote for this instrument...so who will take up the challenge to try and play his music on this instrument?'"(Carson 2008, 103). With careful attention to research, materials, and craft, the architects and creative team behind the new Globe came as close as they could to an authentic replication of the original, considering the limits of the information and resources available to them, but acknowledged that it could only ever be "a shadow, a representation, a laboratory for the player and the theatrical historian" (Mulryne 1997, 147). The architect in charge of the project, Theo Crosby, "shared Sam (Wanamaker)'s vision of the new Globe taking its place within a revitalised Southwark, relating to the community who live beside it, offering educational opportunities to all who work in it and drawing visitors like a magnet" (Gurr 1998, 48).

However, is there more to Shakespeare's Globe? Through the attention paid to Renaissance culture in filling in the research blanks, did the team behind the new Globe in fact create a site worthy of pilgrimage, not just of Bardolatry but a true temple built on the principles of Hermeticism?

The Two Pillars

The Mysteries were enacted in the temples or schools of the Mysteries and one of the main features about the architecture of the dramatic setting was the presence…of two great pillars. The same were represented on the stage of Shakespeare's original Globe Theatre as well as in other Elizabethan theatres, and today are replicated in the new Globe Theatre in London.

—Dawkins 2004, 154

The positioning of the pillars at Shakespeare's Globe is still the subject of debate. It cannot be known for certain whether or not it is the case, as Peter Dawkins implies above, that the pillars in the original Globe alluded to the pillars of the ancient mystery schools and temples. Setting authenticity of reconstruction aside, however, what we do know is that it was a conscious consideration in the construction of the new Globe, and that since Peter Dawkins was involved in the decision over the positioning and size of the pillars (through Mark Rylance), the esoteric symbolism of their presence was a factor in their prominence.

The pillars are a representation of the polarity inherent in the construction of the universe and are variously known as the pillars of Hercules, Joachim and Boaz (meaning "Mercy and Severity," the pillars in Solomon's Temple), or "Mars and Venus," the latter by which they are referred to at Shakespeare's Globe. They are a major symbol of the principles of the Kabbalah, a system of ancient Judaic mysticism that was prevalent in Renaissance philosophy and is often alluded to in Shakespeare's work. That the new Globe embraced this content, at least in the days of Rylance, can be seen even in their brief website promotional blurbs, such as this extract from the page for their production of

Merchant of Venice: "*The Merchant of Venice* compares the Christian, Judaic, and Hermetic traditions of sixteenth-century Italy and England and weighs them in the balance." While it seems possible and even likely that the pillars of the first and second Globe Theatres were there simply for the practical purpose of holding up the heavens, there can be little doubt that Shakespeare's Globe of the modern day has embraced the potential of their sacred symbolism.

The Heavens

The decoration of the stage cover with a celestial
scene resembling a night sky is particularly
appropriate in an iconographical scheme which seeks
to identify the stage as a microcosm of the world…

—Mulryne 1997, 149

One aspect of the Globe's historical reproduction for which there is a reasonable body of evidence is the painted and gilded heavens above the stage. In a far cry from the fibreglass allusions of Disney World, these were painstakingly created using authentic historical methods and materials and are breathtakingly beautiful. The sun and the moon are represented, as is the full circle of the western zodiac in anthropomorphic form. There is also a "supernal fire" painted over a hatch from which gods or other (presumably heavenly) beings can descend. The latter is again a reference to the Cabala, as on the Tree of Life there are ten sephiroth, or "spheres," representing the descent of spirit into matter and manifestation (as we discussed in chapter 3). The three highest spheres on the tree are known as the supernal triad and are thought to be the source of all spirit and beyond mortal comprehension.

Not only does this celestial canopy feed the aesthetic eye of the beholder, but it also provides a tool for actors so they can directly address the heavenly bodies and forces, which is often required in Shakespeare's texts. The painted image of the heavens gives a pictorial gateway to the divine powers as well as a symbolic confirmation of the Globe's nature as manufactured microcosm.

In a continuation of this apparent mapping of the universe, just beneath the heavens, on the wall above the balcony, may be seen anthropomorphised representations of the classical seven planets. From left to right, these are Sol, Luna, Mars, Mercury, Jupiter, Venus, and Saturn. The seven planets not only relate to the seven days of the week but also directly relate to the seven remaining sephiroth of the Kabbalah. Cleverly, they have also been rendered to resemble the seven ages of man as referred to in Jaques' famous soliloquy in act 2, scene 7 of *As You Like It*, which makes the microcosmic parallel blatant: "All the world's a stage."

Beneath the planets, very prominently featured on the walls to either side of the stage, may be found painted representations of the Greco-Roman gods Apollo and Hermes. This represents the next level towards manifestation on the physical plane (the stage itself) of the heavenly powers. Apollo and Mercury/Hermes bring inspiration, illumination, eloquence, and lucidity to creative souls. Between these two figures may be found carvings of the muses, traditionally conveyors of creative inspiration from the divine to mortal artists. In Hermetic tradition (so called as it is said to be passed down to mortals from Hermes), images of the gods can act as conduits for their powers and abilities, so when they are addressed directly in the course of a play, this invokes their energies and adds an extra dimension to the emotional and spiritual experience of the audience.

Connection

We read of audiences being spell-bound
or "ravished" by characters on stage…

—Kiernan 1999, 12

Of course a temple is not created exclusively for the priest/esses, or in this case the actors, but in order to provide the people with a transcendent experience or communion with the divine. This was certainly the intent of Rylance from the start, who in the early days of his office as artistic director said, "I hope we can provide theatrical experiences that reflect and enrich human nature in its many physical, psychological, spiritual and divine forms" (Mulryne 1997, 175).

The open roof of Shakespeare's Globe unites actor and audience under the same sky and surrounds them with the same light. While an allowance is made for evening performances through the use of electric lighting, it is not permitted to use it to create stage effects, but rather to maintain a "universal lighting." This enables the actors to engage

Groundlings viewing a scene from
A Midsummer Night's Dream

on a dynamic level with the audience (and vice versa), which is little-known in modern theatre practice. Actor Jim Bywater, one of the pioneer players of the Globe's first production, observed that "the Globe audience shares the actor's consciousness" (Kiernan 1999, 11). When the audience can become the conscience or part of the soul of the characters they see onstage, truly involved in a spiritual and emotional journey rather than detached observers, the initiatory potential of the theatre is clear.

Vitruvian Proportion

Frances Yates in 1969 attempted to show that
Shakespeare's Globe was a Vitruvian space,
with twenty-four sides. Archaeology proved
her wrong, indicating a theatre of some twenty
sides, a product of standard timber lengths
rather than Renaissance cosmology.

—Wiles 2003, 192

Mark Rylance's first involvement with the reconstruction of the Globe was when he met with Sam Wanamaker to arrange performing his touring production of *The Tempest* on the foundations of the theatre. He had been inspired by the teachings of Peter Dawkins to bring together a group of seven actors (for the number of traditional planets and other mystical resonances), working without a director, to take an alchemical performance of *The Tempest* to sites of key energetic importance on the landscape, most notably the Rollright Stones, in order to balance the energies and bring fertility to the land. When it came to performing in London, he wanted an outdoor space and was attracted to the Globe's foundations as they were the same proportions as the Rollright Stones and Stonehenge.

Sam Wanamaker, a spiritually minded visionary himself, not only agreed to the performance but proceeded to make Rylance part of the artistic directorate who would have input on the construction. Since at the point of planning the new Globe little was known about the original (other than some rough exterior drawings on maps that showed the four main theatres as circular buildings with thatched rooves, and an interior sketch of the Swan Theatre by a Dutchman called De Witt) and what archaeological remains had been uncovered, they were inspired by Renaissance cosmology and the works of Frances Yates to construct the new theatre according to Vitruvian principles. Though it was later discovered that the original Globe was built with the more practical consideration of standard wooden beam-lengths in mind, David Wiles notes that "Despite the collapse of Yates' theory, the classical placing of a square within a circle was found a helpful key to reconstruction" (Wiles 2003, 193).

It is not only the proportions and the sacred geometry of the space that qualify Shakespeare's Globe as a temple, but it is positioned facing northeast, aligned with the rising sun at Midsummer, just as Stonehenge, the Rollright Stones, and other ancient places of apparent worship are. Of this point, scholar Andrew Gurr notes that "While there is no evidence for any particular significance in this fact, it might well be unwise to ignore it" (http://www.edwardfox.co.uk/rylance.html).

Cosmic Harmony

Both in the first Globe and in the present third
Globe, music was placed between the world of
the Gods above, and the earthly stage of mankind,
below. Music is, thus, not only heard but seen as the
expression of the Muses as it transmits heavenly
impulses to Man below on the earthly stage.

—Claire Van Kampen (Carson 2008, 81)

As impressive and significant as the iconography and appearance of the architecture is, one of the effects of its structure according to ancient laws of cosmic harmony is to create an extraordinary acoustic environment. Sound resonates not only through the structure but through each body in the space, actor and audience member alike. This is a physical vibration created by the voices of the actors and the presence of live musicians in the gallery—another feature of the Globe that more recent research shows to have been unlikely at the original—which has the potential to move emotions in a way that transcends rational comprehension. Once again, comparisons can be drawn with ancient sites like Stonehenge, which have been found to have unique acoustic qualities and inherent resonance that are unlikely to be accidental. Like much of the construction of the original Globe, this is likely to remain mysterious.

Hell and the Underglobe

If we were in any doubt as to the intentions of the creative team behind the new Globe's construction to align the theatre with mystical energies, we have only to visit the exhibition centre in the area underneath the stage known as the "Underglobe" with a little esoteric learning behind us. Not only is there a realistic representation of the Tree of Life, but the ceiling is emblazoned with numerous motifs of a Kabbalistic, alchemical, astrological, and Vitruvian nature. There are also alchemical images on embroidered banners and representations of the ancient muses.

Also in the chthonian depths beneath the jewel-like Globe stage, in the area known affectionately as "hell," in keeping with the early modern worldview, is hidden a cigar box left in position by Rylance when he first became artistic director. This contains offerings for the spirits of place, the remains of a shamanic ritual that Rylance conducts with casts of each production (which I have been privileged to participate in), in order to maintain their good will. Whether or not Emma Rice or Michelle Terry share Rylance's mystical beliefs or practices, the cigar box remains.

A Sacred Space

Vitruvius said: "When every important part of the
building is thus conveniently set in proportion by
the right correlation between width and depth, and
when all these parts have also their place in the total
symmetry of the building, we obtain eurhythmy."

—Skinner 2006, 129

From the seeds of one man's vision grew not a tourist-milking machine, nor even a mere museum piece, but a living, breathing temple and cultural icon in its own right, with practices drawn from traditional principles from which theatre draws its ancient roots. Though there can be little doubt that some of this magic became dormant under the more corporate-minded leadership of Dominic Dromgoole (it remains to be seen how it will fare under Michelle Terry), the Globe's sacred nature is inherent in its very structure and foundations, both literal and conceptual. Since they deal with the nature and spiritual journey of humanity, Shakespeare's works are as relevant today as they ever were. However, if we purely focus on the contemporary relevance and ignore the underlying Renaissance philosophy, we deny ourselves an extra depth of appreciation. The Globe provides a bridge of understanding between the modern and the early modern world.

Exercise: Offerings to the Spirits of Place

It's not possible or appropriate to share the specific ceremony that I was fortunate enough to share with Mark Rylance, but it is simple enough to create your own individual practice for connecting with, honouring, and appealing to the spirits of place wherever you are.

Whilst modern thinking might use the term "spirit of place" or *genius loci* (the classical term) in order to simply talk about the character of any given town or location, in magical or spiritual work we use the term to describe the guardian spirits of that place. These may vary in scale from guardians of particular groves, parks, or homes to spirits that watch over whole countries (in a kind of Russian doll arrangement), but we usually only need concern ourselves directly with appealing to guardians over spaces we intend to work or live in.

The intent of presenting offerings to these guardians of place is in order to establish a positive connection with them and, if your magical work develops further, possible cooperation. Especially if you intend to do any outdoor work at all, it is strongly advisable to ask their permission, offer them blessings, and ask for their blessings in return, with a promise that you will do no harm to them or the area over which they govern.

Appropriate offerings are natural food and baked products (preferably home-baked), wine, beer, or devotional song or poetry, which must come from the soul and has the added advantage of leaving no waste product behind. It is a good idea to look at what local produce might be available, and if there are any native or folkloric traditions in the area where you live, ask yourself how you can honour them. It is also important that your offering does not have even a minor negative environmental impact; for example, consider that chocolate is toxic to most animals and should not be left outdoors where it could cause damage to wildlife or pets. Equally be careful with candle use, and always clear remaining food offerings before they rot.

The act of offering itself need not be complex, but the intent, focus, and energy must be pure. Take time simply being and breathing in the space, and reach out with your awareness to see if you can perceive the energies around you. It can be helpful to declare your honourable intentions out loud as you leave your offering. If you are inexperienced in magical practice, the exercises in preceding chapters for establishing sacred space and connecting with the world soul or anima mundi will be helpful for you in order to connect with the space and its guardians.

Whilst it is a good idea for your declaration to come from your own heart, soul, and mind, here is an example using a mash-up technique from different Shakespeare plays:

> Now, ye familiar spirits, that are cull'd
> Out of the powerful regions under earth (Henry VI, Part I)
> Ye elves of hills, brooks, standing lakes, and groves (The Tempest)
> Come you spirits that tend on mortal thoughts (Macbeth)
> My soul the faithfull'st offerings hath breathed out (Twelfth Night)
> Upon this land a thousand thousand blessings (Henry VIII)
> How I do honour thee! (Merchant of Venice)

If working with nature spirits, fairy beings, and spirits of place is an area that particularly interests you, please seek out my earlier work for Llewellyn, Faery Craft.

O ceremony, show me but thy worth!
What is thy soul of adoration?

HENRY V

ACT 4, SCENE 1

TWELVE

Creating Ritual Theatre

This chapter is, in essence, an extended exercise for those who have worked with the rest of the book and wish to combine some or all of these techniques and knowledge by creating a piece of ritual theatre. Western theatre and Western mystery tradition are twin oaks with their roots entwined together deep in the myths and rituals of ancient Greece, where the stories of the gods would be enacted for the people by actor/priests in masks, fully embodying the gods they represented. Today, ritual theatre is less well known, but as we have seen in the previous chapter, there are still people weaving magic in a conscious way through their work in theatre, and many more that we may never hear of quietly making their work, sometimes perhaps not even for any audience other than those who create the piece and whatever invisible forces may witness it.

This book has led you through many insights about Shakespeare's world and work, and also through various magical techniques. Now, if you choose, you may combine some or all of these in creating your own piece of ritual theatre. Ritual theatre does not require trained actors, though it may, of course, include them, but rather that you approach the process with an open heart and a wish to enact those myths that connect us, the divine source that illuminates our inner stars.

What Is Ritual Theatre?

Ritual theatre generally involves the enactment of mythic or allegorical tales as a sacred act of redemption and healing, either performed for an audience or solely for those participating directly. It may also be performed as an act of devotion or offering for an unseen audience of the gods, spirits, land, or whichever forces you wish to be working with. For example, you might wish to perform a piece of ritual theatre to heal a piece of land that has been energetically scarred by war or a tragic occurrence, or perhaps a group may devise a piece for the healing of mankind, even if no one else witnesses it. It is not necessary to be either a trained actor or magician to participate in ritual theatre, but it should be led by someone with a good level of knowledge and experience if it involves a group, and a basic awareness of ritual etiquette and focus is helpful.

Why Create and Perform Ritual Theatre Today?

Our world today may appear to have lost touch with the deep well of myth and divinity, and yet even those who have seemingly lost that connection seek it out in other forms. Popular franchises such as the Marvel and Lord of the Rings movies allow people to access a world of heroes and moral struggles. Sports stars have become the new Achilles or Hercules, and many feel there is something intangible missing from their lives. Humanity needs myth; it's part of how we connect to and make sense of the universe in which we dwell, and it doesn't require any particular religious belief alongside it, although the religions of the world are all formed around their own versions of universal myth. The word *myth* itself has become much misused in modern times, to mean something that is untrue. In fact, myths are stories that tap into our fundamental truths, beyond the limit of actual earthly occurrences.

How Does This Connect to Shakespeare?

Throughout this book we have learned that Shakespeare had a deep awareness of myth, drawing in particular on Ovid (often with very clear references), and wove this throughout his works. The alchemical journey taken through the plays is not dissimilar to the Hero's Journey as made popular by Joseph Campbell in the twentieth century. Most of Shakespeare's plays follow something like a mythic structure and are so much a fixture of our culture now that they can be considered mythic in themselves.

Some plays lend themselves more easily to this interpretation than others. Having so far explored both *The Winter's Tale* (which lends itself to this very naturally due to the Eleusinian undertones) and *The Two Gentlemen of Verona* (a far less obvious choice but a surprising mine of wisdom) in this context with the group led by Mark Rylance and Peter Dawkins, I believe there is scope for any of Shakespeare's plays and indeed the poems to be adapted for this purpose.

How Can We Use Shakespeare in Ritual Theatre?

The short answer to this is up to you! The example at the end of this chapter is fairly complex, using only Shakespearean text from pretty much the whole canon, mashed up and repurposed to tell the myth of light/soul's descent into the world and the cycle of creation, destruction, and rebirth. You may choose to simply use a Shakespearean passage or sonnet within a piece or create a piece around a Shakespearean character or story using your own writing or any manner of other methods and combinations of methods. Shakespeare is wonderful raw material for you to be creative with! Just remember that as with any act of magic, the intent of your ritual theatre must be clear, and it will usually follow a mythic structure. On the most basic level, this would be creation, destruction, and rebirth (or, alternatively, departure, initiation, and return—the key stages of the Hero's Journey). For a more sophisticated approach, you may wish to look back over the chapter on alchemy and the journey through the different states in the process to give you a structural idea.

To begin with a very simple example, say you had created a piece that ended with a union of polarities, or more literally you wished to bless a marriage or partnership: a group of three could enact the following scene from act 4 of *The Tempest*. The only alteration to the text here is that interjections from other characters have been cut out, leaving only the goddesses:

> IRIS: Ceres, most bounteous lady, thy rich leas
>
> Of wheat, rye, barley, vetches, oats and pease;
>
> Thy turfy mountains, where live nibbling sheep,
>
> And flat meads thatch'd with stover, them to keep;
>
> Thy banks with pioned and twilled brims,
>
> Which spongy April at thy hest betrims,
>
> To make cold nymphs chaste crowns; and thy broom-groves,
>
> Whose shadow the dismissed bachelor loves,
>
> Being lass-lorn: thy pole-clipt vineyard;
>
> And thy sea-marge, sterile and rocky-hard,
>
> Where thou thyself dost air;—the queen o' the sky,
>
> Whose watery arch and messenger am I,
>
> Bids thee leave these, and with her sovereign grace,
>
> Here on this grass-plot, in this very place,
>
> To come and sport: her peacocks fly amain:
>
> Approach, rich Ceres, her to entertain.
>
> (Enter CERES)
>
> CERES: Hail, many-colour'd messenger, that ne'er
>
> Dost disobey the wife of Jupiter;
>
> Who with thy saffron wings upon my flowers
>
> Diffusest honey-drops, refreshing showers,
>
> And with each end of thy blue bow dost crown
>
> My bosky acres and my unshrubb'd down,
>
> Rich scarf to my proud earth; why hath thy queen
>
> Summon'd me hither, to this short-grass'd green?
>
> IRIS: A contract of true love to celebrate;
>
> And some donation freely to estate
>
> On the blest lovers.

CERES: Tell me, heavenly bow,

   If Venus or her son, as thou dost know,

   Do now attend the queen? Since they did plot

   The means that dusky Dis my daughter got,

   Her and her blind boy's scandal'd company

   I have forsworn.

IRIS: Of her society

   Be not afraid: I met her deity

   Cutting the clouds towards Paphos and her son

   Dove-drawn with her. Here thought they to have done

   Some wanton charm upon this man and maid,

   Whose vows are, that no bed-right shall be paid

   Till Hymen's torch be lighted: but vain;

   Mars's hot minion is returned again;

   Her waspish-headed son has broke his arrows,

   Swears he will shoot no more but play with sparrows

   And be a boy right out.

CERES: High'st queen of state,

   Great Juno, comes; I know her by her gait.

(Enter JUNO)

JUNO: How does my bounteous sister? Go with me

   To bless this twain, that they may prosperous be

   And honour'd in their issue.

   (They sing)

JUNO: Honour, riches, marriage-blessing,

   Long continuance, and increasing,

   Hourly joys be still upon you!

   Juno sings her blessings upon you.

CERES: Earth's increase, foison plenty,

   Barns and garners never empty,

Vines and clustering bunches growing,

Plants with goodly burthen bowing;

Spring come to you at the farthest

In the very end of harvest!

Scarcity and want shall shun you;

Ceres' blessing so is on you.

IRIS: You nymphs, call'd Naiads, of the windring brooks,

With your sedged crowns and ever-harmless looks,

Leave your crisp channels and on this green land

Answer your summons; Juno does command:

Come, temperate nymphs, and help to celebrate

A contract of true love; be not too late.

(A dance)

This is but one example, and earlier in the book we have already looked at a number of invocations and blessings that could easily be used in a piece of ritual theatre. You may either be inspired by something from one of the plays or sonnets to create a piece around it or choose a theme/intent and then find appropriate material to fill it. Either way, Shakespeare's words are a rich and readily mined resource.

A Step-by-Step Guide

If you are new to ritual theatre and wish to create a piece from scratch, you may be wondering where to begin. In this section I will lead you through the process of creating a piece of ritual theatre, using my own piece, *Hekate: Genesis*, as an example. With reference to my reflective notes from the time of creating the piece and comments from the actors involved, I will also break down the process into its essential building blocks and give notes and suggestions for your work as we go. These steps will be clearly marked.

Genesis

In an experimental fusion of classical theatre and ritual, we will weave a tale of creation, conflict, destruction, and rebirth using text from a number of Shakespeare's plays, including *The Tempest*, *A Midsummer Night's Dream*, *Macbeth*, and

Hamlet. In the beginning, the Universe is created with the words of power…
these words bring the elements into being and through Hekate they face their
darkness and chaos before being brought together into balance and harmony,
revived by her sacred fires. This will be the first production by Emily Carding's Hermetic theatre company, SO POTENT ARTS, who work on the principle that all theatre has the potential to be an act of magic, and that all actors
are magicians.

Thus reads the promotional blurb for *Hekate: Genesis,* a half-hour piece of ritual theatre that I was commissioned to write and perform as part of the Hekate Symposium in
May 2013. It was created using the stitching or "mash-up" technique that we used when
writing our invocations in chapter 9.

Step 1

☞ What is the purpose of your ritual? Will it be dedicated to
a god/myth/planet/star/spirit/otherworldly realm/etc.?
What technique will you use? Will you use a combination of
techniques, i.e., your own writing plus Shakespeare speeches,
mash-up, and maybe work from other sources too?

The overriding aesthetic question today is: what permutations and what contemporary insights can be fashioned from the body of work bequeathed us
over 400 years of Shakespearean history?…it might involve radical reorganisa-
tion of his actual materials—scenes, speeches, characters which are unmistak-
ably Shakespearean but which, taken into other hands, are now transformed
and put to other uses (Marowitz 1991, 30).

The postmodern aesthetic of plundering Shakespeare and creating a mash-up text,
as referred to by Charles Marowitz in the above quote (from a book provocatively titled
Recycling Shakespeare), is usually rendered with an irreverent, humorous, or sacrilegious
intention. With *Hekate: Genesis* it was my intention to use this technique to create something sacred, a technique we have already explored in this book. In order to achieve this,
an established ritual structure had to be in place as the foundation.

You may choose to create yours using different methods, as we have already discussed, either writing your own and inserting some Shakespearean text into it or using
an intact play as a base to start creating from. However you decide to approach it, once
you are clear on your intent, the structure will be most important.

Step 2

☞ What structure suits the theme you have chosen? It should have a clear beginning, middle, and end, and it should end harmoniously.

Inspired by a spiritual pilgrimage to Sicily with Peter Dawkins and Mark Rylance in 2013 that explored the mytho-poetic and esoteric content of *The Winter's Tale*, I was able to use this play's innate magical structure of life, death, and rebirth as a starting point. Then, drawing on the teachings of the Chaldean Oracles, the Bible, and the Qabalah, I slowly started to create a ritual piece from Shakespeare's words.

If you wish to use this approach, keep your focus on your intent and think about which play or plays might best work for your structure. If you want to decide on a structure independently and build from there, use Shakespeare as either all or part of your raw material. What other sources might you draw upon once your structure is in place?

Step 3

☞ Decide on the source materials you want to draw upon and do your research. Also remember the power of music to transform consciousness. How will you use sound and music in your piece?

If you are focusing on a specific deity, is there a myth featuring them that would effectively carry your intent? If you have a more humanist focus or a more general desire of world healing, what myth or text best encapsulates this for you?

I was focusing on Hekate most specifically in her Neoplatonic aspect of world soul and her epithet Soteira, so I looked to the ancient writing that most inspired my work with this aspect of the goddess. The Chaldean Oracles consists of Hellenistic commentary on fragments of a mystery poem. The worldview portrayed within these writings has much in common with Neoplatonism and Gnosticism, but interestingly Hekate takes on the mantle of the animating cosmic soul and Soteira ("saviour") who "ensouls the light, the fire, the aether and the Cosmoi" (Johnston 1990, 62). This "celestial and beneficient" (Ibid., 143) goddess is in contrast to her portrayal in *Macbeth* as the primarily malevolent "Queen of the Witches," Hekate's chthonic form found in folklore and popular mythology. This aspect has been sadly neglected so far by others studying the magical side of Shakespeare's work, who see her only as a dark influence. Jill Line writes about Hekate's dark influence at length, saying that when man

> chooses to ignore natural law and create war, disorder and havoc in himself…
> the binding force of love is forgotten and the chaos of Hekate takes over (Line
> 2004, 31).

Though this may reflect the surface level of Shakespeare's interpretation of this ancient goddess, if we broaden our viewpoint to consider Hekate as world soul (as discussed in chapter 7), then we can see her as Nature herself, who features as a dominant power throughout Shakespeare's plays. It is valuable to consider that rather than influencing the events of the play overtly for the negative, Hekate appears at the moment of choice, illuminating the figurative crossroads. The darkness that makes the choice based on ego and ambition or chaos and destruction comes from within the soul of the anti-hero, which leads to redemption of the land through their eventual destruction. In the end, the greater good of Nature is served, and truth is revealed. Hekate is a multifaceted goddess, and since the Hekate Symposium, for which my performance had been commissioned, was dedicated to her function as Soteira and world soul, this would be my focus for the piece.

There were several places where we used music in different ways. Two sonnets were set to music with backing tracks recorded that were then sung live. There was also a pre-existing music track that was used for the climactic celebratory dancing, and there were various percussion instruments that were played live when needed. I think they were all used at once during the storm scene! This was very free-form.

Step 4

☞ Who will perform your piece? How many actors do you need?

Do your actors need to believe in magic?

Ritual theatre can involve as many or as few people as you wish, but if you are new to it, I highly suggest starting small as managing any group of people, performers or no, and getting them all to stick to a rehearsal schedule (unless you're paying them) can be somewhat akin to herding cats. What best serves your purpose? What's the minimum number of people you could use and be effective? Of course, if your purpose is a large community celebration and you are experienced in running and creating such events, then feel free to think big! However, when thinking big in proportion, it may be best to keep it simple in focus. At any rate, know how many performers you are able to use before you start writing your piece as you need to realistically be able to perform it.

I made a conscious decision to keep the cast as small as possible. I knew I needed at least three actors to portray the triple-formed nature of Hekate, which "emphasised her power over the three realms, these being the heavens, sea and earth" (D'Este 2009, 19), but also that I would need the fourth element of fire, which also encapsulates the power of light and represents soul. Since the four elements in this context related to aspects of the goddess Hekate, I knew these four needed to be female. Since the power of creation is made possible through the energy of polarity, I chose to have a fifth actor who was not only male, but my husband at the time—not a trained actor, but a trained magician. This was part of the experimental nature of my process, as I was curious to see whether it would be more effective in the context of ritual theatre to train actors in magical technique or magicians in theatrical technique.

Working with trained actors over the years, I have found that it is in most of their natures to be able to take on whatever they need to for the work at hand, and because most good actors are instinctive manipulators of the energy within and around themselves, the discipline and exercises required for this work are not a stretch. Magical training and theatre training have much in common!

Step 5

☞ Do the work that's needed to be vocally and physically ready
as well as spiritually prepared.

This relates to the Hermetic principle of "As above, so below." Your body and voice are the instrument on which the song of your work is played, and a tuned instrument will better convey the energy and intent.

This lesson was learned quite early in our process as I discovered in my sole male non-actor participant a reluctance to learn lines, rehearse, or warm up the voice before performance. This highlights the fact that actors, through the practice of transforming themselves through their work, are already partway to becoming magicians and tend to be more open to new techniques. Since this book is aimed primarily at magical practitioners who wish to incorporate theatre (though I hope it will also be of interest to actors), I hope that the reader may have the opportunity to learn through his mistakes and be open to the benefits of proper rehearsal, warm ups, and memorisation. The exercise at the end of chapter 3, "Finding Your Voice," will be very helpful to you here, and it would also be a good idea to find physical exercises that work for you and your limits to incorporate into a warm up. Pick a few tongue twisters to help with diction, and once you've mastered those, learn some new ones so you can keep your essential skills on point. Deep breathing in, holding for a few seconds, and then releasing slowly, repeated a few times, should help with performance nerves. It's not only your physical body but your spiritual that must be prepared, so be sure to practice the world soul awareness exercise at the end of chapter 7 also.

Step 6

☞ Gather your raw material and select what you will use that serves your intent.

Perhaps you are writing yours from scratch or editing a single source to use for your piece, but if you are using multiple sources as raw material, this is a big and time-consuming step.

When creating the text for *Hekate: Genesis*, it was necessary to compile an amount of raw material. This I did by searching Shakespeare's works (using opensourceshakespeare.org) for certain key words that related to the core ritual structure of creation, death, and rebirth, the concept of polarity (male and female, light and dark, order and chaos), and the four elements.

Step 7

☞ Fit your raw material into your planned structure.

In the case of *Hekate: Genesis*, the first stage of the ritual structure would be the first sparks of creation itself: the descent of animating soul, or Hekate's sacred fire, into matter. This involves the division of the unknowable spiritual source into two, akin to the descent of Sophia, Wisdom, the Shekinah, or Holy Spirit, the feminine aspect of God. Using the entirety of Shakespeare's works as a source, it was helpful to use the postmodern resource of the internet to be able to search the texts for keywords that would lead to a selection of phrases and speeches that could be used, arranged, or discarded as necessary. Some came easily without searching. For example, "In the beginning" was always going to be "Words, words, words…" (*Hamlet*), drawing inspiration from the creation myth of the Bible and also representing the three stages of spirit's descent into matter—the Source united and whole, the split into polarity, and the animation of matter with sacred fire, creating the four elements. This also echoes the celestial hierarchy and concept of logos in Neoplatonic philosophy. These three stages were marked in the opening with the three actresses portraying Earth, Sea, and Sky standing in a triple formation, each holding a Tibetan singing bowl and sounding a chime for each repetition. The first "word" was spoken by the actor playing Source, alone. The second was spoken by Source and Light (Fire) together, to represent the initial split of one into two. The third was spoken by the whole cast, representing the division of spirit into the four elements and hence the world's creation.

With this small example of the deconstruction and re-application of text, it is possible to see how a change of context can add new significance to the structure of Shakespeare's language. "Words, words, words" is an iconic quote from *Hamlet* and thus already carries some weight within popular culture and is likely to resonate on some level with any audience member that has a little knowledge of Shakespeare. Its triple structure lends a natural resonance to its new purpose, and as I scoured Shakespeare's works for more synchronous phrases and sections, I discovered not only phrases that could be used in almost direct opposition to their original context with great effect, but also a large amount of material that required little alteration to be used within a sacred context. Searching simply for words about words in Shakespeare led to so much raw material that there was no room in the scope of this text to use the majority of it, but the nature of the extracts illustrated clearly that the author was acutely aware of the potent effect that words could have in and on the world. The most surprisingly rich vein of spiritually significant word ore to be mined was to be found in Shakespeare's sonnets.

Sonnets 29 and 39 provided the majority of the symbolic dialogue between Source and Light during the initial split of one into two. Placing these words into a new context makes the underlying esoteric symbolism more apparent, and rather than reading them as love poetry, they start to take on a deeper meaning for the reader, whether or not the hidden depths were intentional. In *Shakespeare and the Goddess of Complete Being*, Ted Hughes theorises that the Dark Lady of the sonnets is in fact the Dark Goddess, Hekate, in her aspect of Queen of Hell. This is clearly a creative interpretation, which may have no academic justification but is valid within a mytho-poetic context. Inspired by this concept, I used sonnet 130 set to original music as the mystical song that awakens the statue of Light in the final ritual stage of resurrection.

Step 8

☞ Form the spine of your piece.

If you're using more than one source or creating a complex piece, it is helpful to choose the most resonant pieces of source material to give your structure strength; I call this the spine of your piece. Returning to Shakespeare's plays as a source, there were three from which substantial sections formed the backbone of the piece, with smaller chunks of other plays fleshing out the body and most plays at least contributing a line or two. These spinal plays were *The Tempest, A Midsummer Night's Dream*, and *The Winter's Tale*, all of which obviously have an original magical context but brought very different elements to the mix.

The Tempest provided not only the very ending of the piece, with the "Our revels now are ended" speech, but also a Hekate connection through the foundation of Prospero's invocation "Ye elves of hills, brooks, standing lakes and groves" being the invocation to Hekate from Ovid's *Metamorphoses*, as discussed in chapter 9.

The conflict between Titania and Oberon from *A Midsummer Night's Dream* provided the central section of the piece, in which the nature of polarity is explored. Since both Titania and Hekate are strongly linked to Diana, the moon goddess, and also considering that one of Hekate's aspects within British folklore is as a fairy queen, this had a strong resonance with the ritual purpose of the piece. Also used from this play were some of Puck's lines that list the forms he takes, which also happen to be animal forms connected with Hekate: "Sometime a horse I'll be, sometime a hound, a hog, a headless bear, sometime a fire" (act 3, scene 1).

The Winter's Tale, which in itself abides by the ritual structure, provided the rebirth segment of the piece with its final scene in which the statue of Hermione, long presumed dead, is brought to life. Other plays that contributed significant sections of text included *Othello, Hamlet*, and *Titus Andronicus*, which, I was surprised to find, contained some very useful elemental material. Here is an example of how a speech—act 3, scene 1 of *Titus Andronicus*—was broken down into its elemental components and lines assigned accordingly:

DARKNESS: If there were reason for these miseries,

　Then into limits could I bind my woes.

SEA: When heaven doth weep…

EARTH:…doth not the earth o'erflow?

SKY: If the winds rage…

SEA:…doth not the sea wax mad?

　I am the sea.

SKY: Hark, how her sighs do blow!

EARTH: She is the weeping welkin, I the earth:

SEA: Then must my sea be moved with her sighs;

EARTH: Then must my earth with her continual tears…

SEA:…become a deluge, overflow'd and drown'd;

EARTH: For why my bowels cannot hide her woes…

SEA:…but like a drunkard must I vomit them.

SKY: Then give me leave, for losers will have leave

　To ease their stomachs with their bitter tongues.

The cycling through the elements, which is inherent in the text in its intact state, lends itself naturally to a rhythm suited to ritual, and this proved to work well in a number of cases.

Step 9

☞ Rehearse your piece. Find a rhythm and process that works for you and your cast. Inner and outer work are equally important. Alter the piece as necessary when discoveries are made. Find movement and song to fit the words, or rather find how the words express themselves through the whole body and voice. Decide on music, costumes, and props that complement your text, theme, and rehearsal discoveries.

Depending on the size of your cast, finding a way to rehearse and prepare can be quite challenging; after all, we all have other life commitments. Is there a time or pattern of rehearsing that fits with your theme? For example, if it is planetary based, which day of the week would work best, or would a more intensive schedule work best for you? What resources can you draw on for costumes and props, or if your resources are limited, bear this in mind when writing! Rehearsing a piece of ritual theatre involves processes beyond the physical, so find meditations and exercises that will help connect with the energies you wish to work with in your piece. It is a good idea, when possible, to take time over this so that inner processes can work their magic.

The ideal circumstances for rehearsing a piece like *Hekate: Genesis* would include a month (or one full cycle of the moon) of the cast living and working together, in various landscapes and with suitable meditations and exercises. However, due to various mitigating circumstances, we had five days, during which time members of the cast, myself included, also had other commitments. These constraints resulted in the need to distil the experiment and filter ideas down to those that seemed most essential and which it was hoped would work towards the desired effect in as short a space of time as possible. The cast was a mix of abilities. Sea and Sky were played by two fellow theatre students with no previous experience of magical work, Earth was played by a very experienced actress who had worked mostly in the chorus of West End musicals and also had a good deal of magical experience, and I took the role of Light/Fire. Source/Darkness was played by my then-husband, who is magically trained but is not an actor, and due to work commitments he barely participated in the rehearsal process. This meant that the women formed a strong connection through working together and he remained apart, which although not optimum conditions for a good performance (if you watch the performance on YouTube alongside the script, you'll see what I mean) created an interesting energetic dynamic of polarity that worked for the piece.

The rehearsal process for *Hekate: Genesis* can be broken down into the following core elements (and this is but one example; your circumstances are bound to be different, as mine are now—for instance, I would no longer be able to accommodate people under one roof):

COMMUNAL LIVING

The cast all lived under the same roof for the rehearsal process to encourage a strong energetic connection and to enable flexible rehearsal hours. Cast member Sarah Green, who played Sea, reflected back on the process and remarked that "living in close quarters during the process really helped form a quick but healthy bond between performers."

MEDITATION

Guided visualisations were performed with the cast in order to familiarise them with the qualities of the element they would be representing in the piece in order that they might be more readily able to channel that energy in performance. This was particularly aimed at the two most magically inexperienced members of the cast, who were open-minded yet nervous of something so out of the ordinary, as noted by Sarah Green, who recalls:

> I was very unsure on the meditations as I always found myself quite cynical and I was nervous about something I didn't know much about. Once I settled into it, though, it was interesting to see where I rested with my own element and how I subconsciously view water and what water situations I prefer deep down. It was also interesting to note similarities I had with Dana, someone I am close friends with, and what pictures our minds conjured.

These elemental meditations may be found within my book *Faery Craft*.

SACRED SPACE

Each session would begin with a group ritual calling in the seven directions to bless the space and end with thanking them in order to maintain a sacred space through the process and to aid in focus for the short, intensive rehearsal period.

OUTDOOR LOCATIONS

> Given our roles as elements, being close to nature really helped me to engage and explore "water" and its relationship with the other elements. Rehearsing on the beach was especially fun and engaging as it really felt like you were speaking these lines in the elements themselves.—Sarah Green

When you are solely using meditation or visualisation to connect with elemental energies, there is a danger of the experience becoming too intellectualised and "stuck in the head." In order to strengthen the connection with the elements and ground the experience in a more immediate way, rehearsals and movement-devising sessions were held in outdoor locations pertinent to each element. These included the beach, moorland, and local standing stones.

MASK WORK

Masks were utilized in order to free the actors from their usual personas and to aid transformational work and add a ritualised feel. The masks were not neutral but rather particular to each elemental realm of Earth, Sea, and Sky. Cast member Sarah Green noted that the use of masks freed her as a performer, saying that "as someone who can be quite shy in life and as a performer, I found it very liberating to wear the mask and take on the character." In the case of this production, the masks were pre-existing. It would be a powerful exercise for a ritual cast to create masks specifically for a piece whilst in sacred space, perhaps accompanied by a chant appropriate to the deity/theme of the piece.

COLOUR SYMBOLISM AND SPECTACLE

In addition to the masks, each element had a coloured dancing veil that they kept with them at all times during the rehearsal process. These represented the different elemental colours—yellow for air/Sky, blue for water/Sea, and green for Earth—and since they were incorporated into the devised movement, they created a visual spectacle. With the thought of the transportative power of spectacle in mind, we adapted a pair of red Isis wings, a type of veil used in belly dance, by sewing fairy lights into the hem. This created stunning visual effects when used in darkness, which we exploited during the closing resurrection sequence during an improvised dance that we encouraged the audience to join.

DEVISING

Though the creation of the text and rituals was a solo effort, the movement within the piece was group-led and devised. This added a greater sense of ownership of the piece within the cast. It also required a greater depth of familiarity with the meaning of the words in order that the right feeling and energies were conveyed than would be necessary within a more dictated director-led process.

Step 10

☞ Perform your piece!

Most ritual theatre is created to be performed as a one-off event, but of course this may not always be the case. Bear in mind that a run could be energetically quite demanding for your performers. Try to get a date for your performance in place as you start rehearsals so you know what you're working towards, be it a week or a year away!

With *Hekate: Genesis*, due to the nature of the event, there was no time to rehearse in the actual performance space. The rehearsals in different locations had prepared the cast for this, and Sarah Green insightfully noted that "rather than being a hindrance, it made it really feel like this ephemeral one-time piece that was offered to the gathering and was gone."

Hekate: Genesis

Here is the complete text of *Hekate: Genesis* as an example for your inspiration and for your use in performance if you wish. You are welcome to use it, provided you credit the source. There are notes as to the intention and purpose of each section, and if you wish to know where any of the particular lines are from, please search for them on open sourceshakespeare.org as it would be too intrusive to list them all here. You will notice there are minimal stage directions since all movement was devised by the cast, thus making it equal parts creatively belonging to everyone, their energy being even more invested in the performance than if they had been choreographed. Each scene was broken into textual/thematic chunks and devised, often out in locations in nature. If you wish to see the movement we used, please watch the video of the performance on You-Tube. However, it is my hope that you will create your own dedicated sacred theatre in response.

You can view the performance at https://www.youtube.com/watch?v=lxIejl95CZs or simply search for *Hekate: Genesis* on YouTube.

Characters:
Source/Darkness
Lightbringer
Earth
Sea
Sky
(When Earth, Sea, and Sky speak together, it is the Elements.)

CREATION, THE BEGINNING OF TIME AND CREATION OF MATTER

Note: This first section begins with the famous *Hamlet* quote "Words, words, words," moves on to other quotes about words and breath, and then combines two sonnets.

SOURCE: WORDS

S + L: WORDS

ALL: WORDS

SKY: Words be made of breath

E + SEA: And breath of life

SOURCE: The very soul, and sweet religion makes

   A rhapsody of words: heaven's face doth glow:

ELEMENTS: Words of so sweet breath composed

   As made the things more rich

   As fire, air, water, earth, and heaven can make

LIGHT: The fingers of the powers above do tune

   The harmony of this peace,

   This blessed plot, this earth, this realm, this dear dear land.

SOURCE: O, how thy worth with manners may I sing,

   When thou art all the better part of me?

   What can mine own praise to mine own self bring?

   And what is 't but mine own when I praise thee?

   Even for this let us divided live,

   And our dear love lose name of single one,

   That by this separation I may give

   That due to thee which thou deservest alone.

   O absence, what a torment wouldst thou prove,

   Were it not thy sour leisure gave sweet leave

   To entertain the time with thoughts of love,

   Which time and thoughts so sweetly doth deceive,

   And that thou teachest how to make one twain,

   By praising him here who doth hence remain!

> LIGHT: Yet in these thoughts myself almost despising
>> Haply I think on thee, and then my state,
>> Like to the lark at break of day arising
>> From sullen earth, sings hymns at heaven's gate;
>> For thy sweet love remember'd such wealth brings
>> That then I scorn to change my state with kings.

THE SEPARATION OF LIGHT FROM SOURCE AND HER DESCENT INTO MATTER, ENSOULING NATURE

Note: The section fairly intensely combines a number of Shakespeare's invocations and blessings from various plays and then focuses in on *The Tempest*. The repeated "Hear, Nature, hear; dear goddess, hear!" is from *King Lear*, the context shifted from invocation as curse to blessing. This in itself can be seen as an act of transformational healing.

> SOURCE: I see thy glory like a shooting star
>> Fall to the base earth from the firmament.
>> Bright star of Venus, fall'n down on the earth,
>> How may I reverently worship thee enough?
>
> LIGHT: Our separation so abides, and flies,
>> That thou, residing here, go'st yet with me,
>> And I, hence fleeting, here remain with thee.
>
> EARTH: The star is fall'n
>
> SEA: The three-fold world divided
>
> SKY: This is the world's soul
>
> ELEMENTS: And thou, thrice-crowned queen of
>> night, survey with thy chaste eye, from thy
>> pale sphere above. Let her shine as
>> gloriously As the Venus of the sky!
>
> LIGHT: By the sacred radiance of the sun,
>> The mysteries of Hecate, and the night;
>> By all the operation of the orbs
>> From whom we do exist, and cease to be…
>> Hear, Nature, hear; dear goddess, hear!

Note: This next section shows the creation of life as it splits into the four elements and is ensouled by Light.

> EARTH: Earth's increase, foison plenty,
>   Barns and garners never empty,
>   Vines and clustering bunches growing,
>   Plants with goodly burthen bowing;
>   Spring come to you at the farthest
>   In the very end of harvest!
>   Scarcity and want shall shun you;
>   Ceres' blessing so is on you.
> ALL: Hear, Nature, hear; dear goddess, hear!
> SEA: You nymphs, call'd Naiads, of the windring brooks,
>   With your sedged crowns and ever-harmless looks,
>   Leave your crisp channels and on this green land
>   Answer your summons;
> ALL: Hear, Nature, hear; dear goddess, hear!
> SKY: Now, by the burning tapers of the sky
>   We smell the air, we wawl and cry.
>   Where the bee sucks. there suck I:
>   In a cowslip's bell I lie;
>   There I couch when owls do cry.
>   On the bat's back I do fly
>   After summer merrily.
> ALL: Hear, Nature, hear; dear goddess, hear!
> LIGHT: Ye elves of hills, brooks, standing lakes and groves,
>   And ye that on the sands with printless foot
>   Do chase the ebbing Neptune and do fly him
>   When he comes back; you demi-puppets that
>   By moonshine do the green sour ringlets make,
>   Whereof the ewe not bites, and you whose pastime

Is to make midnight mushrooms, that rejoice

To hear the solemn curfew; by whose aid,

Weak masters though ye be, I have bedimm'd

The noontide sun, call'd forth the mutinous winds,

And 'twixt the green sea and the azured vault

Set roaring war: to the dread rattling thunder

Have I given fire and rifted Jove's stout oak

With his own bolt; the strong-based promontory

Have I made shake and by the spurs pluck'd up

The pine and cedar: graves at my command

Have waked their sleepers, oped, and let 'em forth

By my so potent art!

THE CREATION OF THE CONSORT, DARKNESS

Note: For the creation of Darkness, it seemed fitting to use *Macbeth*. Remembering that the witches of *Macbeth* might be considered to represent agents of Fate or aspects of the world soul, this adds special relevance to them putting ingredients together to create the consort for Light.

LIGHT: The dragon wing of night o'erspreads the earth,

Deep night, dark night, the silent of the night,

The time of night when Troy was set on fire;

The time when screech-owls cry and ban-dogs howl,

And spirits walk and ghosts break up their graves,

That time best fits the work we have in hand.

DARK: Are you a god? would you create me new?

Transform me then, and to your power I'll yield.

SEA: Thrice the brinded cat hath mew'd.

EARTH: Thrice and once the hedge-pig whined.

SKY: Harpier cries 'Tis time, 'tis time.

SEA: Round about the cauldron go;

In the poison'd entrails throw.

Toad, that under cold stone

Days and nights has thirty-one

Swelter'd venom sleeping got,

Boil thou first i' the charmed pot.

ALL: Double, double toil and trouble;

Fire burn, and cauldron bubble.

SKY: Fillet of a fenny snake,

In the cauldron boil and bake;

Eye of newt and toe of frog,

Wool of bat and tongue of dog,

Adder's fork and blind-worm's sting,

Lizard's leg and owlet's wing,

For a charm of powerful trouble,

Like a hell-broth boil and bubble.

ALL: Double, double toil and trouble;

Fire burn and cauldron bubble.

EARTH: Scale of dragon, tooth of wolf,

Witches' mummy, maw and gulf

Of the ravin'd salt-sea shark,

Root of hemlock digg'd i' the dark,

Liver of blaspheming Jew,

Gall of goat, and slips of yew

Silver'd in the moon's eclipse,

Nose of Turk and Tartar's lips,

Finger of birth-strangled babe

Ditch-deliver'd by a drab,

Make the gruel thick and slab:

Add thereto a tiger's chaudron,

For the ingredients of our cauldron.

ALL: Double, double toil and trouble;

Fire burn and cauldron bubble.

SEA: Cool it with a baboon's blood,

  Then the charm is firm and good.

LIGHT: O well done! I commend your pains;

  And every one shall share i' the gains;

  And now about the cauldron sing,

  Live elves and fairies in a ring,

  Enchanting all that you put in.

Note: Another sonnet here.

ALL: When most I wink, then do mine eyes best see,

  For all the day they view things unrespected;

  But when I sleep, in dreams they look on thee,

  And darkly bright are bright in dark directed.

  Then thou, whose shadow shadows doth make bright,

  How would thy shadow's form form happy show

  To the clear day with thy much clearer light,

  When to unseeing eyes thy shade shines so!

  How would, I say, mine eyes be blessed made

  By looking on thee in the living day,

  When in dead night thy fair imperfect shade

  Through heavy sleep on sightless eyes doth stay!

LIGHT: I will encounter darkness as a bride,

  And hug it in mine arms. Sometime a horse I'll be,

    sometime a hound,

  A hog, a headless bear, sometime a fire;

ELEMENTS: And neigh, and bark, and grunt,

    and roar, and burn,

  Like horse, hound, hog, bear, fire, at every turn.

EARTH: The king doth keep his revels here to-night:

  Take heed the queen come not within his sight;

  For Oberon is passing fell and wrath,

Because that she as her attendant hath

A lovely boy, stolen from an Indian king;

She never had so sweet a changeling;

And jealous Oberon would have the child

Knight of his train, to trace the forests wild;

But she perforce withholds the loved boy,

Crowns him with flowers and makes him all her joy:

And now they never meet in grove or green,

By fountain clear, or spangled starlight sheen,

But, they do square, that all their elves for fear

Creep into acorn-cups and hide them there.

CONFLICT

Note: This section is long, beginning with the confrontation of Titania and Oberon from A *Midsummer Night's Dream* representing Light and Dark respectively, and then descending into a full on mash-up as Darkness temporarily quashes Light from various tragedies and one comedy. Can you spot which other comedy is quoted?

DARK: Ill met by moonlight, proud Titania.

LIGHT: What, jealous Oberon! Fairies, skip hence:

I have forsworn his bed and company.

DARK: Tarry, rash wanton: am not I thy lord?

LIGHT: Then I must be thy lady: but I know

When thou hast stolen away from fairy land,

And in the shape of Corin sat all day,

Playing on pipes of corn and versing love

To amorous Phillida. Why art thou here,

Come from the farthest Steppe of India?

But that, forsooth, the bouncing Amazon,

Your buskin'd mistress and your warrior love,

To Theseus must be wedded, and you come

To give their bed joy and prosperity.

DARK: How canst thou thus for shame, Titania,

    Glance at my credit with Hippolyta,

    Knowing I know thy love to Theseus?

    Didst thou not lead him through the glimmering night

    From Perigenia, whom he ravished?

    And make him with fair Aegle break his faith,

    With Ariadne and Antiopa?

LIGHT: These are the forgeries of jealousy:

    And never, since the middle summer's spring,

    Met we on hill, in dale, forest or mead,

    By paved fountain or by rushy brook,

    Or in the beached margent of the sea,

    To dance our ringlets to the whistling wind,

    But with thy brawls thou hast disturb'd our sport.

    Therefore the winds, piping to us in vain,

    As in revenge, have suck'd up from the sea

    Contagious fogs; which falling in the land

    Have every pelting river made so proud

    That they have overborne their continents:

    The ox hath therefore stretch'd his yoke in vain,

    The ploughman lost his sweat, and the green corn

    Hath rotted ere his youth attain'd a beard;

    The fold stands empty in the drowned field,

    And crows are fatted with the murrion flock;

    The nine men's morris is fill'd up with mud,

    And the quaint mazes in the wanton green

    For lack of tread are undistinguishable:

    The human mortals want their winter here;

    No night is now with hymn or carol blest:

    Therefore the moon, the governess of floods,

    Pale in her anger, washes all the air,

That rheumatic diseases do abound:

And thorough this distemperature we see

The seasons alter: hoary-headed frosts

Far in the fresh lap of the crimson rose,

And on old Hiems' thin and icy crown

An odorous chaplet of sweet summer buds

Is, as in mockery, set: the spring, the summer,

The childing autumn, angry winter, change

Their wonted liveries, and the mazed world,

By their increase, now knows not which is which:

And this same progeny of evils comes

From our debate, from our dissension;

We are their parents and original.

DARK: Do you amend it then; it lies in you:

Why should Titania cross her Oberon?

I do but beg a little changeling boy,

To be my henchman.

LIGHT: Set your heart at rest:

The fairy land buys not the child of me.

His mother was a votaress of my order:

And, in the spiced Indian air, by night,

Full often hath she gossip'd by my side,

And sat with me on Neptune's yellow sands,

Marking the embarked traders on the flood,

When we have laugh'd to see the sails conceive

And grow big-bellied with the wanton wind;

Which she, with pretty and with swimming gait

Following,—her womb then rich with my young squire,—

Would imitate, and sail upon the land,

To fetch me trifles, and return again,

As from a voyage, rich with merchandise.

But she, being mortal, of that boy did die;

And for her sake do I rear up her boy,

And for her sake I will not part with him.

DARK: Well; go thy way. Thou shalt not from this grove

Till I torment thee for this injury.

SKY: The heavens themselves, the planets and this centre

Observe degree, priority and place,

Insisture, course, proportion, season, form,

Office and custom, in all line of order;

EARTH: And therefore is the glorious planet Sol

In noble eminence enthroned and sphered

Amidst the other; whose medicinable eye

Corrects the ill aspects of planets evil,

And posts, like the commandment of a king,

Sans cheque to good and bad:

SEA: But when the planets

In evil mixture to disorder wander,

What plagues and what portents! What mutiny!

What raging of the sea!

EARTH: Shaking of earth!

SKY: Commotion in the winds! Frights, changes, horrors!

DARK: Blow, winds, and crack your cheeks!

SKY: Rage! Blow!

SEA: You cataracts and hurricanoes, spout

Till you have drench'd our steeples, drown'd the cocks!

SKY: You sulphurous and thought-executing fires,

Vaunt-couriers to oak-cleaving thunderbolts,

Singe my white head! And thou, all-shaking thunder,

EARTH: Smite flat the thick rotundity o' the world!

Crack nature's moulds, an germens spill at once,

ELEMENTS: Let heaven kiss earth! Now let not Nature's hand

    Keep the wild flood confined! Let order die!

    And let this world no longer be a stage

    To feed contention in a lingering act;

    But let one spirit of the first-born Cain

    Reign in all bosoms, that, each heart being set

    On bloody courses, the rude scene may end,

    And darkness be the burier of the dead!

Note: In this following section, Light was represented by myself and a white lantern that was passed between the elements and then blown out.

SKY: The moon's an arrant thief,

    And her pale fire she snatches from the sun:

SEA: The sea's a thief, whose liquid surge resolves

    The moon into salt tears.

EARTH: The earth's a thief,

    That feeds and breeds by a composture stolen

    From general excrement.

DEATH

DARK: Put out the light, and then put out the light:

    If I quench thee, thou flaming minister,

    I can again thy former light restore,

    Should I repent me; but once put out thy light,

    Thou cunning'st pattern of excelling nature,

    I know not where is that Promethean heat

    That can thy light relume.

Note: As we learned in chapter 10, willow is associated with grieving and with rejected or abused lovers. This following section combines two of the most notable willow references in Shakespeare, Desdemona's song in *Othello* and Gertrude's speech upon the death of Ophelia in *Hamlet*.

"There is a willow grows aslant the brook..."

ELEMENTS: [Sung]

    The poor soul sat sighing by a sycamore tree,

    Sing all a green willow;

    Her hand on her bosom, her head on her knee,

    Sing willow, willow, willow.

    The fresh streams ran by her, and murmur'd her moans,

    Sing willow, willow, willow;

    Her salt tears fell from her, and soft'ned the stones,

    Sing willow, willow, willow

[Spoken]

    There is a willow grows aslant the brook,

    That shows his hoary leaves in the glassy stream,

    Therewith fantastic garlands did she make

    Of crow-flowers, nettles, daisies, and long purples

    That liberal shepherds give a grosser name,

    But our cull-cold maids do dead men's fingers call them.

    There on the pendant boughs her coronet weeds

    Clamb'ring to hang, an envious sliver broke,

    When down her weedy trophies and herself

    Fell in the weeping brook. Her clothes spread wide,

    And mermaid-like awhile they bore her up,

    Which time she chaunted snatches of old lauds,

    As one incapable of her own distress,

    Or like a creature native and indued

    Unto that element. But long it could not be

    Till that her garments, heavy with their drink,

    Pull'd the poor wretch from her melodious lay

    To muddy death.

DARK: Too much of water hast thou,

    And therefore I forbid my tears;

I have a speech a' fire that fain would blaze,

But that this folly drowns it.

Note: Here's that comedy play quote…

EARTH: When he shall hear she died upon his words,

The idea of her life shall sweetly creep

Into his study of imagination,

And every lovely organ of her life

Shall come apparell'd in more precious habit,

More moving-delicate and full of life,

Into the eye and prospect of his soul,

Than when she lived indeed; then shall he mourn

Note: Here's that other comedy sneaking in…It's from *Much Ado About Nothing*! Hero and her family must go through their own kind of ritual theatre of death and resurrection in order for Claudio to realize what he has done and that truth and love can be restored.

SEA: If by your art, my dearest father, you have

Put the wild waters in this roar, allay them.

SKY: The sky it seems would pour down stinking pitch,

But that the sea, mounting to th' welkin's cheek,

Dashes the fire out.

DARK: If there were reason for these miseries,

Then into limits could I bind my woes.

SEA: When heaven doth weep…

EARTH:…doth not the earth o'erflow?

SKY: If the winds rage…

SEA: …doth not the sea wax mad?

I am the sea.

SKY: Hark, how her sighs do blow!

EARTH: She is the weeping welkin, I the earth.

SEA: Then must my sea be moved with her sighs.

EARTH: Then must my earth with her continual tears…

SEA: …become a deluge, overflow'd and drown'd.

EARTH: For why my bowels cannot hide her woes…

SEA: …but like a drunkard must I vomit them.

SKY: Then give me leave, for losers will have leave
 To ease their stomachs with their bitter tongues.

EARTH: Nature seems dead, and wicked dreams abuse
 The curtain'd sleep.

SKY: Witchcraft celebrates
 Pale Hecate's offerings, and wither'd murder,
 Alarum'd by his sentinel, the wolf,
 Whose howl's his watch, thus with his stealthy pace.

RESURRECTION

Note: This section draws heavily on the conclusion of *The Winter's Tale*.

 [Light is now wearing a red cape with fairy lights sewn
  around the edges and a crown also of lights—these are not
  yet switched on]

DARK: Look, here comes a walking fire!

ELEMENTS: O for a Muse of fire, that would ascend
 The brightest heaven of invention!

EARTH: As she liv'd peerless,
 So her dead likeness, I do well believe,
 Excels what ever yet you look'd upon,
 Or hand of man hath done; therefore I keep it
 Lonely, apart. But here it is; prepare
 To see the life as lively mock'd as ever
 Still sleep mock'd death. Behold, and say 'tis well.

SEA: Nor shall this peace sleep with her: but as when
 The bird of wonder dies, the maiden phoenix,

Her ashes new create another heir,

As great in admiration as herself.

SKY: So shall she leave her blessedness to one,

When heaven shall call her from this cloud of darkness,

Who from the sacred ashes of her honour

Shall star-like rise, as great in fame as she was.

EARTH: It is required

You do awake your faith. Then all stand still;

On: those that think it is unlawful business

I am about, let them depart.

DARK: Proceed:

No foot shall stir.

ELEMENTS: And thou, thrice-crowned queen of night, survey

With thy chaste eye, from thy pale sphere above…

Music, awake her; strike!

[Music]

Note: It is suggested by some that the Dark Lady of the sonnets is connected to Hekate, hence the inclusion of this sonnet here:

ELEMENTS: (sung) My mistress' eyes are nothing like the sun;

Coral is far more red than her lips' red;

If snow be white, why then her breasts are dun;

If hairs be wires, black wires grow on her head.

I have seen roses damask'd, red and white,

But no such roses see I in her cheeks;

And in some perfumes is there more delight

Than in the breath that from my mistress reeks.

I love to hear her speak, yet well I know

That music hath a far more pleasing sound;

I grant I never saw a goddess go;

My mistress, when she walks, treads on the ground:

And yet, by heaven, I think my love as rare

As any she belied with false compare.

EARTH: 'Tis time; descend; be stone no more; approach;

Strike all that look upon with marvel. Come,

I'll fill your grave up: stir, nay, come away,

Bequeath to death your numbness, for from him

Dear life redeems you. You perceive she stirs:

[Earth switches on Light's fairy lights in the crown and wings; Light unfurls wings]

Start not; her actions shall be holy as

You hear my spell is lawful: do not shun her

Until you see her die again; for then

You kill her double. Nay, present your hand:

When she was young you woo'd her; now in age

Is she become the suitor?

ELEMENTS: Look, here comes a walking fire.

DARK: O, she's warm!

If this be magic, let it be an art

Lawful as eating.

LIGHT: From women's eyes this doctrine I derive:

They sparkle still the right Promethean fire;

They are the books, the arts, the academes,

That show, contain and nourish all the world

ELEMENTS: Praise the gods,

And make triumphant fires!

[Song: "Firebird's Child," freeform dancing and celebration, audience invited to participate. With the end of the song, all become still, audience are returned to seats, lights are dim...]

EPILOGUE

Note: This section is a speech of Puck's from A *Midsummer Night's Dream* split between the different elements, then a speech of Prospero's from *The Tempest*.

EARTH: Now the hungry lion roars

SKY: And the wolf behowls the moon

EARTH: Whilst the heavy ploughman snores

SEA: All with weary task fordone.

LIGHT: Now the wasted brands do glow

SKY: Whilst the screech-owl, screeching loud,

   Puts the wretch that lies in woe

   In remembrance of a shroud.

DARK: Now it is the time of night

   That the graves all gaping wide,

   Every one lets forth his sprite,

   In the church-way paths to glide:

ALL: And we fairies, that do run

LIGHT: By the triple Hecate's team

DARK: From the presence of the sun,

   Following darkness like a dream.

ELEMENTS: Now are frolic: not a mouse

   Shall disturb this hallow'd house:

   I am sent with broom before,

   To sweep the dust behind the door.

LIGHT: Our revels now are ended. These our actors,

   As I foretold you, were all spirits and

   Are melted into air, into thin air:

   And, like the baseless fabric of this vision,

   The cloud-capp'd towers, the gorgeous palaces,

   The solemn temples, the great globe itself,

   Ye all which it inherit, shall dissolve

And, like this insubstantial pageant faded,
Leave not a rack behind. We are such stuff
As dreams are made on, and our little life
Is rounded with a sleep.

[Blow out the crown of light: blackout]

Reflecting on Hekate: Genesis Seven Years On

Hekate: Genesis brought the theatricality many of us crave but rarely get from ritual practice in the modern day. Hearing Shakespeare, rearranged to tell a tale of a goddess's journey, was to be in circle with these fairies and wizard characters. The words resonated with power in the Glastonbury Hall, highlighting a sacred meaning in the speeches, changing them to prayers and invocations. This built to a climax with Goddess (Emily) performing a firebird dance that filled the hall with energy and rebirth. It was exciting and beautiful. The experiencing was like sensing a magic I long knew but did not yet understand how to use. The piece had a long-term impact on my ritual work, as from then on, I have recomposed pieces from different Shakespeare plays to use as a narrative text at each sabbath with my Pagan group.—Fergus Rattigan, audience member, practicing Pagan, and actor

Goodness knows we all have a love-hate relationship with social media, but sometimes it throws up memories that help you identify extraordinary synchronicities, such as the fact that I was working on this chapter of the book exactly seven years on from when we started our intensive week of rehearsals. I posted about this on social media and various people responded with what an impact it had made on them, how they had been moved by the event and even, as with the account above, been inspired to incorporate aspects of it into their own work. I couldn't wish for more. Perhaps I will gather a group together to perform this piece again, perhaps you will, but certainly on the day, as an offering to the goddess and the assembled crowd, it made its mark. So I hope will yours, if you choose to take on this challenge!

Exercise: Create Your Own Piece of Ritual Theatre

It can be as long or as short as you like, for an audience of hundreds or a private performance just for the benefit of the participants. Here are the key stages again and things to bear in mind:

STEP 1: What is the purpose of your ritual? Will it be dedicated to a god/myth/planet/star/spirit/otherworldly realm/etc.? What technique will you use? Will you use a combination of techniques, i.e., your own writing plus Shakespeare speeches, mash-ups, and maybe work from other sources too?

STEP 2: What structure suits the theme you have chosen? It should have a clear beginning, middle, and end, and it should end harmoniously

STEP 3: Decide on the source materials you want to draw upon and do your research. Remember the power of music to transform consciousness. How will you use sound and music in your piece?

STEP 4: Who will perform your piece? How many actors do you need? Do you also need musicians?

STEP 5: Do the work that's needed to be vocally and physically ready as well as spiritually prepared. This is part of "As above, so below." Your body and voice are the instrument on which the song of your work is played, and a tuned instrument will better convey the energy and intent.

STEP 6: Gather your raw material and select what you will use that serves your intent.

STEP 7: Fit your raw material into your planned structure.

STEP 8: Form the spine of your piece, then fit the rest of your material around it.

STEP 9: Rehearse your piece. Find a rhythm and process that works for you and your cast. Inner and outer work are equally important. Alter the piece as necessary when discoveries are made. Find movement and song to fit the words, or rather find how the words express themselves through the whole body and voice. Decide on music, costumes, and props that complement your text, theme, and rehearsal discoveries. If you don't have a date and location sorted for performance, then think about when and where it will be performed and do the work needed to arrange it.

STEP 10: Performance! Break a leg!

Epilogue

'Tis true that a good play needs no epilogue. Yet to
good wine they do use good bushes; and good plays
prove the better by the help of good epilogues…

—*As You Like It*, ACT 5, SCENE 4

THERE ARE PARTS of this book that were written during my studies for my MFA
at Exeter seven years ago. It seems reasonable to suspect that my world would have
changed a lot during that time, which it has—divorce, moving twice, dealing with the
challenges of solo parenthood, and many incredible adventures with my acting career—
but it's not just my world that has changed recently. I am writing these last few words of
the book during the third month of lockdown in the UK due to the global coronavirus
pandemic of 2020. The theatres are all closed, just as they were in Shakespeare's time
with the repeated outbreaks of bubonic plague.

At this point, we don't know what the world will look like on the other side of all this,
and though it's probable that the lockdown will soon be eased in order to try and salvage
the economy, the theatres are likely to remain closed for a long while to come and the
losses will continue. The word *unprecedented* is being overused, simply because it is an
unprecedented challenge that we face. However, in the midst of all this, something that
is very apparent is that people around the world immediately turned to Shakespeare
for inspiration and comfort. There is a huge abundance of performances now available
online, famous actors reading daily sonnets, and the extraordinary phenomenon that
is Shakespeare on Zoom, innovated by companies such as The Show Must Go Online

created by Rob Myles and his partner Sarah Peachey (in which I've so far participated in *Two Gentlemen of Verona* and *Love's Labour's Lost*). This last week Shakespeare's Globe hit the news as it is reliant on private donors and ticket sales for survival, and online reada-thons and appeals are rushing to help save it.

I never could have pictured this with any skills of divination or oracular ability, but I am not surprised to see that Shakespeare is what people turn to in dark times.

In my solo show *Quintessence*, originally written as a commission for London Science Museum in 2018, I imagined a future where humanity was wiped out and had to be rec-reated by an AI who had been programmed with the complete works of Shakespeare in order to give them a sense of that intangible quality, the human spirit.

How I hope that you are reading these words now on the other side of all this. That your losses were not too great, that the world is somehow brighter. How I hope that we have shed the tyrannical leaders and despots who will somehow always surface, as they do in Shakespeare's plays. One thing I know for certain: Whatever the world looks like now, the true beauty and magic of the human spirit will shine through, and I hope this book gives you a way in to explore the full potentials of your own spirit through the works of Shakespeare.

EPILOGUE

Now my charms are all o'erthrown,
And what strength I have's mine own,
Which is most faint: now, 'tis true,
I must be here confined by you,
Or sent to Naples. Let me not,
Since I have my dukedom got
And pardon'd the deceiver, dwell
In this bare island by your spell;
But release me from my bands
With the help of your good hands:
Gentle breath of yours my sails
Must fill, or else my project fails,
Which was to please. Now I want
Spirits to enforce, art to enchant,
And my ending is despair,
Unless I be relieved by prayer,
Which pierces so that it assaults
Mercy itself and frees all faults.
As you from crimes would pardon'd be,
Let your indulgence set me free.
(*The Tempest*, Epilogue)

Acknowledgments

THANKS TO ELYSIA at Llewellyn for infinite patience whilst my acting career got in the way of me being even in the same year as my deadline. Also for infinite patience, Stephen Ball, who has been bombarded with every stage of progress for feedback and has been endlessly supportive as well as an excellent brain to bounce ideas off. Thank you to my gothspring for occasional motivational shouting when I needed it; it really helped!

Huge thanks to the wonderful Caitlín Matthews, who has been an inspiring presence on page and in person for most of my life, for the lovely foreword.

Thank you to Peter Dawkins and Mark Rylance for those amazing pilgrimages in Sicily and Verona, and to Aoife who has walked the Eleusinian path with me these few years, distinct yet parallel, and thanks to all that shared that magical journey.

Thank you to Ellen Kushner, Delia Sherman, Patrick O'Connor, and all from the Zooming Shakespeare group who saw me through the last stages of rewrites and brightened up my lockdown Saturdays!

Sending big love to everyone from my MFA at Exeter University, and to those who showed us the magic of the Globe. Thank you also to Sorita D'Este for commissioning *Hekate: Genesis*, for constant friendship and support, and for #chalkspeare…the legend will return.

Huge thanks to everyone who has been supportive through getting the book finished; you're all wonderful. Thank you.

And thank you, now, for reading. I hope you have found something to inspire you.

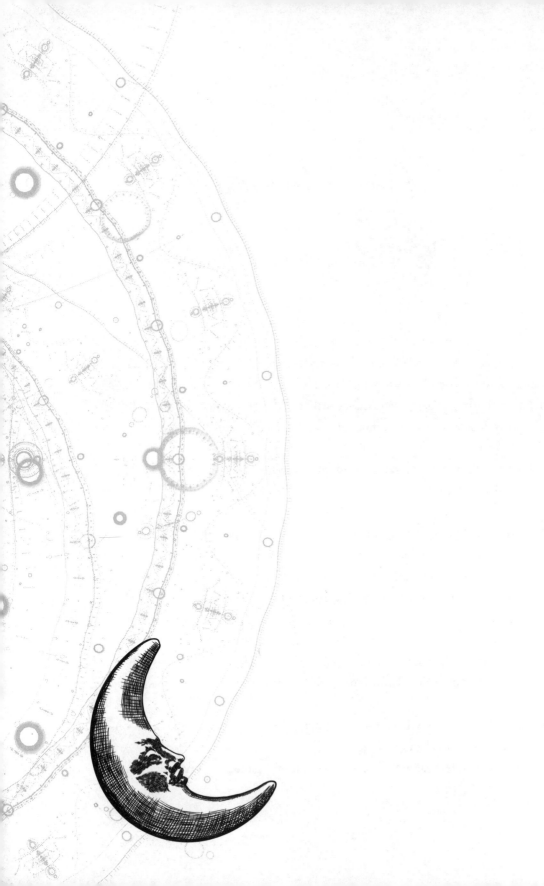

Bibliography

Agrippa. *Three Books of Occult Philosophy.* Llewellyn, 1993.

Apuleius. Translated by Jack Lindsay. *The Golden Ass.* IUP, 2005.

Artaud, Antonin. *Artaud Anthology.* City Lights Books, 1965.

Bacon, Francis. *The Major Works.* Oxford University Press, 2008.

The Ballad of Tam Lin. http://www.tam-lin.org/versions/39A.html.

Bartlett, Robert Allen. *Real Alchemy.* Ibis Press, 2009.

Bate, Jonathan. "Shakespeare's Ghosts and Spirits" lecture. Gresham College, 2018.

Bates, Brian. *The Way of the Actor.* Century, 1986.

Bell, William. *Shakespeare's Puck and His Folklore.* Asher & Co., 1852.

Block, Giles. *Speaking the Speech: An Actor's Guide to Shakespeare.* Nick Hern Books, 2013.

Brook, Peter. *The Quality of Mercy.* Nick Hern Books, 2013.

———. *The Empty Space.* Penguin, 1968.

Bruno, Giordano. *Cause, Principle and Unity.* Cambridge University Press, 1998.

Carding, Emily. *Faery Craft.* Llewellyn, 2012.

Carson, Christie, and Farah Karim-Cooper, editors. *Shakespeare's Globe: A Theatrical Experiment,* Cambridge University Press, 2008.

The Chaldean Oracles. Translated and edited by the Shrine of Wisdom. Shrine of Wisdom, 1979.

Cobb, Noel. *Prospero's Island*. Coventure, 1984.

Copenhaver, Brian P., translator. *Hermetica*. Cambridge University Press, 2002.

Culpeper, Nicholas. *Culpeper's Complete Herbal*. Wordsworth Reference, 2007.

Dawkins, Peter. *The Shakespeare Enigma*. Polair Publishing, 2004.

———. *The Wisdom of Shakespeare in As You Like It*. I C Media, 1998.

———. *The Wisdom of Shakespeare in The Merchant of Venice*. I C Media, 1998.

———. *The Wisdom of Shakespeare in The Tempest*. I C Media, 2000.

———. *The Wisdom of Shakespeare in Twelfth Night*. I C Media, 2002.

D'Este, Sorita, and David Rankine. *Hekate: Liminal Rites*. Avalonia, 2009.

D'Este, Sorita, editor. *The Faerie Queens*. Avalonia Books, 2012.

Green, Robert. 1588. *Pandosto*. http://oxford-shakespeare.com/Greene/Pandosto.pdf.

Greenblatt, Stephen. *Hamlet in Purgatory*. Princeton University Press, 2013.

Grotowski, Jerzy. *Towards a Poor Theatre*. Bloomsbury, 2013.

Gurr, Andrew. *Rebuilding Shakespeare's Globe*. Routledge, 1989.

———. *The Shakespearean Stage 1574–1642*. Cambridge University Press, 2009.

Gurr, Elizabeth. *Shakespeare's Globe: A Souvenir Guide*. Shakespeare's Globe, 1998.

Harms, Daniel, and James Clark. *Of Angels, Demons & Spirits: A Sourcebook of British Magic*. Llewellyn, 2019.

Harms, Daniel, and Joseph H. Peterson. *The Book of Oberon*. Llewellyn, 2015.

Holinshed, Raphael. *Chronicles*. 1577, 1587. http://english.nsms.ox.ac.uk/Holinshed/

Hughes, Ted. *Shakespeare and the Goddess of Complete Being*. Faber and Faber, 1992.

Huson, Paul. *Mastering Herbalism: A Practical Guide*. Madison Books, 2001.

James I. Translated and edited by Brett R. Warren. *The Annotated Daemonologie*. Brett Warren, 2016.

Johnston, Sarah Iles. *Hekate Soteira*. Scholar's Press, 1990.

Keightley, Thomas. *The Fairy Mythology*. William Clowes and Sons, 1870.

Kiernan, Pauline. *Staging Shakespeare at the New Globe*. Macmillan Press, 1999.

Macphee, Wendy Jean. *Secret Meanings in Shakespeare*. M-Y Books, 2018.

Mangan, Michael. *Doctor Faustus: A Critical Study*. Penguin, 1987.

Marowitz, Charles. *Recycling Shakespeare*. Macmillan, 1991.

Mebane, John S. *Renaissance Magic and the Return of the Golden Age*. University of Nebraska Press, 1992.

Monmouth, Geoffrey of. *The History of the Kings of Britain*. Penguin, 1966.

Mulryne, J. R., and Margaret Shewring, editors. *Shakespeare's Globe Rebuilt*. Cambridge University Press, 1997.

Nottingham, Gary St. M. *Ars Alchemica*. Avalonia, 2016.

Orrel, John. *The Quest for Shakespeare's Globe*. Cambridge University Press, 1983.

Paracelsus. Translated by Arthur Edward Waite. *The Hermetic and Alchemical Writings of Paracelsus*. Forgotten Books, 2007.

Pearce, Stewart. *The Alchemy of Voice*. Findhorn, 2010.

Plato. *The Republic*. Penguin, 1955.

Pogson, Beryl. *In the East My Pleasure Lies*. Eureka Editions, 1999.

Quealy, Gerit. *Botanical Shakespeare*. Harper Collins, 2017.

Rankine, David. *The Book of Treasure Spirits*. Avalonia, 2009.

———, editor. *The Grimoire of Arthur Gauntlet*. Avalonia, 2011.

Rankine, David, and Sorita D'Este. *Practical Elemental Magick*. Avalonia, 2008.

———. *Practical Planetary Magick*. Avalonia, 2007.

———. *Practical Qabalah Magick*. Avalonia, 2009.

Rankine, David, and Stephen Skinner. *The Veritable Key of Solomon*. Golden Hoard, 2008.

Rouse, W. H. D., and A. Golding. *Shakespeare's Ovid: Being Arthur Golding's Translation of the Metamorphoses*. At the De La More Press, 1904.

Scot, Reginald. *The Discoverie of Witchcraft*. Dover Publications, 1972.

Shakespeare, William. http://opensourceshakespeare.org/.

———. *The Complete Works*. The Works, 1993.

———. Edited by John Pitcher. *The Winter's Tale*. Arden, 2010.

———. Edited by Kenneth Muir. *Macbeth*. Arden, 1970.

Skinner, Stephen. *The Complete Magician's Tables*. Golden Hoard, 2006.

———. *Sacred Geometry*. Sterling Publishing, 2006.

Stewart, R. J. *The Well of Light*. R. J. Stewart Books, 2006.

Taylor, Thomas, translator. *The Mystical Hymns of Orpheus*. C. Whittingham, 1824.

———. *Proclus' Elements of Theology*. The Prometheus Trust, 1994.

Thiselton-Dyer, T. F. *Folk-lore of Shakespeare*. Okitoks Press, 2017.

Wiles, David. *Greek Theatre Performance*. Cambridge University Press, 2000.

———. *A Short History of the Western Performance Space*. Cambridge University Press, 2003.

Willes, Margaret. *A Shakespearean Botanical*. Bodelian Library, 2015.

Wooley, Benjamin. *The Queen's Conjuror*. Harper Collins, 2001.

Yates, Frances. *The Art of Memory*. Bodley Head, 2014.

———. *Giordano Bruno and the Hermetic Tradition*. Routledge, 2002.

———. *The Occult Philosophy in the Elizabethan Age*. Routledge, 1979.

———. *Shakespeare's Last Plays*. Routledge, 2007.

———. *Theatre of the World*. Routledge, 1969.

About the Author

EMILY CARDING IS an experienced Shakespearean actor, having appeared in versions of over twenty of Shakespeare's plays both on stage and screen. She holds a BA (hons) in theatre arts from Bretton Hall and an MFA in staging Shakespeare from the University of Exeter. Together with independent theatre company Brite Theater, Emily has created a number of challenging and innovative shows including *Hamlet* (An Experience) and *Richard* III (A One-Woman Show), both of which have won awards and rave reviews internationally. Both adaptations use the audience as characters within the play and create a truly immersive experience with very little other than actor, text, space, and audience. Emily is also an accomplished screen actor and played opposite Martin Freeman in the British horror movie hit *Ghost Stories*.

In 2018 Emily was commissioned by London Science Museum to create a solo theatre piece inspired by Mary Shelley's *Frankenstein*. *Quintessence* imagines a future where humanity has become extinct and must be recreated by an AI, using Shakespeare as a guide to the human spirit. This won the outstanding theatre award at Brighton Fringe in 2019. She is hoping to develop this piece further for digital media.

Emily is also a published creator of a number of highly popular tarot decks, including *The Transparent Tarot* and *Tarot of the Sidhe*, and author of esoteric works, including *Faery Craft* and *Seeking Faery*. Trained in a number of magical traditions, she is a priestess of Hekate and a Wiccan initiate.

Index

INDEX